Thomas Hardy
Distance and Desire

Thomas Hardy

Distance and Desire

J. Hillis Miller

The Belknap Press of
Harvard University Press
Cambridge, Massachusetts
1970

In Memory of My Father

Preface

LITERARY CRITICISM IS LANGUAGE about language, or, to put it another way, a re-creating in the mind of the critic of the consciousness inscribed in the texts studied, generated there by the words. To say this is to put in question certain habitual metaphors for what happens in the act of criticism. Among these are all those visual metaphors which set the critic over against the text as a spectator who surveys the literary work as a scientist is sometimes thought to survey the thing he investigates, dispassionately and objectively. Illicit also are the metaphors for criticism which propose to explain the text by something extralinguistic which precedes it and which is its generative source — the life or psychology of the author, historical conditions at a certain time, some event which is the model "imitated" or "reflected" or "represented" in the poem or story. The centuries-old metaphors of mimesis obscure the nature of literary language. The pre-text of a given text is always another text open in its turn to interpretation. There is never an extralinguistic "origin" by means of which the critic can escape from his labyrinthine wanderings within the complexities of relationship among words.

The critic, moreover, does not possess a power of looking from the outside in a sovereign view which sees all the text at once as a spatial design. To understand the text he must be inside it. The means of his entry is language, a medium within which he already dwells. He can insert himself into the text because both he and it are already interpenetrated by their common language. The means of his interpretation is also language, those words of his own which even in the most passive act of reading he adds to the text as he understands it. If there is no escape outside the text, if language is as much the source of consciousness or of history as consciousness or history is the source of language, then far better than any visual metaphor for what happens in criticism is that image employed by Thomas Hardy in *The Dynasts* and elsewhere, the image of the text of history as a woven cloth.[1] A literary text is a texture of words, its threads and filaments reaching out into the pre-existing warp and woof of the language. The critic adds his weaving to the Penelope's web of the text, or unravels it so that its structuring threads may be laid bare, or reweaves it, or traces out one thread in the text to reveal the design it inscribes, or cuts the whole cloth to one shape or another. In some way the critic necessarily does violence of the text in the act of understanding it or of interpreting it. There is no innocent reading, no reading which leaves the work exactly as it is.

---

[1] See below, note 5, and see also Jacques Derrida, "La pharmacie de Platon," *Tel Quel*, 32 (1968), 3-4, for a recent provocative use of this metaphor.

Thomas Hardy
Distance and Desire

Thomas Hardy

Distance and Desire

J. Hillis Miller

The Belknap Press of
Harvard University **Press**
Cambridge, Massachusetts
1970

In Memory of My Father

Preface

LITERARY CRITICISM IS LANGUAGE about language, or, to put it another way, a re-creating in the mind of the critic of the consciousness inscribed in the texts studied, generated there by the words. To say this is to put in question certain habitual metaphors for what happens in the act of criticism. Among these are all those visual metaphors which set the critic over against the text as a spectator who surveys the literary work as a scientist is sometimes thought to survey the thing he investigates, dispassionately and objectively. Illicit also are the metaphors for criticism which propose to explain the text by something extralinguistic which precedes it and which is its generative source — the life or psychology of the author, historical conditions at a certain time, some event which is the model "imitated" or "reflected" or "represented" in the poem or story. The centuries-old metaphors of mimesis obscure the nature of literary language. The pre-text of a given text is always another text open in its turn to interpretation. There is never an extralinguistic "origin" by means of which the critic can escape from his labyrinthine wanderings within the complexities of relationship among words.

The critic, moreover, does not possess a power of looking from the outside in a sovereign view which sees all the text at once as a spatial design. To understand the text he must be inside it. The means of his entry is language, a medium within which he already dwells. He can insert himself into the text because both he and it are already interpenetrated by their common language. The means of his interpretation is also language, those words of his own which even in the most passive act of reading he adds to the text as he understands it. If there is no escape outside the text, if language is as much the source of consciousness or of history as consciousness or history is the source of language, then far better than any visual metaphor for what happens in criticism is that image employed by Thomas Hardy in *The Dynasts* and elsewhere, the image of the text of history as a woven cloth.[1] A literary text is a texture of words, its threads and filaments reaching out into the pre-existing warp and woof of the language. The critic adds his weaving to the Penelope's web of the text, or unravels it so that its structuring threads may be laid bare, or reweaves it, or traces out one thread in the text to reveal the design it inscribes, or cuts the whole cloth to one shape or another. In some way the critic necessarily does violence of the text in the act of understanding it or of interpreting it. There is no innocent reading, no reading which leaves the work exactly as it is.

[1] See below, note 5, and see also Jacques Derrida, "La pharmacie de Platon," *Tel Quel*, 32 (1968), 3-4, for a recent provocative use of this metaphor.

Jude stands alone and in the open, but he is nonetheless bound by the situation he has inherited. Like Pip in Dickens' *Great Expectations,* he is an orphan. Like Pip, he has been told by his foster mother that he is "useless" and would be better dead (JO, 8). Along with so many other heroes of nineteenth-century novels, Hardy's protagonists find themselves "living in a world which [does] not want them" (JO, 11). Though Hardy himself was not an orphan and seems to have had a fairly happy childhood, he too, in the passage from the *Life,* broods over how "useless" he is. The conventional motifs of the orphan hero and the indifferent foster parent express his general sense that no man's situation is of his making or satisfies his desire.

Hardy's response to this experience of life is so instinctive that it is never recorded, but always precedes any record, though it is repeated again and again in his own life and in that of his characters. It precedes any record because it makes consciousness and the recording of consciousness possible. This response is a movement of passive withdrawal. Like a snail crawling into its shell, or like a furtive animal creeping into its burrow, he pulls his hat over his face and looks quietly at what he can see through the interstices of the straw. The gesture objectifies an act of detachment which, for him, is involuntary and antedates any gesture which embodies it. The separation which is natural to the mind may be lost by a man's absorption in the world or it may be maintained by a willful standing back, but initially it is given with consciousness itself. To be conscious is to be separated. The mind has a native clarity and distinctness which detaches it from everything it registers.

Though Hardy finds that his consciousness separates

him from the world, he does not turn away from what he sees to investigate the realm of interior space. He and his characters are distinguished by the shallowness of their minds. They have no profound inner depths leading down to the "buried self" or to God. They remain even in detachment oriented toward the outside world and reflecting it, mirrorlike. Though Hardy remains turned toward the exterior, looking at it or thinking about it, his movement of retraction separates him from blind engagement and turns everything he sees into a spectacle viewed from the outside.

A passage in *The Mayor of Casterbridge* demonstrates further this superficiality of consciousness. The act of coming to self-awareness does not lead to a recognition of the intrinsic quality of the mind. It is a revelation about the outside world, a recognition of the mute detachment of external objects and of the inexplicable fact that this particular power of knowing, which might be anywhere or beholding any scene, happens to be imprisoned by one environment rather than by another. The mind is held entranced by a vision of objects which seem themselves entranced, constrained. The passage describes Elizabeth-Jane Henchard's experience as she sits late at night by the bedside of her dying mother. She hears one of those odd sounds audible in a silent house in the small hours: one clock ticking against another clock, "ticking harder and harder till it seemed to clang like a gong" (MC, 135). This revelation of the fact that a clock's ticking is a mechanical noise, not a natural expression of the passage of time, leads her to recognize the paradoxical nature of her situation. She is both within her immediate environment and outside it. She is in bondage to it in the sense that if she looks at anything she must look at what happens to be there to see. She is free of it in the sense that what she sees has no necessary connection to her watching mind. Seeing this causes her consciousness to spin incoherently with unanswerable questions about why things around her are as they are. Though the passage registers as acute an awareness of self as is expressed anywhere in Hardy's writing, it shows the mind still turned chiefly toward the outside world, still asking why things are as they are rather than why the mind is as it is.[1] The question of the nature of the mind arises only after a confrontation of the helpless objectivity of external things:

> . . . and all this while the subtle-souled girl [was] asking herself why she was born, why sitting in a room, and blinking at the candle; why things around her had taken the shape they wore in preference to every other possible shape. Why they stared at her so helplessly, as if waiting for the touch of some wand that should release them from terrestrial constraint; what that chaos called consciousness, which spun in her at this moment like a top, tended to, and began in. (MC, 135-136)

The spontaneous withdrawal of the mind to a position of detached watchfulness is ratified by an act of will. Rather than choosing to lose himself in one or another of the beguiling forms of engagement offered by the world, Hardy, like many of his characters, chooses to keep

---

1 For a similar passage in the poetry see the beginning of "Nature's Questioning" (CP, 58):

> When I look forth at dawning, pool,
>   Field, flock, and lonely tree,
>   All seem to gaze at me
> Like chastened children sitting silent in a school . . .

his distance. Like Herman Melville's Bartleby, he decides he "would prefer not to" — prefer not to grow up, prefer not to take responsibility, prefer not to move out of his own narrow circle, prefer not to possess things, prefer not to know more people. The young Jude also experiences this desire to remain on the periphery of life. He too pulls his hat over his eyes and lies "vaguely reflecting": "As you got older, and felt yourself to be at the centre of your time, and not a point in its circumference, as you had felt when you were little, you were seized with a sort of shuddering, he perceived. All around you there seemed to be something glaring, garish, rattling, and the noises and glares hit upon the little cell called your life, and shook it, and warped it. If he could only prevent himself growing up! He did not want to be a man" (JO, 15). The motif recurs once more when the speaker in a late poem, a poem characteristically craggy in diction, remembers as a child crouching safely in a thicket of ferns and asking himself: "Why should I have to grow to man's estate, / And this afar-noised World perambulate?" ("Childhood Among the Ferns," CP, 825). The world is noise and glare, the threat of an engulfing violence which will shake and twist a man's life. Only if he can remain self-contained, sealed off from everything, can he escape this violence. He must therefore refuse any involvement in the world. Hardy's fundamental spiritual movement is the exact opposite of Nietzsche's will to power. It is the will not to will, the will to remain quietly watching on the sidelines.[2]

---

2 It is not surprising that Hardy should have spoken of Nietzsche with abhorrence as "a megalomaniac and not truly a philosopher at all" (*Life and Art,* ed. Ernest Brennecke, Jr. [New York: Greenberg, 1925], pp. 137-138). See L, 315, 364, for further negative comments on Nietzsche.

Having given up the virile goals which motivate most men, Hardy can turn back on the world and watch it from a safe distance, see it clearly with a "full look at the Worst" ("In Tenebris, II," CP, 154), and judge it. This way of being related to the world is the origin of his art. Such an attitude determines the habitual stance of his narrators, that detachment which sees events from above them or from a time long after they have happened. Or it might be better to say that these spatial and temporal distances objectify a separation which is outside of life, outside of time and space altogether, as the speaker in "Wessex Heights" seems "where I was before my birth, and after death may be" (CP, 300). The tone of voice natural to a spectator who sees things from such a position imparts its slightly acerb flavor throughout his work as a compound of irony, cold detachment, musing reminiscent bitterness, an odd kind of sympathy which might be called "pity at a distance," and, mixed with these, a curious joy, a grim satisfaction that things have, as was foreseen, come out for the worst in this worst of all possible worlds.

Such a perspective is also possessed by many of the protagonists of Hardy's novels, those watchers from a distance like Gabriel Oak in *Far from the Madding Crowd,* Christopher Julian in *The Hand of Ethelberta,* Diggory Venn in *The Return of the Native,* or Giles Winterborne in *The Woodlanders.* The detachment of such characters is expressed in the recurrent motif of spying in his fiction. He frequently presents a scene in which one character sees another without being seen, watches from an upper window or a hill, peeks in a window from outside at night, or covertly studies a reflection in a mirror.

In the lyric poetry too a stance of detachment is habit-

ual. The speaker of the poems is "The Dead Man Walking," to borrow the title of one of them (CP, 202-203).
He is withdrawn from the present, "with no listing or
longing to join" ("In Tenebris, III," CP, 155). From this
separation he focuses his attention on the ghosts of the
past. He sees things from the perspective of death, and as
a consequence is so quiet a watcher, so effaced, that birds,
animals, and forlorn strangers pay no attention to him,
knowing that his vision is as distant as the stars (" 'I Am
the One,' " CP, 799). This detachment is most elaborately
dramatized in the choruses of spirits in *The Dynasts*.
These spirits, says Hardy, are not supernatural beings.
They "are not supposed to be more than the best human
intelligences of their time in a sort of quint-essential
form." From this generalization he excludes the Chorus
of Pities. They are "merely Humanity, with all its weak-
nesses" (L, 321). The careful attention to details of optical placement in *The Dynasts*, which John Wain has
associated with cinematic technique,[3] is more than a matter of vivid presentation. It is an extension of the implicit
point of view in the novels and in the lyric poems. It has
a thematic as well as technical meaning. The choruses in
The Dynasts are able to see the whole expanse of history
at a glance. When they focus on a particular event they
see it in the context of this all-encompassing panoramic
vision. The spirits in the "General Chorus of Intelligences" at the end of the "Fore Scene" boast that they
are everywhere at once and can contract all time and
space to a single spot of time:

---

[3] See his "Introduction" to *The Dynasts* in the Macmillan paperback
edition of 1965, pp. ix-xix.

> We'll close up Time, as a bird its van,
> We'll traverse Space, as spirits can,
> Link pulses severed by leagues and years,
> Bring cradles into touch with biers;
> So that the far-off Consequence appears
> Prompt at the heel of foregone Cause. — (D, 7)

The narrative voice and perspective in the fiction, the attitude natural to many characters in the novels, the location of the speaker habitual in the poems, the epic machinery of *The Dynasts* — all these express the detachment of consciousness which is fundamental to Hardy's way of looking at the world. Such separation allows him and his spokesmen to see reality as it is. From a detached point of view the environment no longer seems so close that one can only be aware of its dangerous energy, its glare and garish rattling. The man who is pursuing some immediate goal is too close to life to see it whole. Only from a distance are its patterns visible. In *Desperate Remedies,* for example, Aeneas Manston is paradoxically granted by the intensity of his involvement the insight born of a momentary detachment. From the point of view of the man involved in a concrete situation, such a perspective is trivial, a momentary wandering of the mind. The narrator and the reader, however, can see that the character has by a fortuitous inattention been briefly granted a glimpse of the true pattern of existence. Here the view of the protagonist approaches, in a moment of vision which recurs in Hardy's fiction, the wide view of the narrator:

> There exists, as it were, an outer chamber to the mind, in which, when a man is occupied centrally

with the most momentous question of his life, casual and trifling thoughts are just allowed to wander softly for an interval, before being banished altogether. Thus, amid his concentration did Manston receive perceptions of the individuals about him in the lively thoroughfare of the Strand; tall men looking insignificant; little men looking great and profound; lost women of miserable repute looking as happy as the days are long; wives, happy by assumption, looking careworn and miserable. Each and all were alike in this one respect, that they followed a solitary trail like the inwoven threads which form a banner, and all were equally unconscious of the significant whole they collectively showed forth. (DR, 354)

The same image appears in *The Woodlanders*. Though Giles Winterborne and Marty South walking in the early morning are completely "isolated" and "self-contained," their lives form part of the total fabric of human actions being performed all over the globe: "their lonely courses formed no detached design at all, but were part of the pattern in the great web of human doings then weaving in both hemispheres from the White Sea to Cape Horn" (W, 21).

What Manston has for an instant, Hardy and his narrators have as a permanent possession. They see each individual life in the context of the whole cloth of which it is part. This superimposition of the engaged view and the detached, wide view pervades Hardy's writing and is the source of its characteristic ironies.[4] If much of his

---

4 Lucille Herbert, in an interesting essay forthcoming in *ELH*, "Thomas Hardy's Views in *Tess of the d'Urbervilles*," relates this double perspective to the nineteenth-century relativistic sense of history and

work is made up of careful notation of immediate particulars — the weather, the landscape, a house or a room, the colors of things, apparently irrelevant details, what the characters say, think, or do as they seek satisfaction of their desires — the narrative perspective on these particulars, present in the steady and cool tone of the language, is a vision so wide that it reduces any particular to utter insignificance. Such a view reveals the fact that "winning, equally with losing," in any of the games of life, is "below the zero of the true philosopher's concern" (HE, 257).[5]

The nature of the universe seen from this perspective is expressed figuratively in the key images of *The Dynasts*. The motif of the single thread in a cloth reappears there when the Spirit of the Years says that the story of the Napoleonic Wars is "but one flimsy riband" of the "web Enorm" woven by the Immanent Will through "ceaseless artistries in Circumstance / Of curious stuff and braid" (D, 521-522). Along with this image goes another, that of a monstrous mass in senseless motion. The writhing of the whole includes in its random movement all men and women driven by their desires and in-

---

compares it to characteristic strategies in eighteenth-century topographical poetry. Harold Child, in *Thomas Hardy* (London: Nisbet & Co., 1916), long ago saw that this "double vision" is "one of Mr. Hardy's distinctive gifts as novelist and dramatist." "If he sees the littleness," says Child, "he also sees the greatness. Watching from infinity, he sees human life as futile and trivial. Down in the stress and the turmoil, looking out from the very heart of some farmer or milkmaid, he shows human life heroically grand" (p. 21).

5 One might compare with this James Joyce's description of the way Hardy's contemporary, Henrik Ibsen, looked at life: "He sees it steadily and whole, as from a great height, with perfect vision and angelic dispassionateness, with the sight of one who may look on the sun with open eyes" (*The Critical Writings of James Joyce*, ed. Ellsworth Mason and Richard Ellmann [London: Faber and Faber; New York: The Viking Press, 1959], p. 65).

tentions. *Desperate Remedies* anticipates this motif too. In one scene Aeneas Manston looks into a rain-water-butt and watches as "hundreds of thousands of minute living creatures sported and tumbled in its depth with every contortion that gaiety could suggest; perfectly happy, though consisting only of a head, or a tail, or at most a head and a tail, and all doomed to die within the twenty-four hours" (DR, 245). Perfect image of man's life as Hardy sees it! In *The Dynasts,* published over thirty years after *Desperate Remedies,* the image reappears in Hardy's picture of the people of the earth, "distressed by events which they did not cause," "writhing, crawling, heaving, and vibrating in their various cities and nationalities" (D, 6), or "busying themselves like cheese-mites," or advancing with a "motion . . . peristaltic and vermicular" like a monstrous caterpillar (D, 290), or "like slowworms through grass" (D, 454). The actions of man are controlled by the unconscious motion of the universe, "a brain-like network of currents and ejections, twitching, interpenetrating, entangling, and thrusting hither and thither the human forms" (D, 118). Dreaming brain, network, web, mass of writhing, intertwined creatures — these images describe a universe in which each part is a helpless victim of the weaving energy which unconsciously knits together the whole.

Hardy's conception of human life presupposes a paradoxical form of dualism. There is only one realm, that of matter in motion, but out of this "unweeting" (D, 99) movement human consciousness, that "mistake of God's" ("'I Travel as a Phantom Now,'" CP, 429), has arisen accidentally, from the play of physical causes. Though the detached clarity of vision which is possible to the human mind has come from physical nature, it is radically different from its source. It sees nature for the first time as it is, has for the first time pity for animal and human suffering, and brings into the universe a desire that events should be logical or reasonable, a desire that people should get what they deserve. But of course the world does not correspond to this desire. This is seen as soon as the desire appears. Knowledge of the injustice woven into the texture of things does not require extensive experience. The young Jude musing under his hat perceives already the clash of man's logic and nature's: "Events did not rhyme quite as he had thought. Nature's logic was too horrid for him to care for. That mercy towards one set of creatures was cruelty towards another sickened his sense of harmony" (JO, 15). Like little Father Time in *Jude the Obscure,* Hardy is already as old as the hills when he is born, foresees the vanity of every wish, and knows that death is the end of life. To see the world clearly is already to see the folly of any involvement in it.

In Hardy's world there is no supernatural hierarchy of ideals or commandments, nor is there any law inherent in the physical world which says it is right to do one thing, wrong to do another, or which establishes any relative worth among things or people. Events happen as they do happen. They have neither value in themselves nor value in relation to any end beyond them. Worse yet, suffering is certain for man. In place of God there is the Immanent Will, and this unthinking force is sure to inflict pain on a man until he is lucky enough to die. Birth itself is "an ordeal of degrading personal compulsion, whose gratuitousness nothing in the result seemed to justify" (Td, 455). Best of all would be not to be born at all, as Hardy affirms poignantly in "To an Unborn Pauper Child" (CP, 116-117).

Both halves of the term "Immanent Will" are important. The supreme power is immanent rather than transcendent. It does not come from outside the world, but is a force within nature, part of its substance. It is a version of the inherent energy of the physical world as seen by nineteenth-century science: an unconscious power working by regular laws of matter in motion. Though what happens is ordained by no divine law-giver, the state of the universe at any one moment leads inevitably to its state at the next moment. Existence is made up of an enormous number of simultaneous energies each doing its bit to make the whole mechanism move. If a man had enough knowledge he could predict exactly what will be the state of the universe ten years from now or ten thousand. All things have been fated from all time.

The term "Will" is equally important. Hardy's use of this word supports Martin Heidegger's claim that a dualistic metaphysics leads to the establishment of volition as the supreme category of being.[6] Hardy recognizes that his nomenclature may seem odd, since what he has in mind is not conscious willing. Nevertheless he defends "will" in a letter of 1904 to Edward Clodd as the most exact word for his meaning: "What you say about the 'Will' is true enough, if you take the word in its ordinary sense. But in the lack of another word to express precisely what is meant, a secondary sense has gradually arisen, that of effort exercised in a reflex or unconscious manner. Another word would have been better if one could have had it, though 'Power' would not do, as power

---

6 For example, in "Nietzsches Wort 'Gott ist tot,'" *Holzwege* (Frankfurt am Main: Vittorio Klostermann, 1950), pp. 193-247.

can be suspended or withheld, and the forces of Nature cannot" (L, 320). Though the Immanent Will is not conscious, it is still will, a blind force sweeping through the universe, urging things to happen as they do happen, weaving the web of circumstances, shaping things in patterns determined by its irresistible energy.

The only hope for a change from this situation would be a gradual coming to consciousness of the Immanent Will. This odd version of "evolutionary meliorism," which Hardy considered himself to have invented,[7] is expressed in a number of his poems, most powerfully in *The Dynasts,* where the Spirit of the Years, after the reader has been shown all the senseless carnage of the Napoleonic Wars, foresees a time when all will be changed — "Consciousness the Will informing, till It fashion all things fair!" (D, 525). Hardy takes great pleasure in a number of his poems, for example, in "The Blow" (CP, 449), or in "Fragment" (CP, 482-483), in describing the anguish of the Immanent Will if it should become conscious and understand what exquisite tortures of suffering it has unwittingly imposed on man and on the animals over the centuries:

---

[7] In one of the letters to Edward Clodd about *The Dynasts* Hardy says: "The idea of the Unconscious Will becoming conscious with flux of time, is also new, I think, whatever it may be worth. At any rate I have never met with it anywhere" (L, 454). Another letter to Edward Wright, of June 1907, extends this claim of originality to suggest that the coming to consciousness of the Will will be no more than an extension of the consciousness which already exists in man: "That the Unconscious Will of the Universe is growing aware of Itself I believe I may claim as my own idea solely — at which I arrived by reflecting that what has already taken place in a fraction of the whole . . . is likely to take place in the mass; and there being no Will outside the mass — that is, the Universe — the whole Will becomes conscious thereby: and ultimately, it is to be hoped, sympathetic" (L, 335). For Hardy's use of the term "evolutionary meliorism" and a discussion of the idea behind it, see the "Apology" prefixed to *Late Lyrics and Earlier,* 1922 (CP, 526-527).

Should that morn come, and show thy opened eyes
All that Life's palpitating tissues feel,
How wilt thou bear thyself in thy surprise? —

Wilt thou destroy, in one wild shock of shame,
Thy whole high heaving firmamental frame,
Or patiently adjust, amend, and heal?
　　　　　　　("The Sleep-Worker," CP, 111)

"If Law itself had consciousness, how the aspect of its creatures would terrify it, fill it with remorse!" (L, 149). At this point in world history, however, the long expected event has not yet occurred. Mankind is "waiting, waiting, for God *to know it*" ("Fragment," CP, 482). This earnest expectation may or may not be fulfilled. Meanwhile man must endure things as they are. This endurance is made more painful by knowledge that if the Immanent Will does not come to consciousness the best man can hope for is that he will be lucky enough to "darkle to extinction swift and sure" (D, 525). The development of man is a mistake on the part of the vital energy of earth. Man is no more fit for survival than the dinosaur or the saber-toothed tiger.

This vision of the universe is presupposed throughout Hardy's writing. The philosophical passages in *The Dynasts* only make explicit what is implicit in his novels and early poems. His vision of things is one version of a world view widely present in the late nineteenth century. Its sources in his reading of Tyndall, Huxley, Darwin, Spencer, Schopenhauer, Comte, and others have been often discussed. It is impossible to demonstrate, however, that any one of these sources is uniquely important in determining Hardy's view of things. He read many of the writers who formulated the late Victorian outlook, and his notions were undoubtedly also acquired in part from newspapers, periodicals, and other such reading. What matters most is to identify the idiosyncratic emphases in his version of a current view, the personal elements in his response to this view, and the way all the aspects of his world view are involved with one another.

They are involved not in the sense that all flow from some single presupposition, but in the sense that the various elements might be spoken of as implying one another. Beginning with any one of them leads to the others as natural if not inevitable accompaniments. They form a system or structure. If consciousness is a lucid, depthless, anonymous awareness of what is outside it, a "point of view," a reflecting mirror, then the mind sees the world from a distance as something different from it in nature. The wider, the more detached, the more impersonal, the more disinterested, the more clear and objective a man's view is the closer he will come to seeing the truth of things as they are. This is the scientific or historical point of view, a natural associate of the bifurcation of the world into subject and object. Mind is seen as detached lucidity watching a world of matter in motion.

This motion in things appears to be caused by an intrinsic power within them, a power to which Hardy, like Schopenhauer or Nietzsche, gives the name will. If man is separated from the universe by the detached clarity of his mind, he participates in the motion of nature through his body, through the emotions that body feels, and through the energy of desire which engages him in the world. This energy seems to be within his control, but is actually only the working through his body of the universal will in its unconscious activities of self-fulfillment. For Hardy, man has a double nature, a power of thinking and understanding, and a power of doing, feeling, and willing. If through the latter he takes part in the endless physical changes of the world, through the former he recognizes that these transformations, even those "willed" by man, leave nature still indifferent to human needs, unstructured by any inherent system of value. If the world view of nineteenth-century science accompanies naturally the separation of mind from world, along with the scientific view goes that draining of value from the essence of matter of fact which Alfred North Whitehead has described in *Science and the Modern World*. Objects are merely objects. They behave as they do behave, according to universal and impersonal laws. Any human value they may appear to have is a subjective illusion cast over them by man's instinctive desire that the world should provide him with an environment corresponding to his needs.

The emptying of human significance from things is often associated with loss of religious faith. Only a world of hierarchical levels in participation easily allows for a God who is both within His world and outside it. In the dispersal which is likely to accompany the separation of existence into two realms, subject and object, mind and world, God may at first be seen as separating himself from his creation. He withdraws to a distant place and watches the universe from afar. The scientist in his all-embracing objectivity apes this conception of God. If the division of realms of existence appears complete, if there seems no inherence of God in my consciousness, in nature, or in other people, if there remain open no more avenues of mediation by which a distant God may be reached, however indirectly, as in the forlorn echo from an infinite distance in Matthew Arnold's "The Buried Life," then I may experience not the "disappearance of God"[8] but the death of God, that death which Hardy announces in "God's Funeral" (CP, 307-309).

The experience of the death of God seems a natural concomitant of a definition of man as pure consciousness and of everything else as the object of that consciousness. To the "deicide eyes of seers" ("A Plaint to Man," Cp, 306) God seems no more than a "man-projected Figure" ("God's Funeral," CP, 307). God is killed by the attainment of that all-embracing vision which makes man a seer. The span of perfected human consciousness, separate, pure, clear-seeing, is as wide as the infinite universe it beholds, a universe now revealed to be made of blazing suns in a black void. Such a universe is shown to Lady Constantine by the young astronomer, Swithin St. Cleeve, in *Two on a Tower*. "Until a person has thought out the stars and their interspaces," says Swithin, "he has hardly learnt that there are things much more terrible than monsters of shape, namely, monsters of magnitude without known shape. Such monsters are the voids and waste places of the sky" (TT, 33). In such a view the detachment of the watching mind corresponds to the infinite breadth of the universe it beholds. Both are equally null, nullity reflecting nullity, man and all his concerns reduced by the terrible impersonality of space to infinitesimal specks in a measureless hollow. "There is a size," says Swithin, "at which dignity begins . . . ; further on there

8 See *The Disappearance of God: Five Nineteenth-Century Writers* (Cambridge, Mass.: The Belknap Press of Harvard University Press, 1963) for my attempt to investigate this theme in the work of several Victorian poets.

is a size at which grandeur begins; further on there is a size at which solemnity begins; further on, a size at which awfulness begins; further on, a size at which ghastliness begins. That size faintly approaches the size of the stellar universe. . . . [If] you are restless and anxious about the future, study astronomy at once. Your troubles will be reduced amazingly. But your study will reduce them in a singular way, by reducing the importance of everything . . . It is quite impossible to think at all adequately of the sky — of what the sky substantially is, without feeling it as a juxtaposed nightmare" (TT, 34-35).

Such a sense of man's place in the universe is not too different from that of his contemporary, Friedrich Nietzsche, but Hardy's response to this vision is radically different. It is in this response that his special quality must be sought. As a number of critics have seen, his attitude is in some ways strikingly similar to that of Nietzsche's predecessor, Arthur Schopenhauer, the philosopher whose dissertation *On the Four-fold Root of the Principle of Sufficient Reason* Hardy read in 1889 or 1890 in Mrs. Karl Hillebrand's translation.[9] Nietzsche defines man as the will to power. In a world of amoral determinism man should take matters into his own hands, become a center of force organizing the world into patterns of value. The man of relentless will can turn his life from fated repetition into willed repetition and

9 See Carl J. Weber, *Hardy of Wessex,* revised ed. (New York: Columbia University Press; London: Routledge and Kegan Paul, 1965), pp. 246-248, for a description of the marginal notes in Hardy's copy of this book.

so escape into a paradoxical freedom. Hardy, like Schopenhauer's saint or artist who has lifted the veil of Maya, is more passive and detached. Like so many of his countrymen, like Dickens for example, he fears the guilt involved in becoming the value-giving center of his world. Willing means yielding to those emotions which orient a man toward other people. The longing for power and ownership involves a man in the swarming activity of the Immanent Will, and so alienates him from himself, as Napoleon in *The Dynasts,* surely a man of will, is nevertheless only an instrument of impersonal forces working through him.

Each man, in Hardy's view, has a paradoxical freedom. His own power of willing is, as in Schopenhauer's system, only his embodiment of a tiny part of the vast energy of the Immanent Will. Even so, a man's will is apparently under the control of his mind, or at least it expresses the intentions of that mind. This means that if the other powers around him are in a momentary equilibrium he can act freely rather than being pushed by external energies. Hardy returns frequently to this notion and always expresses it in the language of physical forces in interaction, as when he speaks of "the modicum of free will conjecturally possessed by organic life when the mighty necessitating forces — unconscious or other — that have 'the balancings of the clouds,' happen to be in equilibrium" (CP, 527), or as in a stanza from a poem of 1893, "He Wonders About Himself":

> Part is mine of the general Will,
> Cannot my share in the sum of sources
> Bend a digit the poise of forces,
> And a fair desire fulfil? (CP, 480)

The language here reveals how little free Hardy's concept of free will is. As part of the general will his individual will expresses that of which it is a part. It is moved with the whole, even though in unusual circumstances of balance it may be the part of the general will which gives the push to things. His freedom is in fact servitude, as the note of interrogation in this poem suggests. Another text on the theme makes this even clearer. It uses an odd metaphor which suggests that the free will of the individual is no more than his power to move independently, but automatically, according to patterns that have been implanted previously by the "Great Will": "whenever it happens that all the rest of the Great Will is in equilibrium the minute portion called one person's will is free, just as a performer's fingers are free to go on playing the pianoforte of themselves when he talks or thinks of something else and the head does not rule them" (L, 335). Once more the image of the digit occurs. Man is at best no more than a forefinger of the universal sleep-walking giant. Another such text describes the Will as "like a knitter drowsed, / Whose fingers play in skilled unmindfulness" (D, 2). Even when the individual will acts with the paradoxical freedom of a self-acting finger it is still no more than a portion of the universal Will. As a result, the more powerfully a man wills or desires, the more surely he becomes the puppet of an all-shaping energy, and the quicker he encompasses his own destruction. As soon as he engages himself in life he joins a vast streaming movement urging him on toward death and the failure of his desires.

Safety therefore lies in passivity, in secrecy, in self-effacement, in reticence, in the refusal of emotions and of their temptations to involvement. These temptations, however, are almost irresistibly strong, even for a man naturally so clear-headed as Hardy. Though the mind is different in essence from the physical motion of things as they are driven by the Immanent Will, it does not constitute a realm altogether apart. The mind of even the most detached and far-seeing man is still oriented toward the world, watching it, dwelling within it, open to its solicitations, subject to its glare and garish rattling. Like Joseph Conrad in *Victory* and elsewhere, Hardy frequently turns to a theme which is for both writers not without its grimly comic aspects: the story of a man who by luck or by deliberate effort of will has kept himself apart from other men and women, but is in spite of his aloofness lured into involvement and suffering. Boldwood in *Far from the Madding Crowd* is a good example of such a character. Nor was Hardy himself exempt from such experiences, in spite of his reticence and self-control.

In his fiction and in his life this loss of self-possession takes two principle forms: falling in love and yielding to the magical power of music. His love affair with his cousin Tryphena Sparks, if this indeed took place,[10] and his love for his first wife seem to have been, in their ambiguous complexity, the central events of his personal life. These events are reflected with varying degrees of obliquity in his writing, most directly in the poem, "Thoughts of Phena, at News of Her Death" (CP, 55), and in the poems he wrote after the death of his wife, the "Poems of 1912-13." Certainly these infatuations were the most important

10 See Lois Deacon and Terry Coleman, *Providence and Mr. Hardy* (London: Hutchinson, 1966) for an attempt to reconstruct this hidden episode in Hardy's life. It is probably an exaggeration, however, to make so much of his work an oblique dramatization of his love for Tryphena.

cases in which Hardy broke his instinctive reserve. The suffering which seems to have followed in both cases can be glimpsed here and there in the sparse evidence about his private life. This suffering gives his life a pattern much like the recurrent form of his fiction. It was not only Tryphena Sparks or Emma Gifford to whom he responded, however. A number of examples are given in the *Life* of his penchant, as a boy and as a young man, for falling passionately in love with girls he had glimpsed from a distance (L, 25-26). The poem "To Lizbie Browne" (CP, 118-120) commemorates one of these episodes:

> But, Lizbie Browne,
> I let you slip;
> Shaped not a sign;
> Touched never your lip
> With lip of mine,
> Lost Lizbie Browne!

As for Hardy's response to music, a curious passage in the *Life*, a passage almost adjacent to the text describing the young boy's retreat under his hat, shows how he shared with the characters in his fiction a strong susceptibility to it:

He was of ecstatic temperament, extraordinarily sensitive to music, and among the endless jigs, hornpipes, reels, waltzes, and country-dances that his father played of an evening in his early married years, and to which the boy danced a *pas seul* in the middle of the room, there were three or four that always moved the child to tears, though he strenuously tried to hide them. . . . This peculiarity in himself troubled the mind of "Tommy" as he was called, and set him wondering at a phenomenon to which he ventured not to confess. He used to say in later life that, like Calantha in Ford's *Broken Heart,* he danced on at these times to conceal his weeping. He was not over four years of age at this date. (L, 15)

An admirably suggestive and revealing passage! He was of "ecstatic temperament" — the phrase is a strong one. In spite of his self-enclosure, his cultivation of a watchful detachment, Hardy was so subject to the lure of the outside world that music could draw him out of himself, destroy his self-control, and reduce him to helpless tears. His response to music, however, is more than a reaction to the objective beauty of a moving melody. It is also a mediated reaction to other people, those who have invented the tune or who play it. The boy weeping as he listens to music is as much subject to his father as to the melody. It is this double enslavement which so troubles him. The power of music is like the power of a beautiful woman. In both cases an overwhelming emotional reaction draws his soul involuntarily out of his body and makes him the puppet of someone outside himself, as the children were entranced by the Pied Piper of Hamelin.

This association between music and love is dramatized in that admirable short story, "The Fiddler of the Reels" (1893). The Fiddler, "Mop" Ollamoor, plays so magically that he could "well-nigh have drawn an ache from the heart of a gate-post. He could make any child in the parish, who was at all sensitive to music, burst into tears in a few minutes by simply fiddling one of the old dance-tunes he almost entirely affected — country jigs, reels, and 'Favourite Quick Steps' of the last century" (LLI,

167). Mop's power is also sexual, and his sexual magnetism works by way of his music. Like a young girl Hardy once heard whose singing had the power of "drawing out the soul of listeners in a gradual thread of excruciating attention like silk from a cocoon" (L, 118),[11] Mop can "play the fiddle so as to draw your soul out of your body like a spider's thread" (LLI, 170). The story tells how he enthralls a young country girl, Car'line, steals her away from her betrothed, seduces her, and some years later once more hypnotizes her with his playing so that he can abduct the child born of their union. Music and love — both are an irresistible fascination.

Rather than yielding in complete abnegation of will to the lure of music and love, as does Car'line, Hardy fights for his independence. This is not easy to do. It is one thing to withdraw under his hat in a moment of solitude and decide not to involve himself in the world. It is quite another to remain in possession of himself while his father is playing the fiddle or when he sees a pretty girl. In fact it is impossible. The tears flow involuntarily; his soul goes out of his body. The best he can do is to hide his tears, keep his love secret, as he did from the various girls he loved when he was an adolescent.

This hiding takes a curious form. In the passage cited above Hardy dances on to conceal his weeping. The dancing is a response to the emotive power of the music, but it is an indirect, covert response, a transposition of the helpless and self-betraying tears into a more or less impersonal and socially accepted form of behavior. In dancing the uncontrolled tears and the lax flowing out

---

[11] The poem called "The Maid of Keinton Mandeville" (CP, 533-534) is a description of this girl and her singing.

of the soul into the world are turned into the controlled expression of art. This art is a way of being involved in the world and of responding to it without being swallowed up by it. It holds things at a distance and imitates in another pattern the objective patterns in the outside world which have held his attention through their power to generate an emotional fascination. Such an art is at once a reaction to the external world, and a protection against it. It is a transformation of the reaction into a shape which imitates it at a distance.

Exactly this pattern can be seen in another passage from the early pages of the *Life*. Once more there is a strong emotional response to the qualitative aspects of an experience. The experience is accepted and yet held at arm's length through its change into the objective form of a work of art. The text comes between the one about the young Hardy's response to music and the one about his desire not to grow up:

> In those days the staircase at Bockhampton (later removed) had its walls coloured Venetian red by his father, and was so situated that the evening sun shone into it, adding to its colour a great intensity for a quarter of an hour or more. Tommy used to wait for this chromatic effect, and, sitting alone there, would recite to himself "And now another day is gone" from Dr. Watts's Hymns, with great fervency, though perhaps not for any religious reason, but from a sense that the scene suited the lines. (L, 15)

The same elements are here: the bright red wall which draws him to watch for its special intensity at sunset; the holding back from the danger of his response not by destroying the response or by turning away from it, but by transmuting it into another form which matches it at a distance, the fervency of the singing corresponding to the intensity of the red wall at sunset. The fundamental structure of Hardy's relation to the world may be identified through the juxtaposition of these homologous texts. In all of them the mind confronts in detachment a world which is seen as possessing dangerous energies, energies which are yet ambiguously attractive. There is a refusal of direct involvement, but there is also discovery of a means of indirect response. Hardy's preference for such responses may help to explain why he became a writer and what relation to the world his writing expresses.

II

From the Real to the Fictive

THE FACT THAT A GIVEN PERSON becomes a writer is easy
to take so much for granted that it is never put in question. If Hardy had not become a writer students of literature would not concern themselves with him at all. To
our retrospective eyes Hardy the man and Hardy the writer
seem identical. He would not have been himself unless
he had written *The Mayor of Casterbridge,* "Wessex
Heights," and so on. It is also true that there were prac-
tical reasons why he became a writer. He needed to make
a living. Writing was one of the professions open to him.
His early writings showed promise, and he was urged to
continue. Writing was a profession that might win him
social prestige and the acquaintance of interesting people.

This is true enough, and yet it does not seem a complete explanation. There was a time when he was not a
writer, a time when he had a more or less secure career
before him as an architect. The reader of the *Life* will
know that, as in the case of Joseph Conrad's shift from
the sea to writing, Hardy's change of vocation was made
tentatively and slowly, with many waverings and uncer-

tainties. In spite of the social approval writing sometimes receives, it is a particularly lonely and difficult profession. In requires the ability to sit for long hours alone covering blank sheets of paper with words, creating out of the mind's power over the fingers, the pen, the ink, a world which comes into existence only in the words and which, at the time it is written down, has not yet been ratified by any reader as good or bad, authentic or inauthentic. This is so odd a way to spend one's life that it is likely a man will persist in it only if doing so solves some problem for which no better solution can be found.

Jean-Paul Sartre, however, is surely wrong to claim that a novel or a poem is an "unreality."[1] A novel is real enough. It is a physical object which may be held in the hand. It is as real as a road-sign or a road, a chessboard, a hammer, a house, a church, a flower. All things in the human world are both real and unreal, both physical objects and their significances, and the significances cannot be separated from their physical embodiments. As recent philosophers and linguists have argued, a word is not an empty sign to which a meaning is arbitrarily attached from the outside. Language is always already meaningful. Every word has significance only as part of a total structure of language which is implicitly present even for the child speaking his first words. Each utterance has meaning only as part of all the utterances which together form the complete articulation of meanings involved in man's collective inherence in the world. What is true for language is true also for games, tools, artifacts, buildings, and even for natural objects like flowers. Each

---

[1] Jean-Paul Sartre, *The Psychology of Imagination*, trans. anon. (London: Rider & Co., 1950), p. 211.

of these is encountered as already there and as already containing its meaning as an intrinsic part of itself. The ambiguous combination in a word of a physical substratum and an inextricably intertwined meaning provides a model for the way all things exist for man.

The words of a novel have the same kind of meaning as any other kinds of words. The act of reading or writing a novel is therefore no more unreal than the interpretation of a hammer as being of the proper size to drive a certain nail, or than the interpretation of a road-sign as fixing the traveler's location five miles from Penzance, or than the interpretation of the chessmen and chessboard as the scene of a complex conflict of opposing powers. All these acts of interpretation are ways of living in the world, acting in the world, finding significances in the world. The novelist seated at his desk writing *Tess of the d'Urbervilles* or the man in his armchair reading it are as much in the real world as the carpenter, the chess-player, or the motorist. To cover paper with words or to hold a book in one's hand and follow the words with one's eyes is as real an act as to talk to another person, to make love, to till the soil, to operate a machine. All ways of living are modifications of the primordially given human situation, which is to be inextricably involved in the world, participating in it, interpenetrated by it, moving within it from one significance to another, giving it meaning, finding meaning in it, being given meaning by it.

Nevertheless, in spite of the continuity between writing or reading a novel and other human actions, involvement in a fictional world has its own structures, structures which in Hardy's case can be seen to have had special attractions. Just as Conrad, after his experiences in the

Congo, could no longer live an active life as a seaman, but turned to writing as the only safe way of being related to the truth of life, so Hardy's lifelong commitment to writing seems to have been a strategy for dealing with the situation in which he found himself. To choose to be a writer is to go beyond the spontaneous withdrawal from life which has already occurred when he first becomes aware of himself. The position of the silent, detached spectator was as unstable for Hardy as it was for Conrad. Neither man could continue to "look on and never make a sound."[2] Spectatorship is still a mode of involvement. The watcher is still vulnerable to the beckoning solicitations of the world. The logical step beyond detachment, and the only means of preserving it, is the one taken by so many of Hardy's characters when they reach his own wide vision of the way things are. They leave the world altogether. This step is taken by Aeneas Manston, by Eustacia Vye and Wildeve, by Winterborne, by Henchard, by Tess, by Jude. Hardy does not choose death. He becomes a writer instead. Writing is for him a way to accept safely that involvement in the world which is inevitable as long as life lasts.

The writer remains alive, covering sheets of paper with words. His action has a further involvement in reality. A novel is related in one way or another to its author's experience of real people and places. In Hardy's case, in spite of his tendency to deny the connection of his stories with his own life or with people he had known, the relation between his fictional world and the real one is unusually close. This relation is especially evident in topography and setting. "Wessex" is closely modeled on

2 Joseph Conrad, *Victory* (London: J. M. Dent and Sons, 1948), p. 176.

the actual landscapes, towns, houses, and roads of Dorset, Somerset, Cornwall, and Devon. How close is suggested by the photographs included in the definitive editions of his work. There the reader may see a picture of the house in Casterbridge where Lucetta lives in *The Mayor of Casterbridge,* Bathsheba's farm in *Far from the Mading Crowd,* the unoccupied manorhouse where Tess and Angel Clare take refuge after the murder of Alec d'Urberville in *Tess of the d'Urbervilles,* and so on.

Here is an admirable opportunity to explore the ambiguities of fictional realism! The settings of Hardy's novels are as close to reality as a mirror image or a photograph. And yet neither a mirror image nor a photograph is the reality it represents. Both are the transposition of reality not into unreality, but into another form of reality. The same thing may be said of the novels. They are based on reality and depend on it in the same ambiguous way that the name of a thing depends on the existence of the thing for its meaning and yet in a sense brings the thing into existence by assimilating it into the totality of names and meanings. The novels, in a similar way, spring off from the historical and physical reality which was their "source" to create another kind of reality, the kind proper to a work of fiction. The reality of a novel exists only in the words on the page in their interaction. It is brought into existence for the reader through his response to those words, just as a chess game is embodied in the placing of the pieces on the board and is created by the players' interpretation of the configuration of the pieces. For this reason the search for Hardy "originals," like the search for Dickens or Faulkner originals, valuable as it may be for the establishment of historical fact, is of limited value for the understanding of his fiction. The value is in the recognition of the difference between the original and the place or character in the novel. This difference lies not so much in the fact that a creative writer distorts or transforms his sources according to the laws of his imagination as in the fact that the character or place in a novel exists in a different dimension of reality, a dimension purely verbal in nature, but nonetheless real.

The fallacy of the theory of art as an unreal mirror image may be experienced most vividly, perhaps, by a visit to a place which has been transposed into a novel. To visit the Vale of Blackmoor or the Froom Valley after reading *Tess of the d'Urbervilles* is not at all to have a sudden illumination about the meaning of the novel. It is rather to have a curious sense of doubleness which might be expressed by saying, "Yes, I see the similarity, and I see how Hardy based the scenes in his novel on these landscapes, but it is not the same, not the same at all. These hills, villages, and rivers have one kind of reality; the hills, villages, and rivers in the novel have another. To understand *Tess of the d'Urbervilles* I must go back to the novel and read it again with all my attention concentrated there. Only in those pages shall I ever encounter Marlott, Talbothays Dairy, or Welbridge House, or have a chance to understand Tess, Angel, or Alec."

If the value of a visit to the Hardy country lies in the recognition of the difference between the reality of landscape or history and the reality of fiction, the same thing may be said of the relation between Hardy's life and his writing. *A Pair of Blue Eyes* is based in part on his courtship of Emma Lavinia Gifford, and *Jude the Obscure*, it may be, reflects his youthful love affair with Tryphena Sparks. But Emma did not have four lovers, nor did she die soon after her marriage to the fourth, and Hardy's relation to Tryphena did not follow the course of Jude's love for Sue. He has transposed one reality, his own experience of life, into another no less real realm. This second reality is related to the first, but differs from it in substance and structure. His life was incarnated in the acts of real men and women. His fiction is embodied in that other reality of words and is accessible only there. The "sources" of his fiction in his life can no more explain the meaning of that fiction than a photograph of the River Froom can explain the function of the Valley of the Great Dairies in *Tess of the d'Urbervilles*.

The concepts of "reality," of "history," and of "source" are, moreover, extremely problematical. The attempt to explain a novel by means of its sources in history or in the life of its author springs from a desire to avoid the difficulties of interpretation by finding a solid ground outside the text on which it is "based," to which it corresponds in one way or another, and against which it may be measured for its representative adequacy. To find such a source would provide an escape, so it seems, from the complexities of meaning within the text, as each scene, metaphor, or event draws its meanings from other analogous ones, those from the others, and so on indefinitely in a circling of mutually begetting significances. If the distinction between "real" and "fictive" is a false one, however, if things in the real or historical world are already human interpretations of some physical substratum, and if things in the fictive world are no more unreal or imaginary than any other significant things, then the "real world" (that of a historical time or that of the author's experience of life) cannot constitute a base or origin, an unmoving center which will immobilize the ambiguous interplay among meanings in the text and give it a stable, spatialized meaning.

The relation of a novel to its sources is not that of a sign to a referent which is unequivocally factual, but that of one sign to another sign, one human meaning to another human meaning. The facts of Hardy's life or of nineteenth-century European history are not physical objects. They are human significances, interpretations which are themselves in need of interpretation. They can only be interpreted in terms of other significances which are anterior to them, and those anterior ones to others more anterior still, so that a true beginning or source can never be reached.[3] If interpretation of the relation among the various parts of the text of a novel (metaphors,

---

[3] Speaking of the nineteenth-century revolution in the theory of interpretation initiated by Marx, Nietzsche, and Freud, Michel Foucault has described recently this "refus du commencement," the refusal to believe that it is possible to go back to an unequivocal beginning which is the foundation of everything following, its genetic source and explanation. Whenever the interpreter thinks he has reached an absolutely original base, behind which it is impossible to go, he finds himself only face to face with something which is itself already an interpretation, that is, something which refers to something still further back, and so on indefinitely. "There is nothing absolutely first to interpret," says Foucault, "because at bottom everything is already an interpretation, each sign is in itself not the thing which offers itself to interpretation, but interpretation of other signs" ("Nietzsche, Freud, Marx," *Nietzsche,* Cahiers de Royaumont, Philosophie N° VI [Paris: Les Éditions de Minuit, 1967], pp. 188-189, my trans.). This rejection of beginnings was present in the nineteenth century not only in radical philosophers like Nietzsche but as a common late Victorian reaction against the belief in "origins" or the search for them of the mid-century. Opposed to the linear view of history in the geologists and Darwinians (Darwin's great book, after all, is called *The* Origin *of Species*), there is a widespread Victorian commitment to a vision of history as cyclical repetition, as in Arnold and Tennyson. George Eliot in 1876 already makes the "refus du commencement" of Nietzsche or Foucault. In the epigraph to the first chapter of *Daniel Deronda* she "begins" her novel by telling the reader that though "men can do nothing without the make-believe of a beginning," nevertheless Science like Poetry "with his clock-finger at Nought really sets off *in medias res,*" for "no retrospect will take us to the true begin-

characters, scenes, events) is an entry into the endless
spirals of the hermeneutical circle, the interpretation
of the relation between a literary text and its sources is
another example of the same circle. Hardy's poems about
his wife written after her death are an interpretation of
the facts of his life, but his response to Emma Lavinia
Gifford when he first met her was already an interpretation. This response had its analogies in still earlier responses to girls, and each of these needs all the others for
its elucidation. The "factual" descriptions in the *Life* of
these episodes in Hardy's youth were written down long
after the event and are no less imaginary reconstructions
than are the "Poems of 1912-13." In all these cases the
text interprets and clarifies its sources as much as the
sources clarify and interpret the text. Each sustains and
generates the meaning of the other. Each is both real
and unreal.

The reality of a novel, however, is of a special kind.
The nature of the act of writing will determine in part

ning"; *Daniel Deronda*, I, *Works*, Cabinet Edition (Edinburgh and
London: William Blackwood and Sons [1877-1880]), p. 3. Hardy's habitual
strategies in fiction and in poetry are consonant with this late Victorian
atmosphere of thought. He usually begins a novel or a lyric at a moment
when certain determining events have already occurred, and his stories
and poems are structured as a series of repetitions in which no event is
definitively the first. Each event refers to an earlier similar episode which
has happened either to the same person or to some other person, that
episode to one still earlier, and so on, the sequence echoing back into the
mists where man's retrospective knowledge is lost. For Hardy as for
George Eliot or for Nietzsche there is "behind each cave a deeper cave,
. . . a bottomless abyss beyond every 'bottom,' beneath every 'foundation'
[*ein Abgrund hinter jedem 'Grunde,' unter jeder 'Begründung'*]" (*Jenseits
von Gut und Böse*, paragraph 289, *Werke*, ed. Karl Schlechta, II [Munich:
Carl Hanser, 1954], 751; English translation by Marianne Cowan, *Beyond
Good and Evil* [Chicago: Henry Regnery Co., 1955], p. 232).

the nature of its product. Hardy knows that a novel, however directly it may be an interpretation of his response to real people and real places, nevertheless has only a verbal reality. He is making up from sentence to sentence the words which bring the story into being. This act is involved in the real world in three ways, each oriented toward a different dimension of time. The novel grows out of his past experience. As he writes it he is sitting at a certain time in a certain room, at a certain desk, using a certain pen, and so on. The novel is intended for its future readers. It is in a sense written to them and is thereby a form of communication with other people. Hardy writing one of his novels is as much entangled in past, present, and future as he would be in any other way of acting. All these involvements are, however, mediated, indirect, protected. To change the real world as he has experienced it into a fictional world is to nullify it, to hold it at a distance, to make it over into a linguistic form which renders it less dangerous. The real world is a glare and garish rattling, mysteriously threatening. A novel is only words. The act of writing a novel is the covert exercise of a sovereign power over the world. It neutralizes it. To write or to read a novel presupposes the absence of the real events or places the novel is "based on" and their replacement by a new reality of words.

Moreover, writing a novel is a solitary act. The writer has withdrawn from direct engagement. He sits alone, safe in his study, protected from the eyes of others and from the dangers of direct involvement. Though he is in a real room and performing the physical act of covering paper with words, he is turned away from what is immediately before him and dwells in the imaginary realm his words create. His words fall lightly on the paper and change it into a means of access to a new world which is visible nowhere in the room. This new realm is generated in an act which pays little attention to the room as a place in which to live. In the same way the reader of a novel, sunk in his armchair, is both within his immediate surroundings and outside them. Turning the pages of a book and following the words with attentive eyes is as real a form of behavior as any other, and yet the reader dwells apart, turned away in absence of mind to a place which exists only in the subtle pages of his book. Though a novel is written for others, it is an indirect form of communication with them. The novelist does not know his readers or confront them directly. Hardy's early work, like that of many other Victorian novelists, was first published anonymously. Moreover, in his fiction he speaks not in his own voice but in that of a narrator he has invented. In all these ways the act of writing has the evasiveness or insulation which he seems instinctively to have desired. Writing ratifies and preserves his spontaneous withdrawal to the periphery of things without pushing it to the ultimate withdrawal of death.

Here the necessity of a distinction between Hardy and his narrators has special force. If he knows that the novel, though to some degree an interpretation of real scenes and people, exists only in words, the narrators of his novels speak as though the events and characters were historical happenings, as if they had taken place before the eyes of a spectator who records what he has seen with the fidelity of an objective witness. Hardy's novels have little of the reflexive quality of Thackeray's fiction. *Vanity Fair,* for example, is often "anti-fiction" in the sense that it confesses to the fact that it is fiction, the puppet show and the puppeteer juxtaposed to reveal the illusory quality of the former. Hardy on the other hand almost always preserves the illusion. Only in the brief prefaces affixed to later editions of his novels does he speak in his own voice as Thomas Hardy and recognize explicitly that the novel is something which he has made up. An example is the first sentence of the preface to *Far from the Madding Crowd*: "In reprinting this story for a new edition I am reminded that it was in the chapters of 'Far from the Madding Crowd,' as they appeared month by month in a popular magazine, that I first ventured to adopt the word 'Wessex' from the pages of early English history, and give it a fictitious significance as the existing name of the district once included in that extinct kingdom" (FFMC, vii). To move from such brief, dry speeches of the puppeteer to the first words of the novel proper is to leap from one dimension of reality to another. In an instant the reader has gone to the other side of the looking-glass and is listening to another voice, a voice speaking as though the events of the story had a physical rather than a verbal reality. Most often this voice places the story in a specific place and time, introducing characters moving within a historical scene:

On an evening in the latter part of May a middle-aged man was walking homeward from Shaston to the village of Marlott, in the adjoining Vale of Blakemore or Blackmoor. (Td, 3)

One evening of late summer, before the nineteenth-century had reached one-third of its span, a young man and woman, the latter carrying a child, were approaching the large village of Weydon-Priors, in Upper Wessex, on foot. (MC, 1)

The narrative voice of Hardy's novels is as much a fictional invention as any other aspect of the story. In fact it might be said to be the most important invention of all, the one which generates the rest and without which the rest could not come into existence. The narrator of *The Mayor of Casterbridge* or *The Return of the Native* is a role Hardy plays, just as the characters of Pompilia, Caliban, or Fra Lippo Lippi are roles Robert Browning plays, placing himself in imagination within their experience and speaking for them. If the act of role-playing and its characteristic form, the dramatic monologue, are of fundamental importance for the development of nineteenth-century poetry, role-playing is no less important in the development of fiction. The novel depends, like the poetry of the dramatic monologue, on a man's power to enter into the lives of fictional characters and speak for their private experience, and just as Henry James was right to speak of "The Novel in *The Ring and the Book*,"[4] so it would be proper to speak of the dramatic monologue in *David Copperfield*. A third-person novel, however, is also a dramatic monologue and depends on a power of impersonation. The narrator of *Under the Greenwood Tree* is as much an invented character as is Bishop Blougram, as much to be distinguished from Hardy as Blougram is from Browning. Both "Bishop Blougram's Apology" and *Under the Greenwood Tree* are the self-expressions of their authors, but in both works the self-expression is disguised, indirect, covert. Just as it is a mistake to oppose nineteenth-century fiction to nineteenth-century poetry, labeling one realism and the other

---

4 *Notes on Novelists* (New York: Scribner, 1914), pp. 385-411.

an outgrowth of romanticism, so it is a mistake to oppose the "objective" fiction which is told by an omniscient narrator to "subjective" fiction which is told by a character involved in the events. Both *David Copperfield* and *The Return of the Native,* both the first-person subjective novel and the third-person objective novel, are objective and subjective at the same time. Or rather they put in question the distinction between subjective and objective. Both express in their narrators' points of view indirect ways of taking possession of the world. The omniscient narrator no less than the first-person narrator is an invented role which expands certain aspects of everyday ways of being related to the world and excludes others. Just as Guido Franceschini is an extension of attitudes Browning could imagine or understand, and therefore is in a sense Browning's expression of himself, so the omniscient narrators of Hardy's novels, with their godlike powers of detached insight, are an extension of his relation to other people and to the world. They emphasize certain aspects of that relation and avoid others. Like the poetry of the dramatic monologue, Victorian fiction, whether written from an omniscient or from a limited point of view is a response to a nineteenth-century atmosphere of concern for the perennial problems of literature, for epistemological questions (What is real?), for questions about selfhood and interpersonal relations (Who am I? Who are you? How can we know one another or love one another?), and for questions about perspective or point of view (How do I know what is real?).

Hardy's way of experiencing these questions and his use of the strategy of role-playing are, however, peculiar to him. They differ from those of other novelists as well as from those of the poets of the dramatic monologue. Though Browning, for example, like Hardy, was a man of reticence who sought to hide himself as well as express himself in his poetry of impersonation, the fundamental aim of his poetry was to explore as many as possible of the ways of feeling and being in the world, thereby transcending man's natural finitude and approaching, as curve its asymptote, the infinite plenitude of God. Hardy had no such metaphysical aim. His goal seems to have been to escape from the dangers of direct involvement in life and to imagine himself in a position where he could safely see life as it is without being seen and could report on that seeing. To protect himself and to play the role of someone who would have unique access to the truth — these motives lie behind Hardy's creation of the narrative voice and point of view which are characteristic of his fiction.

This may be seen not only in the special privileges he accords his narrator, but also in the scattered remarks he makes about point of view, particularly in his repeated affirmation that his work makes no claim to philosophical consistency, but is a series of "seemings," a reflection of the way things have appeared to him at one time or another. "The sentiments in the following pages," he says in the "General Preface to the Novels and Poems," "have been stated truly to be mere impressions of the moment, and not convictions or arguments" (Td, xii). The same thing is said repeatedly in the various prefaces to the books of poems. Even the most apparently auto-biographical portion of *Poems of the Past and the Present* "comprises a series of feelings and fancies written down in widely differing moods and circumstances, and at various dates," and therefore will "possess little cohesion of thought or harmony of colouring" (CP, 75). One of the volumes of verse is called *Moments of Vision*. In the preface to another he says that his work is "a series of fugitive impressions which I have never tried to co-ordinate" (CP, 527). In the final preface, that to the post-humously published *Winter Words*, Hardy is still affirming "that no harmonious philosophy is attempted in these pages — or in any bygone pages of mine, for that matter" (CP, 796).

Partly such assertions are a way Hardy forestalls hostile criticism, but the way in which he defends himself is revealing. It is a mistake, he says, to seek a coherent philosophy of life in his writings or to hold a single man responsible for this view of things. There is no single man behind what he has written. As he affirms in a late poem called "So Various," he is not one man but a multitude of men, brisk and old, a faithful lover and fickle, happy and sad, enterprising and unadventurous — "All these specimens of man, / So various in their pith and plan, / Curious to say / Were *one* man. Yea, / I was all they" (CP, 832). Hardy has no permanent personality, but changes from moment to moment according to his mood or his experience. His writing can therefore be nothing more than a discontinuous sequence of moments of vision, written as things seem first one way to him and then another.

This dispersal of the self into a multitudinous series of fugitive selves shifts over easily into the claim that the poems are not the direct expression of Hardy himself, but are dramatic monologues. There is in fact no "Hardy himself," only the series of momentary roles he plays as he gives voice to one or another of the ways things have seemed to him. The claim that his poems are dramatic monologues even where they do not seem to be so echoes through the prefaces to the various volumes. The *Wessex Poems* are "in a large degree dramatic or personative in conception; and this even where they are not obviously so" (CP, 3). Almost the same words are used in the preface to *Poems of the Past and the Present*, with a substitution of "impersonative" for "personative" (CP, 75). The poems in *Time's Laughingstocks* "are to be regarded, in the main, as dramatic monologues by different characters" (CP, 175).

What Hardy affirms so explicitly for the poems is no less true of the novels. They too are the expression of an assumed voice and attitude, for all his voices are assumed. He has no permanent character and must make the best in both fiction and poetry of a situation in which he can speak only in the person of the character who is appropriate to a temporary and fleeting way of looking at things. Any point of view is only one moment of vision among many.

The point of view Hardy in fact chooses for the narrators of his novels and for the speakers of his poems allows him to enjoy surreptitiously certain special privileges through the guise of an invented character. Here, as in most ways, the poems are continuous with the novels, and either may be used to cast light on the other.

Poem after poem sets a past event when the speaker was happily engaged in life against a present detachment when he has lost that happiness and looks back in retrospective meditation on the past. He sees that past now in the perspective of what followed it, and this double vision gives him a wisdom of disengagement. Such a relation of the self to itself combines closeness to experience and distance from it, blind absorption in life and withdrawn contemplation of a past self as if it were another person. This juxtaposition of past involvement and present reminiscent isolation is the characteristic structure of the poems. The irony of this juxtaposition is often generated by a return to the scene of the speaker's former happiness. The place is the same, but the speaker's situation is now radically different, and the persistence of the scene leads to a painful recognition that the past is irremediably past. In "Where the Picnic Was," for example, the last of the "Poems of 1912-13," the speaker returns to the scene of the previous summer's picnic. The charred sticks are still there, and the sea still "breathes brine," just as it did then, but the four people who shared the picnic are now separated forever:

> . . . two have wandered far
> From this grassy rise
> Into urban roar
> Where no picnics are,
> And one — has shut her eyes
> For evermore. (CP, 336)

In the same way, the speaker in "An Anniversary" (CP, 441-442) returns to a place at the same time of year a remembered event took place. He finds everything the same and yet not the same, for the tree then young is now old, new moss covers a wall, new headstones a cemetery, and "the man's eyes then were not so sunk that you saw the socket-bones." In "Paths of Former Time" (CP, 496) the speaker refuses to return to a scene once familiar because the person with whom he walked there is now dead. In "The Man Who Forgot" (CP, 503-504) the speaker thinks momentarily that it is forty years ago, and then is returned to the bareness of the real present. In "She Revisits Alone the Church of Her Marriage" (CP, 604-605) a woman finds the "fateful chancel" the same as it was long ago, and this sameness seems ironically disproportionate to the long years of change which were initiated there. In "The Old Neighbour and the New" (CP, 639) the speaker visits the new rector, but sees the old one, dead since the last September, as a ghostly presence in the parsonage.

All these poems, and many others, have the same form. The outside world remains much as it was in the past. This persistence gives the speaker power to be both within the past and outside it, simultaneously re-enacting a former involvement in life and seeing it from the cool perspective of a knowledge of what followed, enchanted and disillusioned at once. A few lines from "Under High-Stoy Hill" express with concentrated intensity the ironical combination of presence and absence which such poems express, and the brooding pain of reminiscence the experience generates:

> The moon still meets that tree-tipped height,
> The road — as then — still trails inclined;
>   But since that night
> We have well learnt what lay behind!
>
> For all of the four then climbing here
> But one are ghosts, and he brow-lined . . . (CP, 749)

"What lay behind!" The phrase is an odd one. The future, the words suggest, lay not *before* the four walkers as an unpredictable set of events, but *behind* the scene they walked in, as a latent presence within it. The landscape seems to be transtemporal. It contains past, present, and future, as the road connects the beginning and ending of the journey. The future lies hidden behind that part of the road the walkers have not yet reached, just as it now lies behind, in another sense, for the retrospective panoramic view of the speaker who looks back to see the particular "tree-tipped height" in the perspective of the whole span of the road where the four persons walked toward death. The poem juxtaposes present and past, proximity and distance, blind engagement in the part and clear knowledge of the whole.

This pervasive double vision in the poems is a more personal and compact version of the point of view habitual in the fiction. In the novels too the way of seeing is double, but the two perspectives are divided between the vision of the narrator and the vision of the characters rather than being expressed as the past and present attitudes of the same character. Between the narrator and the protagonist there is a distance, but the field of consciousness established within this distance has a structure similar to that of the relation of past involved self and present detached self in the poems. This doubleness is both temporal and spatial.

The past tense of the narrative in Hardy's novels is more than a convention. The events are placed firmly and precisely in a specific time in the past. As commentators have noted, his fiction covers the whole span of the nineteenth century, from the Napoleonic Wars to later decades which he had experienced in his own life, but there is always a gap between the narrator's time and the character's time. The nominal distancing of the past tense is reinforced by references to differences in customs, dress, and speech between past and present. The narrator constantly calls attention to his own location long after the events and to the perspective on the past this gives him. Sometimes this contrast between past and present gives an explicit dramatic form to the narrative, as in the "frame-story" of *A Few Crusted Characters* (LLI, 189-259). The protagonist of this collection of anecdotes returns to his native village after a long absence, intending to resettle there. He hears a sequence of stories told by the villagers, then reflects that the people about whom he has heard now all lie in the churchyard. This contrast between past and present realities shows the visitor that you can't go home again, or, as Hardy puts it in a poem, "nought happens twice" ("On the Departure Platform," CP, 206). The visitor is a revenant, a walking ghost, and he has no more place in the village than the dead men and women in the stories he has heard. When he recognizes this he leaves the village for good.

On the other hand, if the past tense and its various reinforcements function in Hardy's fiction to place the events at an unattainable distance in time, the mode of telling allows the narrator to enter into the experience of the characters and present these from the inside as if they were happening now. Often, as with most novels, the reader forgets that the past tense places the story at a distance and responds to it as if it had a present immediacy. The reader is both close to the action and far away from it in time.

The same doubleness exists in the spatial location of the narrator. The distancing of the choruses of spirits in

The Dynasts and the presentation of bird's-eye views of the events is present in the cinemalike attention to details of optical placement by the narrators in the fiction. The fiction often presents things in visual terms. The reader is usually placed in a specific location in space, often some distance from the events being described, as in the panoramic view of Casterbridge in *The Mayor of Caster-bridge* (MC, 29-30). The narrator tells the reader what was there to be seen and records this as a dispassionate spectator or camera-eye, occasionally calling attention to his detachment by saying something like: "an attentive observer would have noticed" (WT, 165), or "an acute observer might have noticed" (UGT, 131). There *is* an observer, of course, the invisible narrator, that privileged spectator who is a character in the story and yet not a character, a witness who can see and judge the other characters, even in their most private moments, but who can never be seen or judged by them in return.

The Mayor of Casterbridge provides examples of the cinematic technique of Hardy's fiction. He tends here, as throughout his work, to present each scene from a specific optical location and often goes out of his way to express meanings in terms of visual signs rather than in terms of explanation. The fact that Mrs. Newson is a widow, for example, is shown by the black-bordered card her daughter carries (MC, 21-22). The bad bread made from Henchard's wheat is shown in a brief vignette (MC, 33). A disastrous change in the weather is shown by a "shot" of the weathervanes swinging to a new direction (MC, 215).

The optical detachment of these spectator narrators is often sustained by a superimposition of the small and the large — a woven cloth with human history; worms, caterpillars, and cheesemites with the Napoleonic Wars; a living brain with the motion of the universe. The annihilating objectivity of his separation does not necessarily involve a physical distance from events as great as that possessed by the choruses in *The Dynasts*. The events may still be seen as if they were close by. Hardy is adept at making sudden relatively small shifts in perspective which put his reader virtually, though not actually, at an infinite distance from events — as if they were suddenly seen through the wrong end of a telescope. The reader is made aware that there are two ways of seeing events, a way which takes what is seen as the whole span of reality, and one which sees any perspective as only one among many possibilities and therefore as relative in the value it gives to things. To embrace any view of things with a wider, more inclusive view, or even one merely different, is to put both views in question. Even the widest vision is still limited and may be seen as large or small, inclusive or exclusive, depending on how one looks at it. What matters is not how much is included in the span of attention, but the way what is included is seen. There is a way of seeing which views both the activities of an anthill and the whole span of history as equally small and unimportant. Any number divided by infinity is zero, and Hardy's shifts of perspective are made on the basis of an infinite detachment which, in his arithmetic of vision, shows both the widest and the narrowest views as equally null. There are worlds within worlds within worlds, and to move from one to another is to recognize that the smallest world means as much as the largest and may be taken as an emblem of the pointless movement of the whole. Just as what Aeneas Manston watches in the rain-water-butt is a microcosm of the world of *Desperate*

Remedies and allows the reader to see it momentarily as a whole, so, in *The Return of the Native,* the "never-ending and heavy-laden throng" (RN, 343) of ants Mrs. Yeobright watches just before her death functions as a powerful symbol of human life in its aimless search for happiness. In a passage in the *Life* Hardy escapes from loneliness by shifting to a microscopic view of things: "I sit under a tree, and feel alone: I think of certain insects around me as magnified by the microscope: creatures like elephants, flying dragons, etc. And I feel I am by no means alone" (L, 107). These cases depend on a shift from large to small, as does the comparison of the English army to crawling caterpillars in *The Dynasts.* Other texts move from small to large, as when Hardy claims that mature wisdom involves the recognition "that all things merge in one another — good into evil, generosity into justice, religion into politics, the year into the ages, the world into the universe. With this in view the evolution of species seems but a minute and obvious process in the same movement" (L, 111). Or perhaps it would be better to say that such shifts in perspective involve seeing things simultaneously from close-to and from a distance.

The significance of the double perspective governing Hardy's point of view in his writing is given in a passage from the "General Preface" to his collected works: "by surveying Europe from a celestial point of vision — as in *The Dynasts* — that continent becomes virtually a province — a Wessex, an Attica, even a mere garden — and hence is made to conform to the principle of the novels, however far it outmeasures their region" (Td, xi). An ant hill, a garden, Wessex, all Europe — each is both small and large at once, small in relation to the infinity which surrounds it, large in that, however small it may be, it expresses the universal laws which govern the universe everywhere at all times. Hardy is always a local writer, in the sense that he concentrates on the particulars of gesture, speech, and event, but at the same time he sees any locality, however small or large, as representative of the whole. The people of Wessex are "beings in whose hearts and minds that which is apparently local [is] really universal" (Td, ix).

This universality is not left to the reader to discover for himself. The spatial and temporal detachment of Hardy's narrator manifests itself as a cool self-possession which allows him to make generalizations on the basis of some particular event in the story. Such generalizations explain the constant laws of which these events are a unique case. They place the particular in a context as wide as all time and space. The punctuation of his narrative with such objective generalizations is as important as the optic detachment of the point of view in establishing the distancing of the narrator from the events he describes. In *The Woodlanders,* for example, the narrator stops for a moment to say: "The petulance that relatives show towards each other is in truth directed against that intangible Cause which has shaped the situation no less for the offenders than the offended, but is too elusive to be discerned and cornered by poor humanity in irritated mood" (W, 95). Or he explains Eustacia Vye's renewed interest in Wildeve after he has deserted her for Thomasin by a generalization valid for innumerable such cases: "Often a drop of irony into an indifferent situation renders the whole piquant" (RN, 109). Or in "Barbara of the House of Grebe" he steps back from the story to tell the reader that "there is no more indiscreet mood than that of a woman surprised into talk who has long been imposing upon herself a policy of reserve" (GND, 70). In such texts the narrator's habitual spatial distance is strengthened by the psychological reserve this physical separation makes possible.

Though the narrator is spatially and psychologically detached, he can also present events from close to. This is evident partly in the careful notation of delicate details of sight and sound which runs through Hardy's fiction and through his poetry: "the flap of the flame, / And the throb of the clock" ("A New Year's Eve in War Time," CP, 516), the creak of the wind in a tree, the movement of an eyelid in a covert glance, the look of a closed window, the sound of running water in a brook, drops of water on a gate in February, the wayward indirection of conversation, details of domestic arrangement or farming practice — Hardy's writing is full of precise registration of fact. These are shown with great immediacy, as though they were just before the reader's eyes or ears. Such a power of close approach is also present in the way the subjective feelings, thoughts, and experiences of Hardy's characters are expressed. Like the narrator's observation from a distance, this gift of the introspection of others is an elaboration of powers possessed by human beings in the real world. If a man can see his fellows from the outside as a detached spectacle, he also has a power of sympathy which allows him on the basis of what he sees to enter into the life of another and share his experience. Seeing another person, his body, his gestures, his behavior, hearing his speech, a man knows something of what that other person is thinking and feeling. The reader has no sense that the narrator of *The Return of the Native*, for example, is claiming extraordinary powers when he presents from the inside Eustacia's feelings and thoughts or Clym Yeobright's yearnings. All men live in an intersubjective world. The existence of this realm makes fiction possible, for the novel is a form of literature which takes as its central theme the various ways in which minds may interact with one another.

At a distance in time and yet present as the events occur, a cold observer, spatially detached, seeing without being seen, and yet at the same time able to share the feelings of the characters, see with their eyes, and hear with their ears — a paradoxical combination of proximity and distance, presence and absence, sympathy and coldness, characterizes the narrator whose role Hardy plays.

All his life Hardy hated to be touched.[5] To be touched is to be incarnated, to cease to be a spectator, and to be brought physically into the world of others, to become vulnerable to their energy and will. He wanted to remain invisible, untouchable, a disembodied presence able to see without being seen or felt. This desire is expressed in a curious passage of 1888 in the *Life*. "For my part," Hardy says, "if there is any way of getting a melancholy satisfaction out of life it lies in dying, so to speak, before one is out of the flesh; by which I mean putting on the manners of ghosts, wandering in their haunts, and taking their views of surrounding things. To think of life as passing away is a sadness; to think of it as past is at least tolerable. Hence even when I enter into a room to pay

---

[5] See *Life*, 25: "He tried also to avoid being touched by his playmates. One lad, with more insight than the rest, discovered the fact: 'Hardy, how is it that you do not like us to touch you?' This peculiarity never left him, and to the end of his life he disliked even the most friendly hand being laid on his arm or his shoulder."

a simple morning call I have unconsciously the habit of regarding the scene as if I were a spectre not solid enough to influence my environment; only fit to behold and say, as another spectre said: 'Peace be unto you!' " (L. 209-210). Like the resurrected Christ, who said to Mary Magdalene in the garden, "Touch me not; for I am not yet ascended to my Father" (John 20:17), Hardy is a ghostly presence, a dead man who has not yet left his body or the world, and who yet is a specter not solid enough to touch his surroundings or to be touched by them. Like a ghost, he looks at the present not as a flowing sequence of vanishing moments with an unpredictable future, but from the perspective of death, as if it had long ago happened. This ghostlike view of things qualifies him to say, as the risen Jesus said to his disciples on two occasions, "Peace be unto you" (John 20:19, 26). Viewing things from the perspective of death takes away the pain of their passing and the uncertainty of their future by seeing them as if they had already joined the other things which make up the inalterable past. Best of all, this way of seeing things ensures the intangibility of the seer.[6]

The narrator Hardy invents for his novels is a projection into the realm of fiction of the way of seeing things he describes in this text. The narrator attains in fact (that is, as fact within the fiction) the invulnerability the author has in real life only in the mode of "as if." The narrator is within life and outside it. He can see everyone, but can be seen or touched by none of the other characters. Whatever happens to him, he remains safe,

[6] I have discussed this important text in the *Life* from a somewhat different perspective in " 'Wessex Heights': The Persistence of the Past in Hardy's Poetry," *The Critical Quarterly* (Winter 1968).

an intangible power of looking. This odd form of inherence in the world determines the quality of the narrator's language and the tone of voice the reader hears telling the story. It is present in one form or another in every paragraph Hardy wrote.

❦

A few pages of *Far from the Madding Crowd* offer an opportunity to watch in detail the advance and retreat of the narrator's consciousness as he identifies himself with his characters or moves so far away in time and space that the story he tells seems only an arbitrary example of laws valid everywhere at all times.

Chapter 22, "The Great Barn and the Sheep-Shearers," is memorable for its lively description of a sheep-shearing in a southwestern county of England. As Mario Praz might put it, the chapter forms a genre picture rich in precise detail, carrying a stamp of authenticity no reader can question.[7] Hardy has obviously seen what he describes, and the re-creation by his narrator of this high point in the sheep farmer's year is a good example of what is meant by "realism" in Victorian fiction — the more or less photographic representation of a specific historical reality. Against this background a certain moment of rearrangement in the relations of Bathsheba, Oak, and Boldwood takes place. My interest here is in the constant shifts of temporal and spatial perspective which form the narrative rhythm of the chapter. At one moment the

---

[7] For Praz's exploration of the parallel between Victorian fiction and genre-painting, see *La crisi dell'eroe nel romanzo vittoriano* (Florence: G. C. Sansoni, 1952); trans. Angus Davidson, *The Hero in Eclipse in Victorian Fiction* (London and New York: Oxford University Press, 1956).

reader is sharing a close observation of the events and an identification with the characters. At the next he is so far away in time and space that the events are seen from a godlike distance and with a godlike objectivity. Sometimes the reader is explicitly put in both these positions at once. In fact the alternation is so constant that the effect of the narrator's language is to maintain the reader simultaneously both close and distant throughout. As soon as the reader seems about to relax in his closeness, the narrator says something which throws him off to a great distance again, and like a juggler keeping two balls in the air, the narration sustains both points of view at once.

Though the narrative technique of a novel like *Far from the Madding Crowd* is a complex matter, making use of many conventions and habits of language inherited from earlier fiction, the reader of novels becomes so agile in the changes of point of view demanded of him that he is usually not aware of the imaginative gymnastics he is performing. Only if he makes an act of reflection on his experience as he reads, holds his experience at arm's length and looks at it, will he notice the complex superimposition of perspectives which structures a chapter of apparently straightforward realistic narrative. In order to make the reading of chapter 22 of *Far from the Madding Crowd* an experience at the second power, an experience conscious of its quality as experience, the reader must ask himself throughout the reading where he is being placed as a watcher and what is being presented to fill up the span of his attention.

The chapter opens with a generalization valid for all men in all times and places: "Men thin away to insignifi-

cance and oblivion quite as often by not making the
most of good spirits when they have them as by lacking
good spirits when they are indispensable" (FFMC, 163).
The reader at this point is nowhere and at no specified
time, looking at no particular scene in the novel. He is
merely listening to the disembodied voice of the narrator.
After the narrator's expression of a universal judgment
three sentences follow describing Gabriel Oak's habitual
state of mind and habitual action at this time of his life:
"But this incurable loitering beside Bathsheba Everdene
stole his time ruinously" (FFMC, 163). There is still no
particular scene to put before the mind's eye. The universal generalization has led to specific generalizations located in no particular place or action, but covering an
entire period of Gabriel's life. It is impossible to tell
whether Gabriel's "loitering" is to be thought of literally
or figuratively, though it appears to be the latter — a way
of saying that Gabriel spent much time thinking about
Bathsheba.

The next paragraph moves finally to a specific scene
located definitely in time and space. This scene is
initially, however, the landscape of a whole region. The
first sentence ("It was the first day of June, and the sheep-
shearing season culminated, the landscape, even to the
leanest pasture, being all health and colour" [FFMC, 163])
is followed by a list of flowers, "flossy catkins," "fern-
sprouts like bishops' croziers," and so on. These flowers
are either given in the plural or are collective names
("the toothwort"). The reader still has no local scene to
imagine, but has only been told the sorts of flowers he
would have encountered at that time on a walk through
the countryside of Wessex. Only at the end of this para-

graph, in a list of the men engaged in the sheep-shearing and in a description of their clothes, does the point of view narrow to a particular scene.

This narrowing leads to an elaborate picture of the shearing-barn in the next two paragraphs. Here at last the reader stands in imagination before a scene which he might view in one look if the novel were the real world or a stage set. This focusing of the point of view, however, is qualified by language which gives the reader a temporal perspective on the barn which no physical vision, cinema, or stage set could provide. The barn as it presently looks is placed in the context of the mind's knowledge of its four centuries of existence. The reader sees the present in the perspective of the past, with that double vision so characteristic of Hardy: "Standing before this abraided pile, the eye regarded its present usage, the mind dwelt upon its past history, with a satisfied sense of functional continuity throughout" (FFMC, 165).

The beginning of the next paragraph returns the reader firmly to the present: "To-day the large side doors were thrown open towards the sun to admit a bountiful light to the immediate spot of the shearers' operations" (FFMC, 165). This is followed by the detailed description of the sheep-shearing which occupies much of the remaining nine pages of the chapter. This presentation is so direct, so immediate in time and space, that it falls naturally at one point into the historical present, a narrative tense Hardy does not often use: "Cainy now runs forward with the tar-pot. 'B.E.' is newly stamped upon the shorn skin" (FFMC, 168). Nevertheless, such immediacy and precision of representation, which makes this part of the chapter read like a motion picture scenario, is held within the wide temporal and spatial context established at the beginning of the chapter and sustained by echoes of this distancing throughout the direct reporting. An example is the narrator's reminder to the reader that the dress and speech of the rustics are as traditional as the barn is old and make of their actions something approaching a timeless ritual. The peasants have little awareness of historical time; the narrator is vividly aware of it: "This picture of to-day in its frame of four hundred years ago did not produce that marked contrast between ancient and modern which is implied by the contrast of date. . . . Five decades hardly modified the cut of a gaiter, the embroidery of a smock-frock, by the breadth of a hair. Ten generations failed to alter the turn of a single phrase. In these Wessex nooks the busy outsider's ancient times are only old; his old times are still new; his present is futurity" (FFMC, 166).

Another example of the maintaining of narrative distance in the midst of close-up reporting is the description of Maryann, who, "with her brown complexion, and the working wrapper of rusty linsey, had at present the mellow hue of an old sketch in oils — notably some of Nicholas Poussin's" (FFMC, 173). None of the characters of the novel is thinking of Poussin at this moment, and most of them have never heard of him. The comparison establishes the narrator as a knowledgeable man of culture watching the scene with the detachment of a connoisseur, as if it were a painting. He places it in a historical and cultural context of which the participants in the scene are unaware. The presentation of the scene as though it were being recorded objectively by a camera is reinforced by various statements establishing a wide temporal and spatial perspective for it, the whole Wessex landscape in June, the four-hundred-year history of the barn, the context of European painting. To watch the scene with cool detachment as an invisible spectator is already to be more separated from the scene than any participant in it, and the interspersed notations preserving a wider mental withdrawal help to sustain this uninvolved observation of what is there to be seen and heard. The reader is held simultaneously within and without, close and distant.

The closeness, however, is more than that attainable by an imaginary spectator crouched in the rafters of the barn and watching the sheep-shearing below. Against the background of the rural ritual which is represented with such photographical fidelity is performed one of those dramas of self-consciousness and consciousness of others which make up the texture of Hardy's fiction. Such a texture means that much of his writing presents careful notation of what his characters think, do, or say as they live from moment to moment. More precisely, the characters are conscious of themselves in terms of their consciousness of others. This interaction between minds is not shown from the outside as something the narrator watches in detachment. It is presented from within, as something experienced directly. If the picture of a Wessex sheep-shearing is embraced within a context of knowledge implicitly as wide as all history, that picture in its turn embraces the inside of the inside, three of the central characters of the story in a crucial moment of their awareness of one another. This awareness is not fully shared by any of the other characters, but they are shown as in part sensitive to what is going on. The sensitivity of Bathsheba, Oak, and Boldwood to one another, and the narrator's power to enter into this sensitivity are made plausible by their emergence from a milieu of sympathetic understanding within which all the characters dwell. In varying degrees all the characters possess a power of intuitive knowledge of others. So Bathsheba stands over Gabriel as he shears, and Gabriel silently enjoys the blissful feeling "that his bright lady and himself formed one group, exclusively their own, and containing no others in the world" (FFMC, 167). His silence and her evasive chatter are the outward signs of an intense flow of emotion between them, a pressure of mutual awareness generated by his love for her and by her unwillingness to recognize or return that love. "There is," says the narrator, "a loquacity that tells nothing, which was Bathsheba's; and there is a silence which says much: that was Gabriel's" (FFMC, 167).

The lines of force created by this communication beyond words or beside words is interrupted by the entry of Boldwood. Boldwood's presence, even before he speaks, magically alters the pattern of interpersonal awareness within the barn, not only for Gabriel, but even for the relatively uninvolved rustics. Hardy is aware as much as George Meredith or Henry James of the power which the entry of another person may exert on an individual or on a group: "Boldwood always carried with him a social atmosphere of his own, which everybody felt who came near him; and the talk, which Bathsheba's presence had somewhat suppressed, was now totally suspended" (FFMC, 168-169). If all the people in the barn respond to Boldwood's presence, Bathsheba and Oak are even more sensitive to it. Boldwood's coming changes them not only in their relation to him, but in their relation to one another. The narrator offers the reader an exact registration of the dynamics of these changes. Bathsheba responds to Boldwood by altering her way of speaking:

"she instinctively modulated her own [tones] to the same pitch, and her voice ultimately even caught the inflection of his." The narrator then gives the general law of which this change of behavior is an example: "woman at the impressionable age gravitates to the larger body not only in her choice of words, which is apparent every day, but even in her shades of tone and humour when the influence is great." Gabriel's reaction to Boldwood's entrance is given not through a description of changes in his overt behavior, but by a penetration directly within his mind. The chapter here approaches as close as it has yet come to indirect discourse: "Standing beside the sheep already shorn, they went to talking again. Concerning the flock? Apparently not. Gabriel theorized, not without truth, that in quiet discussion of any matter within reach of the speakers' eyes, these are usually fixed upon it" (FFMC, 169). The narrator's point of view here coincides with Gabriel's, and the reader momentarily sees through Gabriel's eyes as he watches without being watched — that activity so often performed by Hardy's protagonists.

Gabriel is so upset by what he sees that he accidentally cuts the sheep he is shearing and is rebuked by Bathsheba. This episode leads to the most complex recording of the interaction between minds given in this chapter, a recording which includes five persons in their reactions to one another. There are references to an hypothetical unknowing outsider, to Oak's sensitive awareness of Boldwood and Bathsheba, to her awareness of him, to his awareness of her awareness of him, and the omniscient narrator embraces all these interactions in a single view. If the novel is a form of literature developed to explore the nuances of interpersonal relations, so adept do writers and readers become at following the complexities of such relations, perhaps because they are so expert at it in real life, that only a somewhat artificial interrogative stepping back brings to the surface the echoing crisscross of responses, mind answering to mind, recorded in an apparently simple passage: "To an outsider there was not much to complain of in this remark [Bathsheba's remonstrance]; but to Oak, who knew Bathsheba to be well aware that she herself was the cause of the poor ewe's wound, because she had wounded the ewe's shearer in a still more vital part, it had a sting which the abiding sense of his inferiority to both herself and Boldwood was not calculated to heal" (FFMC, 170).

The chapter then proceeds to note the general comprehension among the shepherds of Boldwood's love for Bathsheba. Though Gabriel's feelings are hidden from them, they have understood part at least of the significance of the scene enacted before their eyes: " 'That means matrimony,' said Temperance Miller, following them out of sight with her eyes" (FFMC, 170). This insight is echoed by other characters, but their attention drifts conversationally away to other matters, and the chapter ends with a counterpointed harmony made up of the juxtaposition of Gabriel's thoughts about Bathsheba presented as indirect discourse ("He adored Bathsheba just the same" [FFMC, 174]), and the irrelevant talk of the rustics which he and the narrator hear as a ground bass to the melody of his suffering. The continuo persists and gets the last word, which returns the reader to the objective watching of the invisible narrator:

"And there's two bushels of biffins for apple-pies," said Maryann.
"Well, I hope to do my duty by it all," said Joseph

Poorgrass, in a pleasant, masticating manner of anticipation. (FFMC, 174)

☙

The language of chapter 22 of *Far from the Madding Crowd* constantly moves the reader back and forth between proximity and distance. There is, however, a final form of distancing, one functioning implicitly throughout the chapter. I have said that the events are placed in a particular moment in the past. This seems to be no more than another way to hold the story at arm's length and see it in the perspective of the centuries which preceded it. There are, however, further implications of this.

Hardy's specification of the time in the past when the events took place establishes the novel as, like most fiction, an expression of the historical imagination. *Far from the Madding Crowd* re-creates sympathetically a particular time in the past and a particular culture flourishing in Wessex at that time. "At the dates represented in the various narrations," he says in the "General Preface to the Novels and Poems," "things were like that in Wessex: the inhabitants lived in certain ways, engaged in certain occupations, kept alive certain customs, just as they are shown doing in these pages" (Td, ix). The conventional past tense of the narration is a way of expressing the separation of the narrator from the culture he describes. He sees it in the perspective of history, as relative to its time and place. This distancing undercuts the assumptions and values which the characters share. It suggests that they might have been otherwise and implies the narrator's awareness that people at other times and places lived by other standards. Sympathetic re-creation is balanced by a recognition of the relativity of the culture which is so vividly brought back to life.

The temporality of the narrative in *Far from the Madding Crowd* is, however, more complex still. Though a particular moment of the action is often presented with great immediacy, so that it fills up the whole span of the reader's attention, the events are given as part of the flowing of time, that flowing which is suggested by the image of a man or woman moving across the landscape. This image is frequent in the poems and in the initial chapters of the novels. Each moment has an immediate past and an immediate future. As the reader watches Gabriel snip the sheep by accident, he remembers the silent happiness Gabriel enjoyed a few moments ago, before Boldwood entered, and he looks forward with indistinct anticipation to what will happen next, knowing that in all probability it will be brought into being by the motive power of the tension between the three main characters. Surrounding the reader's awareness of the immediate past and future is a vaguer memory of all that has preceded in the action and an indistinct anticipation of the future course of events which lies hidden from the present. As in real life, the present moment does not exist alone. It is surrounded by the other dimensions of time, permeated by them, and the reader's awareness reaches out toward past and future in an attempt to obtain a unified apprehension of present, past, and future in a single glance.

This presentation of the temporality of experience could, however, be made just as well through a present-tense narration. The use of the past tense serves to throw the immediate experience of each moment, with its particular reaching out toward past and future, back into the past as part of a completed sequence. The past tense constantly and unobtrusively reminds the reader that the narrator is in a radically different situation from that of any of the characters. They are living in a flowing present which has an uncertain and unpredictable future. He not only locates the events in the past, but enjoys by way of this placement the privilege of already knowing how the story came out. He tells the story not just from the perspective of a later time, but from the perspective of an explicit knowledge of what was for the characters hidden in the mists of the future. The reader can have both these experiences at once, in a paradoxical closeness and distance of relation to the present which is impossible in real life and which is one of the special privileges the reader of a past-tense novel shares with its narrator. The reader can put himself fully in this double position by reading the novel a second time. He is virtually in it even in the first reading, both because he holds the completed book in his hand and because he is constantly hearing a narrator who speaks as someone who already knows the story to the end. Both the first and second readings are valid, for the reader must maintain a sympathetic identification with the characters' experience of a present which as yet has only a potential future, and at the same time he must experience those moments as over. He must experience them as having already been followed by the events which completed them, the events which formed the sequence which was the ineluctable destiny of the characters. Hardy's concern for the fated, the sense of a cruel inevitability in his novels, is perhaps partly a product of his theoretical determinism, but it is also a natural consequence of the kind of narrator he chooses for his stories. From the point of view of a narrator who looks back at the completed pattern of events from a time much later in the future, those events appear as a necessary sequence. The reader who shares this perspective is led in his turn to see the events as fated.

Occasionally the fatalizing perspective built covertly into the form of the narration comes explicitly to the surface. When this happens the reader is made momentarily aware of the fact that the narrator is both close to the events in time and seeing them from long after. An example of this occurs in the chapter of *Far from the Madding Crowd* which follows the one I have analyzed. Bathsheba sings at the shearing-supper a song about a lady who marries a soldier, and the narrator, knowing of Sergeant Troy and his future relations to Bathsheba, comments: "Subsequent events caused one of the verses to be remembered for many months, and even years, by more than one of those who were gathered there" (FFMC, 179). Events which are not yet even dreamed of by the characters are seen simultaneously as the unborn future and as the fated past. The form of the narration at such moments becomes a powerful shaping force determining the meaning of the events.

This double temporal perspective is one expression of the open structure of human temporality. Human time is not a linear series with a beginning, middle, and end laid out in a spatial row. It is a present which moves toward a future which will be a perfected assimilation of the past and therefore make the life into a whole. Until life ends, however, this totality is not complete. Literature may express this structure in various ways. A novel told in the past tense by an anonymous narrator, like *Far from the Madding Crowd,* is one such way. The characters advance from moment to moment through time toward an unpredictable future. The narrator relives from within the present experience of the characters.

At the same time he sees that experience in retrospect. He sees each moment as part of the total life of the character. The narrator moves forward in his own time as he repeats in language the past experience of the characters. In this moving he approaches toward that moment when the experience of the protagonist will be complete in his retelling of it, a final wisdom attained, and the point of view of the character will coincide with that of the narrator. Whether that coincidence is ever attained in Hardy's novels remains to be determined, but as long as the novel continues, its temporal form remains open.

Hardy's narrative technique in chapter 22 of *Far from the Madding Crowd*, in its dependence on a gap between the narrator's point of view and the characters' points of view, is characteristic of his general practice in his fiction. The combination of proximity and separation, time present and time past, in one mixture or another, can be identified in any given passage from his novels. When he plays the role of the narrator he is already fulfilling that desire he expresses in a poem of 1915, the desire to "Travel as a Phantom Now" and to "visit bodiless / Strange gloomy households often at odds" (CP, 429). The narrator is the central figure in a structure of interpenetrating minds and multiple locations in time and space. The reader, the characters, Hardy himself — all these minds are brought together in the words of the text and held there in a complex relation by the guiding voice which tells the story.

A question remains unanswered. What need is satisfied by this invention of an unseen seer and of a world for him to see? If Hardy understands the nature of the world as soon as he steps back from it, and if he has made on the basis of this insight a firm decision to remain as uninvolved as possible, why does he not stay altogether detached? Why does he not remain a passive silent watcher, looking on without breathing a word, a meditative Buddha like that ideal spectator of Schopenhauer who, having lifted the veil of Maya, annihilates things by dreaming on them, frees them from the pain of their involvement in the universal will by absorbing them into his silence and inactivity? Hardy's career as a writer was an indirect form of involvement, certainly, but far from annihilating things through forgetful silence it preserved them indefinitely by representing them in words. His work is a verbal repetition and prolonging of reality.

The choice Hardy did not make is expressed with great power, curiously enough, in the last poem of the *Collected Poems*. The poem is called "He Resolves to Say No More," and the echoing repetitions of the last line of each stanza are a haunting refrain expressing Hardy's decision to let the reticence which has been covertly present in the tone of all his speech win out at last in the ultimate reserve of silence: "Yea, none shall gather what I hide!"; "What I discern I will not say"; "What I have learnt no man shall know" (CP, 887). The final stanza iterates once more his decision. His wide vision of life allows him to see the truth hidden from those blinded by their involvement, but this knowledge of the truth teaches him the wisdom of silence. His vision should perish with him, and so he resolves to say no more:

> And if my vision range beyond
> The blinkered sight of souls in bond,

> — By truth made free —
> I'll let all be,
> And show to no man what I see. (CP, 887)

The irony of this poem lies in the fact that though it was followed by silence, a silence imaged in the blank page at the end of the *Collected Poems,* and though it was published only after Hardy's death, nevertheless it comes at the end of eight hundred and eighty-seven pages of lyric poetry. The poems themselves were preceded by the many volumes of fiction. Hardy was anything but silent during most of his life, and it seems a grim joke for him to promise he will tell no man what he sees when he has been full and explicit for so many years in telling his readers exactly how life looks to him. Why did he spend his life in this telling?

The full answer to this question will emerge only through interpretation of further aspects of his work, but a preliminary hypothesis may be suggested here. Hidden in the disguise of a narrator with the special privileges I have described and turned in this disguise not toward the dangerous real world but toward a verbal reality which exists with physical solidity only for the imagined narrator, Hardy can explore in safety the various kinds of involvement which have been a temptation to him in spite of his fear of them, his suffering from them, and his foreknowledge of their defeat. His involvement in life when he writes is at a double remove. Imagining himself in the place of the narrator he can through that narrator share vicariously in the experience of the characters and allow those characters to test for him various ways of seeking happiness in the world. This indirect exploration of life is undertaken on the basis of a prejudgment which assumes that all forms of engagement lead ultimately to disaster, but at the same time he hopes his prejudgment may be mistaken. Perhaps somewhere, somehow, there is a way of direct involvement which will bring happiness. The lure of the world is so great, especially the lure of other people, women in particular. A glimpse of them seems to promise so much. Surely this beguiling promise is not illusory, and yet his instinct and his past experience tell him that it *is* false. The writing of fiction is a way of testing the validity of this instinct without risk. Hardy's work might be defined as a putting in question of the attitude of passive detachment by experiencing indirectly its opposite. If involvement turns out to be folly, then he is vindicated in his detachment. If not, then the folly is his.

He is therefore fascinated by the theme of fascination, not just a disinterested spectator of the drama of love. Novel after novel tells the story of someone who falls in love and then concentrates his life on attaining possession of the "well-beloved." The looking or spying which so often constitutes the drama of Hardy's scenes makes many of his characters like the narrator, but there is an all-important difference. His watchers at a distance, Gabriel Oak or Giles Winterborne or Elizabeth-Jane Henchard, are almost always infatuated with another person. Their watching has a focus. The person they love has become a center of the world for them. If love can be shown to lead to happiness, then it will constitute the only guiltless escape from the poverty of detachment. If a man becomes his own source of order, imposing himself on other people, creating patterns, and establishing relative values, he is implicitly recognizing that the world as it is has no given order or value. It is better not to act at all.

Hardy seems condemned to this form of nihilism. He has neither faith in a benign spirit in nature, nor faith in society as the expression of a providential power, nor faith in a personal God manipulating the lives of his people for good ends. If he is to avoid the bad alternatives of either having no order or making one for himself, he can do so only by finding a source of order in the one place it may remain: in another person. This is precisely what love means for him. It means finding someone who appears to radiate life and energy around him, establishing a measure of the worth of all things. If I can possess the person I love, then I can, without guilt, escape the world of flat desolation in which I began. But I must not take possession through an act of willful appropriation. I must stand back passively, watching and loving at a distance, as Gabriel Oak does or as Diggory Venn does. I must wait until the loved one willingly returns my love, so closing the distance between us.

Hardy's work is a good illustration of the connection between the development of fiction as a dominant literary form and the attenuation of belief in God as an effective power sustaining each individual in his identity and available in prayer, present in nature, or present as the providence directing human history. "I have been looking for God 50 years," writes Hardy in 1890, "and I think that if he had existed I should have discovered him" (L, 224). When God comes to be seen as an illusion created by man, a "man-projected Figure," then each person is likely to turn to other people as the best possible source of value or meaning. The novel's concentrated focus on relations between persons is not the result of a detached interest in morality or in social laws. It is one response to a situation in which relations between man and God seem to be losing their validity, and in which nature is also apparently being drained of that spiritual presence many of the romantic poets find in it. In the novel the disappearance of God often becomes the death of God, and Hardy, not only in his overt statements about religion but in the way his fiction is a long, patient exploration of the varieties of intersubjectivity, is an example of this. For him, as for Angel Clare, "God's *not* in his heaven: all's *wrong* with the world!" (Td, 324). His vision of human life depends on this assumption. When God seems dead, man turns to his fellows in a different way. Hardy's lyric poetry accompanies the exploration of this turning in his fiction and grows out of it. The major theme of the poetry too is relations between persons in a world without God. In this it provides a brilliant extension or commentary on the nature of living together as it is presented in the fiction.

III

What the Narrator Sees

LIVING TOGETHER takes fixed forms in Hardy's work and is expressed in motifs which recur so frequently that they assume a structuring role. They bind his world together and make it one. The possible ways in which men and women can be related are determined in part by the nature of the physical and social worlds which form a context for these relations. These too take constant forms.

The disengaged observer Hardy invents as his narrator does not see a world entirely alien to man. This is true in spite of the division between mind and world which seems implied in his assumption that the mind can separate itself so that a man becomes a detached viewer of life. Even such a spectator is still involved in the world, subject to it, permeated by it. The assumption of an ambiguous interpenetration of each man and his enviroment governs Hardy's representation of life in all its dimensions. Each man, for him, is both identified with what is around him and yet free of it. He participates intimately in his social and physical surroundings, is determined by them, and yet they are alien to him and have nothing to do with his real life. Happiness might be possible if he were either wholly separate or wholly involved, but he is both within and without at once. Since he cannot escape this situation, he seems destined to be unhappy. The various forms of dramatic irony which structure the fiction derive from this incomplete inherence of man in his milieu.

Each action a man performs enters into a complex stream of natural and social events. This means that what he does often has a result out of tune with its intention. A willed intention, aimed at some specific outcome, becomes as soon as it is launched into the outer world no more than one force or event in the tangled web of events caused by the actions of others and by the movements of nature. An omniscient man could forsee all, for all is fated to happen as it does happen, but usually ordinary men and women are blind to the future, absorbed in their own narrow desires and goals. They often do not know what other men are thinking, cannot foresee what others will do, what the weather will be like, and so on. It continually happens that the actions they direct toward one outcome have exactly opposite results, or at any rate results ironically different from the ones they intend. When an action becomes part of the web of circumstances it is alienated from the man who performs it and often has unexpected effects. The hideous ironies which make Hardy's stories and poems so often tales of "It might have been!" or "if I could only / Have known what I know now" ("Known Had I," CP, 767), or "If I had only done so and so, rather than what I did do!" are not the product of "some mean, monstrous ironist" (D, 304). They happen naturally, as an explicable sequence of physical and human actions mixed. This is what makes them so painful. Things happen as they happen, and only man, with his desire that events should correspond to some abstract idea of justice, or to some providential or human design, finds them ironically cruel. Tess's confessional letter to Angel Clare slips under his carpet rather than on top of it according to universal physical laws, laws which are altogether impersonal, neither malign nor benign. Or, to give another example out of many possible ones, "A Sunday Morning Tragedy" (CP, 188-191) is a distressing poem about a mother who procures an abortifacient for her unmarried daughter only to find, when the daughter has died from the drug, that the seducer has decided to marry the girl after all.

Just outside each man are the people immediately around him. Beyond them is the whole community of which he is a part, with all its ties to other communities and to history. Beyond other people is the natural world which is the scene of their actions, intervening at every point to limit what they can do. The individual, other people, physical nature — these form a complex spatial and temporal contiuum, overlapping and interacting in many ways without ever becoming wholly unified. Within this context each man must live.

Hardy has a strong sense of the way a man's life is conditioned by his natural environment. The relations between persons which make up the central action of his stories are always placed in the context of a careful and exact description of the landscape, the weather, the season. The poems also often describe weather, season, and place. Nor are these merely background to give the story realistic vividness. Natural forces enter into the story, limit it, and determine it at crucial points. The events could have happened as they did only in this enviroment, and the dramatic action often follows closely the rhythm of nature.

Many of the novels have a seasonal pattern. Beginning at one time of the year or another, the changing relations of the characters are matched by the progression of the seasons. The climax of the story has a definite relation, often ironic, to the season in which it occurs. *Under the Greenwood Tree*, for example, has five sections, "Winter," "Spring," "Summer," "Autumn," and "Conclusion." The courtship of Dick Dewy and Fancy Day proceeds through the round of the seasons to their marriage in the middle of the second summer. *The Woodlanders* begins on a winter's day, moves through Winterborne's death in the autumn rains (his name suggests his seasonal orientation), and concludes in the late spring with Grace back in Fitzpiers' arms, and Marty South able to stand by Winterborne's grave to say, "Now, my own, own love . . . you are mine, and only mine" (W, 444). A phrase describing Grace's remorse for Winterborne's death is a good example of the way the human drama is counterpointed by the progression of the seasons: "her simple sorrow for his loss took a softer edge with the lapse of the autumn and winter seasons" (W, 404).

The relationship between natural change and human change goes beyond direct or ironic echoing at a distance. Man participates in natural rhythms and is subject to them. The shift in the weather which ruins Henchard's investments, the rain which causes Grace Fitzpiers to stay in Winterborne's hut and so causes his death, the fine moonlight night which gives Alec d'Urberville an opportunity to seduce Tess — these are examples of the interpenetration of man and nature which functions throughout Hardy's work. The dramatic structure of *Tess of the d'Urbervilles* is perhaps the best example of this. The novel begins on an evening in late May, and the succession of seasons is followed through the many months of the action to the warm July morning when Tess is executed. This correspondence of event and season is an important thematic strand in the novel. Tess's seduction follows a law of nature, as does her ensuing pregnancy, and one theme of the story is the tragic incompatibility between social convention and doing what comes naturally. By way of their bodies and in particular their sexual desires men and women are part of nature, driven by the same energies which lead to the growth of plants and animals. Tess dwells in both worlds, the natural and the social, and must suffer for their incompatibility, just as Jude Fawley has two loves, Arabella for the body, Sue for spirit, and can never reconcile his two ways of loving. Tess's participation in the life of nature is powerfully dramatized in the scene in which she pauses in her binding of the harvested corn to suckle her child (Td, 113). A moment before she has been shown "holding the corn in an embrace like that of a lover" as she binds the sheaves (Td, 112). Her child seems part of the general fecundity of nature and is ironic proof of a generalization the narrator has made a little earlier: "a field-woman is a portion of the field; she has somehow lost her own margin, imbibed the essence of her surrounding, and assimilated herself with it" (Td, 111). Though Tess is "maiden no more," unfit for honest society, she is no less what the subtitle of the novel calls her, "a pure woman," as pure as any other expression of nature's will to life and reproduction. This argument is given universality in the description of the dairymaids at Talbothays, all hopelessly in love with Angel Clare, all filling the fecund summer night with sighs of frustrated desire (Td, 187, 188).

Tess's story is not peculiar to her, but is an example of a general human law, and the Talbothays section of *Tess of the d'Urbervilles* is an admirable example of Hardy's insight into the way the life of a whole community is determined by a place and a season. The growing passion of Angel and Tess follows exactly the progress of the summer, from the humid early days, when they are "converging, under an irresistible law, as surely as two streams in one vale" (Td, 165),[1] to the hot and dry season of August: "And as Clare was oppressed by the outward heats, so was he burdened inwardly by waxing fervour of passion for the soft and silent Tess" (Td, 190).

This correspondence between seasonal change and the growth of love between Angel and Tess is only the most dramatic example in *Tess of the d'Urbervilles* of man's participation in the season and the landscape. The novel is more than most of Hardy's stories structured around a contrast of landscapes which recalls the juxtaposition of Loamshire and Stonyshire in George Eliot's *Adam Bede*. From Marlott in the Vale of Blackmoor, the Vale of the Little Dairies, where Tess is born, to The Chase, near Trantridge, where she is seduced, to the rich summer rankness of the Froom Valley, the Valley of the Great

---

1 Two passages in George Eliot's *Adam Bede*, one for the bad lovers and one for the good, use the same image to express the ambiguity of the relation to nature of human sexual desire. Arthur Donnithorne and Hetty Sorrel "mingle as easily as two brooklets that ask for nothing but to entwine themselves and ripple with ever-interlacing curves in the leafiest hiding-places" (*Adam Bede*, I, *Works*, Cabinet Edition, p. 196). Adam Bede and Dinah Morris "approach each other gradually, like two little quivering rain-streams, before they mingle into one" (*ibid.*, II, 310).

Dairies, to the wintry barrenness of Flintcomb-Ash, on to the final dawn at Stonehenge — each place and season in Tess's pilgrimage is carefully described, and each has a determining influence not only on her life, but on the life of the other people living there. One example of the recurrent notation of this will suffice. Tess is returning from Trantridge to Marlott after her seduction by Alec d'Urberville:

> The ascent was gradual on this side, and the soil and scenery differed much from those within Blakemore Vale. Even the character and accent of the two peoples had shades of difference, despite the amalgamating effects of a round-about railway; so that, though less than twenty miles from the place of her sojourn at Trantridge, her native village had seemed a far-away spot. The field-folk shut in there traded northward and westward, travelled, courted, and married northward and westward, thought northward and westward; those on this side mainly directed their energies and attention to the east and south. (Td, 95)

"The natives of the rain are rainy men"[2] — Wallace Stevens' adage about the influence of environment on character is also a presupposition underlying Hardy's fiction. The relation between man and his physical surroundings, however, is an interaction, not just an irresistible effect of nature on man. The immersion of

---

2 Wallace Stevens, *The Collected Poems* (New York: Alfred A. Knopf, 1954), p. 37.

Hardy's people in their environment gives them, especially those who are farmers and woodsmen, a power to read nature as if it were speaking a human language. Far from being impersonal and alien, nature is for Gabriel Oak or Giles Winterborne, for all those who live amid fields and pastures or under the greenwood tree, something close and friendly, a companionable background for their labors. Nature for such people is thoroughly humanized, not because it is the dwelling place of a personal spiritual presence, but because man has so assimilated himself to nature and dwells so in harmony with it that he can interpret it as though it were speech.

There are many examples in the fiction of this power to read the language of nature. The opening of *Under the Greenwood Tree,* for example, tells the reader that trees "whisper" to man's intelligence: "To dwellers in the wood almost every species of tree has its voice as well as its feature" (UGT, 3). In the second chapter of *Far from the Madding Crowd* the reader is asked to stand on Norcombe Hill with Gabriel Oak and listen to "learn how the trees on the right and the trees on the left [wail] or [chaunt] to each other in the regular antiphonies of a cathedral choir" (FFMC, 9). Perhaps the most elaborate of such texts is a paragraph in *The Woodlanders* describing the ability of Giles Winterborne and Marty South to understand the Hintock woods:

They had been possessed of its finer mysteries as of commonplace knowledge; had been able to read its hieroglyphs as ordinary writing . . . [T]ogether they had, with the run of the years, mentally collected those remoter signs and symbols which seen in few were of runic obscurity, but all together made an

alphabet. From the light lashing of the twigs upon
their faces when brushing through them in the dark
either could pronounce upon the species of the tree
whence they stretched; from the quality of the wind's
murmur through a bough either could in like manner name its sort afar off. (W, 399)

So close are such people to nature that they seem to
have grown naturally from it and to have remained part
of it. Man here is not opposed to nature as the human
to the inhuman, but the two together form a continuum
without division or seam. Just as Tess's power of reproduction makes her already like the animal she comes to
resemble as she crouches on the Stone of Sacrifice at Stonehenge ("[H]er breathing now was quick and small, like
that of a lesser creature than a woman" [Td, 505].), so
Gabriel, Giles, or Marty have not yet detached themselves altogether from their origin in nature. If they can
understand the voice of nature, their own speech seems
to have its source in this mute alphabet. Such passages
suggest a homogeneity between man's language and
nature's. If a man can read the hieroglyphs of the woods,
he can also express himself with a speech not detached
from its sylvan source. His language is not arbitrary labels
imposed on nature from the outside by the sovereign
reason, but is a further articulation of the murmuring
words already spoken unconsciously by shrubs and trees.
Man and his speaking are not alien presences in nature,
but an extension of nature whereby it becomes conscious
and its stammering whisper reaches the clarity of human
speech. The self-expression which constitutes human
culture is also an expression of nature. In this expression
the secret workings of the Immanent Will are brought

into the open, and it is for this reason that the speech of a region is tainted with the flavor of a local soil, the speech of the Vale of Blackmoor differing from that of The Chase.

The relation between man and nature is a reciprocal one. If the natives of the Froom Valley are as rank and earthy as the word "Froom," and also as rank and earthy as the place this word names, at the same time the speech and the culture which grow out of a region are as different from the region as articulation, clarity, and consciousness are different from the elemental muteness which they rise from and yet transform by configuring. The word "Froom" might be taken as an emblem of human culture as Hardy sees it. The word, like the other elements of a culture, is the meeting place of an interchange between man and his enviroment which goes in both directions, the land giving its weight and fecundity to the sound of the word, the word being a manmade embodiment of the essence of the region. Nature without man is the blank, neutral presence of things as they are, that presence which is glimpsed in the poems when the speaker so effaces himself that it is as if he were not there at all, but were seeing the landscape as it might be if man had never evolved out of it.

Hardy's characteristic scene is a wet, dreary expanse of "Neutral Tones" (CP, 9). This "sad-coloured landscape" ("The Lacking Sense," CP, 106) is caught seemingly in a numb quiescence, rapt in an unconscious stillness and "Suspense" (CP, 851) which seems like a plea for release. The meditative, broken rhythms, as of a man musing quietly to himself, reinforce the sense of desolate solitude in such poems, as does the speaker's power to focus on tiny details which a busy passerby would miss. The fact that he lives "in quiet, screened, unknown" ("A Private Man on Public Men," CP, 885) means that he is a man who can "notice such things" ("Afterwards," CP, 521):

> The bars are thick with drops that show
>   As they gather themselves from the fog
> Like silver buttons ranged in a row,
> And as evenly spaced as if measured, although
>   They fall at the feeblest jog.
>
> They load the leafless hedge hard by,
>   And the blades of last year's grass,
> While the fallow ploughland turned up nigh
> In raw rolls, clammy and clogging lie —
>   Too clogging for feet to pass.
>   ("At Middle-Field Gate in February," CP, 451)

If natural objects, in these somber landscapes, are a mysterious hieroglyphic which those learned in such language can read, these signs do not speak for some inborn pattern in things, nor are they emblems of a transcendent reality which they stand for at a distance by analogical resemblance. For Hardy there is neither a transcendent nor an immanent conscious force sweeping through nature and expressing itself there. In a number of early poems he laments his inability to see nature as a religious man or as a romantic poet would see it. He would confirm their vision if he could, but he cannot, and so asks for the pity of those who believe, as in "The Impercipient (At a Cathedral Service)," with its explicit echo of Wordsworth's "Immortality Ode":

> I am like a gazer who should mark
>   An inland company

> Standing upfingered, with, "Hark! hark!
>   The glorious distant sea!"
> And feel, "Alas, 'tis but yon dark
>   And wind-swept pine to me!" (CP, 60)

This negative religious experience is very different from Matthew Arnold's belief in a God who exists but who has withdrawn from the world and can be heard at intervals in the form of "airs, and floating echos," "as from an infinitely distant land."[3] Hardy's earth is only earth, and the wind sweeping through the pine is not the breathing of a secret spiritual presence. It is only air in motion. His nature is matter moved by an impersonal, unthinking energy, and in this it is unlike the nature of Coleridge, Wordsworth, or Hopkins. Even in the passages which approach closest to a romantic personification of nature there is nothing like Wordsworth's "characters of the great Apocalypse," or Coleridge's "esemplastic" force, or Hopkins' inscapes of a nature which is "news of God."

❦

The description of Egdon Heath at the beginning of *The Return of the Native* is a case in point. This is Hardy's most elaborate description of nature before man or without man, and the personifications in the description have led some critics to speak of the heath as the chief character in the novel, not its scene but its protagonist. Though this is in my view the wrong way to put it,

---

3 Matthew Arnold, *The Poetical Works,* ed. C. B. Tinker and H. F. Lowry (London: Oxford University Press, 1957), "The Buried Life," ll. 75, 74, p. 247.

the language of the first chapter of *The Return of the Native*, "A Face on which Time Makes but Little Impression," is curious in a number of ways. There is an odd alternation between describing the heath as if there were no one there to see it and more or less surreptitious references to a spectator. The novel begins with a sentence which is, like those at the beginning of so many other novels by Hardy, the description of a wide expanse of landscape. The difference is that in this case there is no figure in the scene: "A Saturday afternoon in November was approaching the time of twilight, and the vast tract of unenclosed wild known as Egdon Heath embrowned itself moment by moment" (RN, 3). The effect of this sentence is peculiar. It suggests that no one is there to watch what is going on. It is as if man had not yet evolved to become conscious of the scene and so bring suffering into the world. The title of the second chapter confirms the fact that the reader is to think of the first chapter throughout as a description of the heath without man: "Humanity Appears upon the Scene, Hand in Hand with Trouble."

Humanity, however, has already been present covertly throughout the previous chapter, even though it is supposed to be absent. This appears in many details: "Looking upwards, a furze-cutter would have been inclined to continue work" (RN, 3); "when night showed itself an apparent tendency to gravitate together could be perceived in its shades and the scene" (RN, 4); "It was a spot which returned upon the memory of those who loved it with an aspect of peculiar and kindly congruity" (RN, 4); "To recline on a stump of thorn in the central valley of Egdon, between afternoon and night, as now, where the eye could reach nothing of the world outside the summits and shoulders of heathland which filled the whole circumference of its glance" (RN, 6-7); "On the evening under consideration it would have been noticed that" (RN, 7). It would have been noticed, if anyone had been there to notice, but no one is there. Yet someone is there: the narrator. It is precisely his vision of things, his ambiguous presence in the world and absence from it, which is expressed by the chapter in its continual references to a spectator who is there and not there.

As a kind of reflex or mirror image of this point of view there arises a vision of the heath as unchanged from prehistoric times and as like the spectator-narrator in its cold detachment and watchful waiting. Hardy is no more able than anyone else to imagine what the world would be like if man were not in it. It is like trying to imagine what it would be like to be dead, if death is the obliteration of consciousness. In order to think at all a man must be alive, and to be alive is to experience one or another of the innumerable ways man can be present to the world. The best that can be done is to reduce oneself to a neutral power of watching. What the world looks like from such a perspective is expressed admirably in the first chapter of *The Return of the Native*. When a man is least present as an active force shaping nature, he is most present, present not as a subjective power of transformation, but as a manlike presence in the landscape reflecting his own detachment and expressing it.

The personifications in Chapter 1 of *The Return of the Native*, like the personifications in the poems ("All seem to gaze at me" ["Nature's Questioning," CP, 58]), or in other similar texts in Hardy's writing, do not express the presence in nature of a conscious spiritual presence. The personifications are projected into nature by

man's presence in the world. By a paradoxical interchange between spectator and scene which is easier to
feel than to express, the personification of nature arises
most intensely when the spectator most effaces himself
and looks at nature as if he were not there to disturb it
from being itself. The personifications indicate the appropriateness of the heath to a detached spectator. When
a man has withdrawn himself from engagement in a
particular social role, his perspective, in its neutral embrace of time and space, coincides with the neutrality and
enduring persistence of nature and can give a voice to
nature, or can hear nature speak. In these extraordinary
passages man becomes conscious for nature rather than
imposing one of his own patterns on it. The attitude of
detached watching is justified as the one most in tune
with nature, therefore closest to the truth of things. Far
from presupposing a separation of spectator and scene,
these texts, and others like them in the poems, express a
strange union of subject and object in which the spectator's passive neutrality allows the passive neutrality of
nature to manifest itself and to speak for the spectator's
vision of things in speaking for itself. If the spectator
were not there to hear this speech, it could not exist. The
heath would remain mute and without meaning. Though
the heath has waited in vain through innumerable centuries for the awakening of the Immanent Will to consciousness, man has in the interval appeared on the scene,
and Hardy in these sentences describes one form of the
relation between them, a relation which is a revelation
of man's nature as much as a revelation of the nature of
the heath:

The place became full of a watchful intentness
now; for when other things sank brooding to sleep

the heath appeared slowly to awake and listen. Every night its Titanic form seemed to await something; but it had waited thus, unmoved, during so many centuries, through the crises of so many things, that it could only be imagined to await one last crisis — the final overthrow.

It was at present a place perfectly accordant with man's nature — neither ghastly, hateful, nor ugly: neither commonplace, unmeaning, nor tame; but, like man, slighted and enduring; and withal singularly colossal and mysterious in its swarthy monotony. As with some persons who have long lived apart, solitude seemed to look out of its countenance. It had a lonely face, suggesting tragical possibilities. (RN, 4, 6)

The function of Egdon Heath throughout *The Return of the Native* must be understood in the context of the first chapter. The heath is neither a character in itself nor merely a dark background against which the action takes place. The heath is rather the embodiment of certain ways in which human beings may exist. Diggory Venn and Eustacia Vye rise out of the heath as versions of two of these ways, Diggory the detached waiting and watching expressed by the heath, Eustacia the tragical possibilities of violence and infinite longing the heath contains. The relation between these characters and the heath is a reciprocal one, like the relation between the heath and the narrator. The heath comes into specifically human form in its native men and women, but they are swayed by its influence, as Clym Yeobright loses all his ambition for wealth and social advancement when he returns to the heath. He reaches a point of wise indifference in which he can be happy in the monotonous and almost unconscious action of furze-cutting. In the stories of Diggory, Eustacia, and Clym the potentialities of the heath are enacted in a human drama. At the same time, their proximity to the heath makes it possible for them to live outside the usual restraints of society and therefore, in their different ways, closer to the truth of things.

The relation of the narrator, Diggory, Clym, and Eustacia to Egdon Heath is an extreme version of that interchange between man and nature which is assumed throughout Hardy's writings as the permanent condition of man. It is extreme both in the union of man and nature it presupposes and in the detached consciousness of the heath the narrator enjoys. More usual is an overlapping between man and nature which is not quite an identity between them, but has become so unconscious or habitual that it is taken for granted, though the narrator brings it back to light. Hardy's subject is never man alone or nature alone, but always man in nature, "The Background and the Figure," or "The Figure in the Scene," to borrow the titles of two of his poems (CP, 426, 447). He never doubts that it is the presence of man which gives interest and meaning to nature. The scene without the figure is a nullity, as he says explicitly in several texts in the *Life*. "An object or mark raised or made by man on a scene is worth ten times any such formed by unconscious Nature. Hence clouds, mists, and mountains are unimportant beside the wear on a threshold, or the print of a hand" (L, 116). The method of Boldini and Hobbema in their paintings is "that of infusing emotion into the baldest external objects either by the presence of a human figure among them, or by mark of some human connection with them" (L, 120). The method of Boldini and Hobbema is Hardy's method too.

In the fiction this appears in his loving attention to the details of Wessex culture, ways of farming, raising sheep, milking cows, or making butter, in the careful description of the traditions of the church choir which forms a background for *Under the Greenwood Tree*, or of the mummer's show of St. George and the dragon which provides a dramatic scene in *The Return of the Native*, or of country rituals of wedding, funeral, or dance in so many of the novels. Most important, perhaps, is Hardy's exact notation of the physical embodiments of West Country life, the houses, roads, clothes, utensils, implements, and vehicles which play such important roles in his fiction. These physical objects are parts of nature which have been made over by man to his own uses. He has yielded to nature in the sense that, for example, his way of cultivating the land is determined by the soil in that region, but at the same time he has made his own mark on nature, a mark which gives it importance and infuses emotion into it. Even Egdon Heath, older than human history and almost unchanged through so many centuries, is traversed by the white surface of a road, built over an old Roman *via* and reaching from one edge of it to the other (RN, 7). Much more completely is any farmstead, house, or town the place of an elaborate humanization of nature, a humanization which is concretely present, for example, in the expert list of things for sale in the shops in Casterbridge:

Scythes, reap-hooks, sheep-shears, bill-hooks, spades, mattocks, and hoes at the ironmonger's; beehives, butter-firkins, churns, milking stools and pails, hay-rakes, field-flagons, and seed-lips at the cooper's; cart-ropes and plough-harness at the saddler's; carts, wheel-barrows, and mill-gear at the wheel-wright's and machinist's; horse-embrocations at the chemist's; at the glover's and leather-cutter's, hedging-gloves, thatchers' knee-caps, ploughmen's leggings, villagers' pattens and clogs. (MC, 32)

The language of this text is made up of the names of utensils, the names of their uses, the names of their users, the names of their makers and the characteristic acts of those makers. The leather-cutter cuts leather for the glover to make hedging-gloves which the hedger uses in his hedging, knee-caps which the thatcher uses in his thatching. The many hyphenated terms in the passage, as well as the overlapping of words for maker, utensil, user, and function, put concretely before the reader the intimate connection of man, implement, and environment in Casterbridge. A sheep-shear is a scissors for shearing sheep; a reap-hook is a hook for reaping. The function of the tool is built into its name, just as utensil and use are inseparable in reality. The intention of the hay-rake, that it should be used for raking hay, is encountered as an inextricable part of the rake. To see it as a disconnected "object" is an artificial and derivative way of seeing it, for the rake by way of its use reaches out toward all the surrounding items in the community and can only by abstraction be detached from them. Each element in the collection, whether maker, tool, or user, is part of a complex totality of involvements which is a certain way of appropriating the environment and living within it.

Hardy's world is thick with such utensils and his

writing is thick with notations of the way these manmade objects bind their makers to the physical world. He is aware, however, that human artifacts are not the signs of an unequivocal marriage of man with his environment. They are rather the location of an incomplete inherence of man in nature. In rake, wheelbarrow, or seed-lip matter as it is in itself is partially made over by man's use of it, but still it is not wholly transformed or dominated. A passage in the *Life* shows his insight into this. A note of 1873 describing a visit to Tintern Abbey ("But compare the age of the building with that of the marble hills from which it was drawn!") is followed by a comment made by Mrs. Hardy as the nominal authoress of the *Life:* "Here it may be stated, in relation to the above words on the age of the hills, that this shortcoming of the most ancient architecture by comparison with geology was a consideration that frequently troubled Hardy's mind when measuring and drawing old Norman and other early buildings" (L, 93-94). Well might he be troubled! What really exists in a church is the shapeless and ageless stone of the hills. The imposition of a pattern on the stone by the carvers of Norman churches is only the superficial laying on of an evanescent design, just as the old road is only a slender white scar inscribed across the age-old monotony of Egdon Heath. This is a perfect expression of Hardy's sense of the paradox of culture. The stone is the source of the church and is expressed by it, brought out in the open by it. The carving has lain from all time in the stone, and the stone of a region determines to some degree the architecture possible there. At the same time the stone in its shapeless muteness is immeasurably older than the carving and is veiled by it, traduced by it. The culture which developed this mode of architecture uses the stone as a means of embodying itself, but at the same time its characteristic forms are a thin veneer on the surface of the eternal stone, as evanescent as foam and as fragile. This idea of a merger and yet distance between a culture and its physical incarnation runs all through Hardy's work.

The power man has to transfigure nature by turning it into artifacts and implements is assumed as a given. Hardy's characters are born into a world which has already been made over by past generations. All men must live out their lives in a place full of houses, roads, and tools. The parts of nature which man has reshaped in this way are the sedimentation of history. Without the physical world history might disappear without a trace, but as long as any relics of the past remain history need not be dependent on memory or on books. Hardy's people are surrounded by objects which embody the past and bring it before them. In one poem, for example, a collection of old musical instruments is played again by the ghosts of the people who once played them in the past ("Haunting Fingers: A Phantasy in a Museum of Musical Instruments," CP, 559-560). In another beautiful poem the speaker lovingly describes how the dead are still present in the things they used. The caressing meditative rhythm, like the movement of hands touching an old clock or an old violin, carries much of the emotion here:

I see the hands of the generations
That owned each shiny familiar thing

> In play on its knobs and indentations,
>   And with its ancient fashioning
>   Still dallying:
>
> Hands behind hands, growing paler and paler,
>   As in a mirror a candle-flame
> Shows images of itself, each frailer
>   As it recedes . . . ("Old Furniture," CP, 456)

In an other poem an old house boasts to a new house of "the Presences from aforetime that I hold," and predicts that though "a new house has no sense of the have-beens," still a time will come when the dwellers in the new house will "print on thee their presences as on me":

> Where such inbe,
>   A dwelling's character
> Takes theirs, and a vague semblancy
> To them in all its limbs, and light, and atmosphere.
>   ("The Two Houses," CP, 563-565)

These presences are not subjective inventions. The people who played on the instruments, or used the old furniture, or lived in the old house have instilled their lives into the physical objects they have used, so transforming them that the objects remain permeated with their presence and can liberate them in afteryears, like an aroma freed from a sealed vase. This theme, so Proustian in idea and treatment, echoes through Hardy's poems. For him, as for Proust, an event which includes strong emotional involvement with a scene is not just the subjective shadowing of inner feelings against a neutral background. The background lends its part to the feelings and embodies them, in an inextricable merger of inner and outer. While the event was going on feeling and gesture were objectified in the scene.

This theme is important evidence for Hardy's instinctive rejection of a firm division of mind and world. Just as there is no such thing as a completely detached consciousness for him, so there are no detached feelings, feelings which are purely subjective. The emotions people feel, the actions and gestures they perform, transfigure the scenes around them, even though they do not intend this. The scene remains pervaded by the emotion, stores it up, and may release it long after to those who are sensitive to such intangible presences. So in "The Strange House" Hardy imagines two people living in his own house at Max Gate in the year 2000. Though the new couple do not know that he and his wife have lived there a hundred years earlier, the more sensitive of the new dwellers is disturbed by their presence and finds difficulty in living an independent life in a house which has old dreams "imprinted . . . on its walls" (CP, 550). The same theme appears in "The Re-enactment" (CP, 339-342). A love scene so permeates a room and has so "enghosted" its walls that it is not only periodically repeated there, but keeps new lovers from fulfilling their love within the same house, for the "intenser drama" of the old love "fill[s] the air" and "[leaves] no room for later passion anywhere" (CP, 342).

The accumulation of history in the physical world is not an objective fact which people who come afterward can behold from the outside with dispassionate impunity. The past embodied in the physical scene has a coercive power. It creates a complex cultural environment made of the persistence of the past generations. This can impose itself on the people of the present and determine their lives, sometimes without their knowledge. Caster-bridge, with its Roman amphitheater and its Roman skeletons in every garden and field, is an example of the tangible presence of history which Hardy so often finds in his Wessex. Dwellers in Casterbridge are "quite un-moved" by these "hoary shapes." "They had lived so long ago, their time was so unlike the present, their hopes and motives were so widely removed from ours, that between them and the living there seemed to stretch a gulf too wide for even a spirit to pass" (MC, 80). Nevertheless, in spite of their insensitivity to influences from the past, the citizens of Casterbridge are so much aware of the sinister events which have taken place over the centuries in the amphitheater, events which have deposited themselves layer by layer there, that they use the spot only for "appointments of a furtive kind" and never for love meetings (MC, 81). Even now, events which long ago took place in the amphitheater have so impregnated the scene that they are periodically re-enacted there in a repetition like that in certain folk beliefs or like that in Yeats's "Crazy Jane on God" and *The Words Upon the Window-Pane:* "at certain moments in the summer time, in broad daylight, persons sitting with a book or dozing in the arena had, on lifting their eyes, beheld the slopes lined with a gazing legion of Hadrian's soldiery as if watching the gladiatorial combat; and had heard the roar of their excited voices" (MC, 82). When Henchard meets his estranged wife in the amphitheater what takes place between them adds itself to the long sequence of such events, and it is as if their interview takes some of its somber fatefulness from its placing.

The references to Job, to Faust, to King Lear, and to Saul which run through *The Mayor of Casterbridge* function in the same way.[4] The narrator makes these references, not Henchard himself, until the end of his life. Their cumulative effect is to suggest that Henchard, without at first being aware of it, is in his life repeating certain archetypal patterns of tragic experience which have echoed through the centuries incarnating themselves now in this person, now in that. Henchard is not living his life freely, but is determined in his actions by the irresistible force of universal patterns of recurrence. The strength of these lies partly in the fact that until the end of his life he is ignorant of them. This theme is reinforced by the way Henchard in his own life repeats compulsively the same movements of approach toward another person followed by rejection of him. Character may be Fate, according to the aphorism from Novalis which is quoted in *The Mayor* (MC, 131),[5] but Henchard's character seems fateful in that it forces him to relate himself to other people in a way which will make his life a variation on that of Cain, Saul, Job, Oedipus, Samson, or Lear. *The Mayor of Casterbridge* may be defined as a demonstration of the impossibility of escaping from the past. Though Henchard tries to free himself,

[4] See Julian Moynahan, "*The Mayor of Casterbridge* and the Old Testament's First Book of Samuel: A Study of Some Literary Relationships," *Publications of the Modern Language Association*, LXXI (1956), 118-130.

[5] Hardy's source here is apparently George Eliot's somewhat modified version in *The Mill on the Floss* of Novalis' text. In *Heinrich von Ofterdingen* Novelis says, "Ich einsehe, dass Schicksal und Gemüt Namen eines Begriffes sind." This becomes in *The Mill*, " 'Character,' says Novalis, in one of his questionable aphorisms — 'character is destiny.' " See Gordon S. Haight's note in the Riverside Edition of *The Mill on the Floss* (Boston: Houghton Mifflin Co., 1961), p. 351, and W. E. Yuill, " 'Character is Fate': a Note on Thomas Hardy, George Eliot, and Novalis," *Modern Language Review*, LVII (1962), 401-402.

his own past actions, as well as the universal patterns he unwittingly incarnates, come back to destroy him.

This notion of the fatefulness of character is reinforced by the fact that so many of Hardy's protagonists have already inextricably involved themselves in determining situations when the reader first encounters them. Like many of William Faulkner's characters, Joe Christmas, for example, or Bayard Sartoris, his heroes and heroines have often made fateful commitments or choices, or had fateful experiences, long before the first scene of the story. The action of the novel is in a sense the working out of a destiny which has long since been fixed. At the beginning of *The Return of the Native,* for example, Diggory Venn has long been in love with Thomasin, though rejected by her, and Eustacia's first liaison with Wildeve is already a thing of the past. Only the return of Clym Yeobright is needed to establish a tangle of thwarted desires, each character loving someone but not being loved in return. At the beginning of *The Woodlanders,* to recall another example, Marty South is already in love with Giles Winterborne, though his marriage to Grace Melbury is already planned, and Fitzpiers' affair with Mrs. Charmond is already past. The same sort of crisscross of four mismatched lovers as in *The Return of the Native* is already latent in the situation. The scene of the wife-selling in *The Mayor of Casterbridge* is in effect a direct presentation of what becomes Henchard's fatefully determining past, since it is followed by a gap of eighteen years and a new beginning in the story which presupposes the wife-selling as a distant and yet ominous background. Even when the reader first encounters Henchard his marriage to Susan and his ensuing disgust with

her, the first such sequence in his life of which the reader
is told, has already happened. Hardy's novels rarely begin
with their true beginnings, but open in the midst of the
action, with the characters already entangled in situations
which hold their futures in predetermined suspension.

Tess of the d'Urbervilles might seem to contradict
this generalization. In fact it is centrally concerned with
the way the human past determines the present. Though
Tess is apparently free at the beginning of the story and
only caught in a tragic sequence of events after her seduction by Alec, nevertheless she is never really free. Her
life follows from her inheritance of a place as a member
of the much decayed family of d'Urbervilles, with "a-gr't-
family-vault-at-Kingsbere — and knighted-forefathers-in-
lead-coffins-there," as her father sings in his grotesque
drunkenness after an afternoon at The Pure Drop Inn
(Td, 12). The idea of a present which is a repetition or
reincarnation of the past recurs through the novel like
a refrain with many variations. The narrator at his first
introduction of Tess tells the reader that, "for all her
bouncing handsome womanliness, you could sometimes
see her twelfth year in her cheeks, or her ninth sparkling
from her eyes; and even her fifth would flit over the
curves of her mouth now and then" (Td, 13). When she
meets Alec d'Urberville she expects to see "an aged and dig-
nified face, the sublimation of all the d'Urberville linea-
ments, furrowed with incarnate memories representing
in hieroglyphic the centuries of her family's and England's history" (Td, 45), and when Alec has seduced
her the narrator sourly comments that "doubtless some
of Tess d'Urberville's mailed ancestors rollicking home
from a fray had dealt the same measure even more ruth-
lessly towards peasant girls of their time." He adds bitterly

WHAT THE NARRATOR SEES | 103

enough: "But though to visit the sins of the fathers upon
the children may be a morality good enough for divin-
ities, it is scorned by average human nature; and it therefore does not mend the matter" (Td, 91).

The sins of her fathers are inflicted upon Tess in a particularly unpleasant way. The nature she inherits forces
her to enact involuntarily a new version of a life which
has been lived over and over again by her ancestors, as
if she were no more than a puppet of history, or an actor
in a play already performed a thousand times before,
just as Henchard repeats the life of Saul or Cain. Tess is
to some degree aware of this destiny. In a speech to Angel
Clare she expresses her repudiation of history and her
unwillingness to study it. In the perspective of the end of
the novel what she says has great pathos: "what's the use
of learning that I am one of a long row only — finding
out that there is set down in some old book somebody just
like me, and to know that I shall only act her part; making
me sad, that's all. The best is not to remember that your
nature and your past doings have been just like thousands'
and thousands', and that your coming life and doings
'll be like thousands' and thousands' "(Td, 162).

So strong is Tess's conviction of the irresistible coercion
of history that she does not believe she can avoid repeating the past. The best she can hope for is not to know it
or remember it. Her forebodings are fulfilled when she
kills Alec, performing again the act which has been predestined by "the family tradition of the coach and
murder." She shares in that "obscure strain in the d'Urberville blood" which predisposes members of her family to
such violence (Td, 492). The murder is not her act, but
is performed by her ancestors acting through her. It is
appropriate that when Tess is captured she should be in

a posture and place which suggest that she is re-enacting the pagan sacrifices once supposedly performed at Stonehenge. The "heathen temple" is "older than the centuries; older than the d'Urbervilles" (Td, 502). The form of repetition in her capture is a fitting climax for a novel which has been dominated by a brooding sense of man's atavistic kinship with what is oldest, darkest, and most irrational in nature. The last chapter continues the theme of repetition in its suggestion, by way of references to Giotto's "Two Apostles" (Td, 507) and to Aeschylus, that Tess's execution is a re-enactment of the crucifixion or of the death of a Greek tragic hero. This reinforcement of the theme of repetition may be the major function of the famous sentence at the end of the novel: " 'Justice' was done, and the President of the Immortals, in Aeschylean phrase, had ended his sport with Tess" (Td, 508). The idea of a malign god who sports with man (as much reminiscent of *King Lear* as of Aeschylus[6]) is neither integral to the text of *Tess* nor reinforced by the rest of Hardy's work. The notion is in fact explicitly denied in all those poems which express his belief that the Immanent Will is not yet conscious. In "The Blow" (CP, 449), for example, the speaker rejoices that his unmerited suffering has at least not been caused by an "aimful author," but is "the Immanent Doer's That doth not

---

6 "As flies to wanton boys, are we to th' Gods;/They kill us for their sport" — the terrifying lines from *King Lear* (Arden ed., IV, i, 36, 37) are quoted in the preface to the fifth edition of *Tess of the d'Urbervilles* (Td, xix), and as David Lodge has noted (*Language of Fiction* [London: Routledge and Kegan Paul; New York: Columbia University Press, 1966], p. 174) the lines may be echoed in the novel in the description of Tess standing in the Valley of the Froom "like a fly on a billiard-table of indefinite length" (Td, 136), or in the parallel description of Tess and Marian "crawling over the surface of [Flintcomb-Ash] like flies" (Td, 364).

know." In a letter quoted in the *Life* Hardy affirms that in the passage in *Tess* "the forces opposed to the heroine were allegorized as a personality," although in fact they were not personal at all, but were "inanimate" (L, 244). The allusion to Aeschylus functions most powerfully as a suggestion that Tess reincarnates a pattern of tragic experience already present in the earliest masterpieces of Western literature.

In all Hardy's work, then, history is present not just objectively in old roads, houses, utensils, the debris of past generations, but is also able to enter into the lives of people living in the present, to force them to act and feel in ways it imposes. There is one more important form of this coercive presence of the past in the present: human speech. I have said that a place name like "Froom" is the meeting point of a people and its environment. This union of man and nature in a word took place long ago. The use of the name today therefore carries the past alive into the present. Hardy's characters never encounter a bare, nameless river, heath, hill, or wood, but always find themselves in places which have already been named. This naming has assimiliated these places into the continuity of human history. The places carry their past with them as a living presence.

What is true of place names is true also for human speech in general. Language is another of those givens which the newborn find already there when they enter the world. In the speech which surrounds a child the indifferent outer world has been appropriated by the life that is lived in it and elaborately structured in ways which make some actions and judgments easy, others hard. The coercive power of language manifests itself in Hardy's fiction in the rustic choruses which constitute a kind of background or context for the experiences of the central characters, a context as circumscribing and limiting as the natural scene, or as the houses and roads which man has constructed within the scene.

The language of Hardy's peasants is a thick network or texture of speech which has assimilated nature and preserves the past, including both in a rigid framework of traditional meanings and attitudes. His rustics do not so much act as talk. The function of their talking is to express a verbalization of the world which is so completely taken for granted that such characters can hardly be said to be individualized or conscious at all. Certainly their qualities of individuality and consciousness are very different from those of the main characters. The community speaks through the rustics, speaks for its collective memory and collective interpretation of the world. Scenes of echoing stichomythic dialogue between such characters often take place in the warm cosiness of a tavern. Such a scene is appropriate. The rustics are passive, static, without longing for anything beyond the daily repetition of agricultural tasks which have been repeated for so many generations that they have a ritualistic fixity. Their voices, as the collective wisdom speaks through them, have a semiconscious, dreamy quality, like a man talking in his sleep, or like a medium possessed by a spirit. The rustics speak continually of the past and keep it alive in a language which is embodied memory, haunted by years gone by, a language as nostalgic, musing, or reminiscent as Hardy's own voice in many of his poems or as Falstaff's "We have heard the chimes at midnight, Master Shallow."[7]

A Group of Noble Dames and *A Few Crusted Characters* are each a series of reminiscent anecdotes told in turns by a group of friends in whose retrospection the past is resurrected. In *Far from the Madding Crowd* or in *Under the Greenwood Tree* or even in *The Mayor of Casterbridge* the protagonists, with their acute self-consciousness and longing for some higher joy, detach themselves from immersion in a thick background of speech and live out their more dramatic lives in the context it provides. The refrain of "Do ye mind?" echoes ominously through the talk of the rustics and, together with their exact memory for seemingly trivial details of bygone events, suggests the difficulty the main characters will have in freeing themselves from the past:

> " — And so I used to eat a lot of salt fish afore going, and then by the time I got there I were as dry as a lime-basket — so thorough dry that that ale would slip down — ah, 'twould slip down sweet! Happy times! heavenly times! Such lovely drunks as I used to have at that house! You can mind, Jacob? You used to go wi' me sometimes."
>
> "I can — I can," said Jacob. "That one, too, that we had at Buck's Head on a White Monday was a pretty tipple." (FFMC, 67-68)

> "And dostn't mind how mother would sing, Christopher?" continued Mrs. Cuxsom, kindling at the retrospection; "and how we went with her to the party at Mellstock, do ye mind? — at old Dame Ledlow's, farmer Shinar's aunt, do ye mind? — she

[7] II *Henry IV*, Arden ed., III, ii, 209, 210.

we used to call Toad-skin, because her face were so yaller and freckled, do ye mind?"

"I do, hee-hee, I do!" said Christopher Coney. (MC, 97)

In roads, houses, clothes, and furniture, in traditional ways of farming and cooking, in language, that most powerful of tools for humanizing nature, Hardy's people find themselves living within a ready-made culture which exerts its influence over them from every side. The isolation of his narrators from the world they behold at a distance and the separation of his characters from one another might be expected to lead to a presentation of other people as a mysterious spectacle which can be interpreted only with difficulty. Assumptions like this about the way people are related to one another are, for example, the basis of Jane Austen's art. Hardy's vision is different. In spite of the objectivity and detachment of his people, in spite of his emphasis on seeing as the chief way a man is related to others, he often grants his characters spontaneous access to the minds and feelings of others. Just as they can read nature, so they can read one another. The other person's clothes, the disposition of his furniture, his body, his gestures, his facial expression, the way he walks or works — all these are signs which may be read intuitively, so that a man is an open secret to his neighbors. The collectively humanized world is a kind of medium or milieu which absorbs a person and brings what he is thinking or feeling into the light where it is accessible to all.

Many passages in Hardy's fiction testify to this open-

man must live out his life in a milieu of determining forces woven out of the crisscross of relations between these various elements. Together these make up a world rich in history, a strongly integrated community sustained by a highly articulated web of language. These together endow people with an intuitive understanding of one another and with a great power of turning physical objects into utensils and signs. The world Hardy's characters find themselves in has already been disclosed, structured, and understood, and other people are included in this all-inclusive pattern of understanding.

In all these interactions the notion of an imperfect interpenetration returns. The social, natural, and historical worlds overlap but are not identical. Landscape and topography determine the kind of life which can be lived in a region. Man can never escape the biological inheritance which makes him part of nature. Nevertheless, man gives names and meanings to a scene and transforms it by living in it. Men and women understand one another instinctively on the basis of bodily gestures and expressions, and yet another person may also remain in part a mystery, have secret thoughts and a hidden past. An old house stores up and preserves the living which has been done in it. Nature sustains history, keeping the past alive. Yet beneath the thin patina which man has spread over nature by his use of it, a church, a house, Egdon Heath, or the River Froom remain as mute and indifferent as they were before human history began.

❧

It would seem that Hardy's characters might find everything they want in a world of this sort. His rural communities, "sequestered spots outside the gates of the world," would seem, "by virtue of the concentrated passions and closely-knit interdependence of the lives therein" (W, 4, 5), to fulfill the definition of a proper society as provided by nineteenth-century humanists like George Eliot or Auguste Comte. The main characters of his novels, however, are not satisfied by the life that is natural in their communities. They are tormented by unassuaged longings for something more. The conditions of their existence alienate them from a better life which exists in their dreams.

There are a number of related reasons for this. To the degree that man is part of nature he is determined by it, yet its movements do not correspond to his needs or aims. A man's inherence in nature is constantly frustrating his intentions. The same thing may be said for his inherence in society. Tess is the powerless victim of conflicting natural and social forces which make her life a vain repetition, one of a long line of identically futile lives. The unreflecting absorption of Hardy's rural characters in traditional forms of speech, habits of acting, and ways of judging leads them to accept their society as the only proper one. This is a multiple form of alienation. The rustics do not know that their view of things is relative, not absolute. The wide view of the narrator is required for that knowledge. The narrator's detachment shows Wessex society as local and temporary, one way of living among thousands, but Mother Cuxsom or Christopher Coney are so immersed in their community that they are unable to see it from the outside. This unselfconscious immersion in a community keeps people from seeing that man and nature are moved alike by the rapt, unknowing impulsions of the Immanent

Will. Such people are unable to see that their society is a manmade mirage. It projects certain values on nature, but the amoral force within nature remains all-determining and offers no support to those values. Man has created the society within whose structure he is caught. This means both that his society hides the truth from him and that it is as evanescent and uncertain as human life itself.

The theme of social change and its power to destroy the old rural ways of life runs through Hardy's fiction as an undertone of pathos giving the narrator's loving re-creation of country ways the nostalgia and insubstantiality of a dream of childhood. Industrialization, economic changes creating an itinerant farm-working population, new methods of farming — these are irresistibly destroying the folkways of even the most sequestered nooks in Wessex. Even if the life there were altogether good, it is destined to pass away, like everything else in human history, for "slow effacement / Is rife throughout" ("The Ageing House," CP, 461). *Under the Greenwood Tree,* for example, is the most idyllic of Hardy's pastoral novels, yet the story of Dick Dewy's courtship of Fancy Day takes place against a nostalgic account of the displacement of the old "Mellstock Quire" by the single organist of modern churches.

The given conditions of Wessex life are unsatisfactory in another way. They fail to satisfy the yearnings of certain more highly endowed characters. If the members of the rustic chorus remain absorbed in their culture, half-consciously repeating its traditions, fixed in their places and without desire for anything more, the protagonists possess, unhappily for them, self-consciousness and longings for larger satisfactions. Only a man or a woman who for some reason is detached from immersion in the collective life of the community has a chance to attain a proper existence, an existence open to the truth of things. Like the heroes of so many other nineteenth-century novels, for example those of Flaubert or of George Eliot, Hardy's heroes have religious desires in a world which offers no satisfaction for such desires. Their lives are spent in the attempt to find a substitute for God in a world without God. This search must take place within the given human world as Hardy sees it, but it is a search which reaches beyond what is given toward something more, toward some limitless joy. In a world without deity they turn toward the only thing which seems a possible substitute for it, someone who exists within the everyday social world, but who radiates a seemingly divine light upon it. It may be that in a Godless world another person can play the role of God. Hardy's fiction has a single theme: "fascination." Novel after novel tells the story of a love affair which emerges from the dreaming background of Wessex life and is followed to its predestined end. Though there is great variety in his treatment of this theme, there is also a recognizable pattern which governs this variety. Universal laws of human relationship are exemplified in his love stories. These laws bind his lovers irresistibly and are specified anew in each lover's life. Each story is a variation on a melodic sequence which has a rigorous power to determine the stages of love.

IV

Falling in Love

BEFORE FASCINATION, and presupposed by it, is boredom. Hardy's protagonists are usually encountered at a time when they have already committed themselves in marriage or in love but have tired of this commitment. Like all men, they live within the coercive context of nature and society. They have also before the reader meets them chosen one person out of all the world to be the focus of their lives. This relationship has gone awry, leaving them in a situation of exasperated boredom. They are encumbered by a great reservoir of unused emotions ready to precipitate itself on the first attractive person who comes along. Dissatisfaction and ennui have separated them from unselfconscious absorption in society. Seeing the community from the outside, they find it does not answer to their needs. It seems to impose a circumscribed life of petty concerns which offers no fulfillment to their large souls. Like Emma Bovary, Hardy's characters dream of some other place, some other person, some distant source of radiance for their lives. Even if they have never loved before, they have an unsuspected susceptibility to a sudden crystallization of desire around someone they encounter.

Boldwood, in *Far from the Madding Crowd*, is a man of great reserve. He has habitually enclosed himself in himself and has resisted all the lures offered him by women. Bathsheba's ill-considered valentine tears down this reserve, and Boldwood becomes the victim of an irresistible passion: "The insulation of his heart by reserve during these many years, without a channel of any kind for disposable emotion, had worked its effect. It has been observed more than once that the causes of love are chiefly subjective, and Boldwood was a living testimony to the truth of the proposition. No mother existed to absorb his devotion, no sister for his tenderness, no idle ties for sense. He became surcharged with the compound, which was genuine lover's love" (FFMC, 139).

Henchard is another such man. At the beginning of *The Mayor of Casterbridge* he has grown so tired of his marriage that he is ready to commit the strange and shocking act of selling his wife. His posture as he walks along the road in the first pages of the novel is a memorable emblem of that "atmosphere of stale familiarity" which most marriages, for Hardy, quickly generate: "his taciturnity was unbroken, and the woman enjoyed no society whatever from his presence. Virtually she walked the highway alone" (MC, 2). Yet Henchard is by no means unemotional or habitually reserved. He is "the kind of man to whom some human object for pouring out his heat upon — [be] it emotive or [be] it choleric — [is] almost a necessity" (MC, 142). He has "an emotional void . . . that he unconsciously crave[s] to fill" (MC, 169). This void and the longing it generates drive him compulsively again and again to try to seek happiness through possession of another person.

Mrs. Marchmill, in "An Imaginative Woman," one of the stories in *Life's Little Ironies*, is another such person. She is "an impressionable, palpitating creature," given to "letting off her delicate and ethereal emotions in imaginative occupations, day-dreams, and night-sighs" (LLI, 4). The boredom created by her husband's stolidity and indifference leads her to an odd form of infatuation. She falls in love with a poet she has never met. The contagion of living in his room when he is absent inflames her with desire: "being a woman of very living ardours, that required sustenance of some sort, they were beginning to feed on this chancing material" (LLI, 12).

Lady Constantine, in *Two on a Tower*, is another variation on this theme. Deserted by her husband, she suffers from "an almost killing *ennui*" (TT, 3). The handsome young Swithin St. Cleeve is "a new and unexpected channel for her cribbed and confined emotions" (TT, 53). In the same way Henry Knight's proposal to Elfride Swancourt in *A Pair of Blue Eyes* comes "with all the ardour which [is] the accumulation of long years behind a natural reserve" (PBE, 315). Edward Springrove, in *Desperate Remedies,* has "an impressionable heart" which has for years "been distracting him, by unconsciously setting itself to yearn for somebody wanting, he scarcely [knows] whom" (DR, 200), and Eustacia Vye, having tired of her liaison with Wildeve, drops into a state of "mental vacuity" (RN, 127) which prepares her, "perfervid woman" that she is (RN, 139), for the sudden orientation of her passion toward the figure of Clym Yeobright.

Again and again the same pattern manifests itself. Ennui, lassitude, an inner emptiness, and a vague yearning for some grand adventure — these negative qualities predispose Hardy's characters to the fateful beginning of a new infatuation. In *The Well-Beloved,* the most elaborate dramatization of the mechanism which governs loving in his world, Jocelyn Pierston's many love affairs are always preceded by a period of dullness when the glory fades from the world and specifically from the body of the woman who has been the most recent incarnation of the Well-Beloved. "Each shape, or embodiment," he explains, "has been a temporary residence only, which she has entered, lived in awhile, and made her exit from, leaving the substance, so far as I have been concerned, a corpse, worse luck!" (WB, 33).

Fitzpiers in *The Woodlanders* is a final case in point. He gives the most explicit formulation of the law of falling in love which operates throughout all Hardy's stories of fascination. Love, Fitzpiers says, is a projection outward from a man's affective nature, not a response to anything objectively present as a spiritual essence in the loved one. Love begins in an ennui which makes possible the dangerous building up of unexpended emotion. This emotion discharges itself suddenly and irrationally on almost any person who appears at the right time. There is something pathetic in the randomness with which the lightning of love strikes:

> . . . people living insulated, as I do by the solitude of this place [says Fitzpiers], get charged with emotive fluid like a Leyden jar with electric, for want of some conductor at hand to disperse it. Human love is a subjective thing — the essence itself of man, as that great thinker Spinoza says — *ipsa hominis essentia* — it is joy accompanied by an idea which we project against any suitable object in the line of our vision, just as the rainbow iris is projected against an oak, ash, or elm tree indifferently. So that if any

other young lady had appeared instead of the one
who did appear, I should have felt just the same interest in her. (W, 137-138)

❧

What causes the sudden flowing out of stored-up emotion? Here is encountered one version of a theme which
occurs in a great variety of forms in Hardy: the look.
Many poems or scenes in his fiction are organized as a
system of looks. This theme is sustained by the motif of
eyes which recurs in the poems and fiction. A person's
eyes are his chief means of being related to the world.
The "animated eye" ("To an Impersonator of Rosalind,"
CP, 218) of the other is the center of his power, the place
where the mysterious recesses of his personality are open
to the observer's gaze. The eyes of the loved one are his
most dazzling and fascinating part, the visible aspect of
him closest to his secret consciousness and most exposing
that secret to the lover's look. The drama of fascination
begins with a look, "the lust of the eyes" (1 John 2:16),
and the eyes of the other are the ultimate goal of that
looking. They are the focus of the beloved's life and
lead the lover back recess after recess into the infinite
depths of promised richness, like a landscape without
verge. The eyes of Paula Power in *A Laodicean,* for
example, are of "a bottomless depth" (La, 100), and
Elfride Swancourt's eyes, which give a title to *A Pair of
Blue Eyes,* are "a sublimation of all of her": "it was not
necessary to look further: there she lived" (PBE, 1). Her
eyes are "blue as autumn distance — blue as the blue we
see between the retreating mouldings of hills and woody
slopes on a sunny September morning. A misty and shady

blue, that had no beginning or surface, and was looked *into* rather than *at*" (PBE, 1-2).

The direct encounter, eye to eye in open reciprocity, is often only the final stage before sexual possession in a drama of looks which begins with some form of spying or the look unreturned. This play of glances includes a great variety of mediated ways of looking: the look at a distance; the look at the house of the loved one or at one of his possessions; the look at the person reflected in a mirror; the look at him sleeping.

Love begins most often for Hardy's characters with the view at a distance of a person never seen before. So susceptible are his lovers to the mysterious lure of another person that one glimpse is enough to cause an outpouring of bottled-up emotions. The other person is not known at all, only seen as image, but his clothes, hair, or posture seem to promise so much that the ennui of undirected passion becomes focused in an instant in a fascination which may last a lifetime. I have referred to the passage in the *Life* which tells how Hardy as a youth would fall passionately in love with girls he glimpsed in a lane or at church. His heroes and heroines have the same propensity. A stranger is desirable precisely because he is unknown and therefore may possibly be more interesting than prosaic and familiar neighbors. The pleasure of looking at a stranger who does not know he is being watched is conducive to the beginning of love. It also exacerbates love if it has already begun, as does the inaccessibility of the other, his prior commitment to another person, his association with unknown and distant places, or the fact that he is already loved by someone else. Distance, unfamiliarity, inaccessibility, connection with something more distant which he may provide a means

of reaching — the object of love for Hardy is never desired in a direct encounter of one person with another,
but is always approached indirectly, in one form or another of mediated access, or as a way of reaching something else. He shows great inventiveness in imagining
circumstances of this sort.

Simplest is the falling in love by way of a distant
glimpse, often by a surreptitious and unreturned look.
Somerset's infatuation with Paula in *A Laodicean*, for
example, begins when he looks unseen through a window
into the interior of a Baptist chapel where Paula is re-
fusing to be baptized: "The stranger's girlish form
stamped itself deeply on Somerset's soul" (La, 19).
A Laodicean, like *The Hand of Ethelberta* or *Desperate
Remedies*, is structured around the same motifs which
organize Hardy's more famous novels. Often these motifs
may be isolated in the lesser work in forms which are
purer or simpler, perhaps closer to what is most spontaneous and most idiosyncratic in his imagination. Of all
the scenes in his work describing the moment of falling
in love, none is odder than the one in *A Laodicean* which
shows Captain de Stancy peeping through a hole in the
wall of Paula's summer house gymnasium as she swings
through the air creating "a sort of optical poem": "Paula,
in a pink flannel costume, was bending, wheeling and
undulating in the air like a gold-fish in its globe, sometimes ascending by her arms nearly to the lantern, then
lowering herself till she swung level with the floor"
(La, 195). The motif of the fascinated spy in this curious
scene is characteristic of Hardy, as is the fact that De
Stancy's watching Paula without her knowledge is
doubled: his illegitimate son William Dare and Mr.
Havill are watching him watching, seeing his reaction

to Paula's "sportive fascination" (La, 196) mirrored on his face: "To precisely describe Captain de Stancy's admiration was impossible. A sun seemed to rise in his face. By watching him they could almost see the aspect of her within the wall, so accurately were her changing phases reflected in him. He seemed to forget that he was not alone" (La, 197). A passing reference to the fact that De Stancy's actions "would have been comical to an outsider" (La, 195) shows the reader that Hardy is not being too solemn about this scene. It also reminds him that there is another spectator here, more an outsider than Dare or Havill: the narrator. The narrator is watching Dare and Havill watch De Stancy watch Paula, just as in a melodramatic scene in *Desperate Remedies,* Hardy's first published novel, Anne Seaway watches Miss Aldclyffe watch a detective watch Aeneas Manston (DR, 408-414): "The four persons proceeded across the glade, and into the dark plantation, at equi-distances of about seventy yards" (DR, 414). The latter scene is absurd enough too and is doubtless borrowed from the conventions of sensational fiction on which Hardy depended for this novel. Nevertheless the convention is made over in a way which makes it uniquely his. For a moment, in scenes like these, scenes in which "Night herself seem[s] to have become a watcher" (DR, 414), the reader feels like a spy himself, the first in a repeating series of spies. He becomes aware of himself as an invisible intruder watching the narrator watching the characters watch one another.

The beginning of love in such secret watching can be observed repeatedly in the fiction: Grace Melbury, in *The Woodlanders,* becomes fascinated by Fitzpiers as she watches his house from a distance; Anne Garland, in

The Trumpet-Major, at different times becomes fascinated by John and Bob Loveday when she sees them from
her bedroom window in their fine uniforms; the hero of
"On the Western Circuit" falls in love with a girl he
sees whirling by on a merry-go-round, and then is over-
looked in turn in his lovemaking by the girl's mistress,
who "observe[s] the pair from a screened nook" (LLI,
116).

Perhaps the best example of this motif is the admirable
opening of *Far from the Madding Crowd.* Here Gabriel
Oak watches unseen over the hedge as Bathsheba,
adorned in her crimson jacket and perched on the sum-
mit of her wagon load of furniture, looks at herself in a
looking-glass and smiles: "What possessed her to indulge
in such a performance in the sight of the sparrows, black-
birds, and unperceived farmer who were alone its specta-
tors, — whether the smile began as a factitious one, to
test her capacity in that art, — nobody knows; it ended
certainly in a real smile. She blushed at herself, and seeing her reflection blush, blushed the more" (FFMC, 5).
An extraordinary text! It shows Hardy's great insight
into the nuances of interpersonal relations and also his
ability to embody these relations in concrete gestures
which objectify them. So objectified, they are compre-
hensible to the reader without commentary or analysis.
Bathsheba's charming vanity, smiling at herself, blushing
at the smile, and blushing more at her perception of the
blush, in echoing self-reflection, brings into the open the
hidden intimacy of her relation to herself. The act is
more provocative even than seeing her unclothed would
be, for it reveals a spiritual rather than a physical mystery. It is irresistible to the watching Gabriel. Practicing
the smiles which are designed to captivate men, the vain

Bathsheba safely enjoys both the pleasure of attracting and the power over herself which an outsider might have in beholding her smile. The sense of shame when she sees she is seen causes her to blush, and the recognition that she herself is the seer doubles the blush once more, in an endless play between reflection and reflected which is a short-circuited intersubjective relation. Bathsheba plays the role of both lover and beloved, seer and seen. Gabriel, meanwhile, like the narrator and the reader, has been watching her all along, as David in the biblical story watched Bathsheba bathing (2 Samuel 11:2). Gabriel has been stealing from her that sovereignty over herself she has thought she has been enjoying in secrecy and security. It is not surprising that Gabriel is entranced by his unintentional entry into this arcanum of the feminine nature. Enjoying the delicate peeping-Tom pleasure of seeing without being seen, a pleasure tantalizingly attractive to Hardy's people, Gabriel is captivated in an instant, and the permanent structure of his relation to Bathsheba is etablished. For most of the novel he watches over her from a distance as her servant and unrequited lover.

Sometimes even a distant look at another person is not required to set in motion the sequence initiated by the act of falling in love. Hardy's characters live in a world haunted by the presence of other people. Anything which is a true or false sign of the existence of another may be a means of enticing the lover into fascinated longing. Grace's interest in Fitzpiers is focused on the distant glimmer of his lighted window. She watches this as the sign of his presence there, allowing "her reasoning fancy to play in vague eddies that shaped the doings of the philosopher behind that light" (W, 56). In the same way, Jude Fawley's fascination with his miragelike vision of the distant Christminster acquires "a tangibility, a permanence, a hold on his life, mainly from the one nucleus of fact that the man for whose knowledge and purposes he had so much reverence [Phillotson] was actually living there" (JO, 20). Another example of mediated desires is the way the loving initiated by a look in "On the Western Circuit" is sustained by the letters which the girl's mistress writes for her, pretending they come from the girl herself. I have already referred to "An Imaginative Woman," where the bored wife falls in love with a poet by way of his room. Hardy's description of this strange fascination specifies admirably the irresistible lure the signs of another person's existence may have. It also offers an example of the spontaneous precipitation of latent emotion not directly on the loved one but on the mute evidence that he somewhere exists: "The personal element in the magnetic attraction exercised by this circumambient, unapproachable master of hers was so much stronger than the intellectual and abstract that she could not understand it. To be sure, she was surrounded noon and night by his customary environment, which literally whispered of him to her at every moment; but he was a man she had never seen, and that all that moved her was the instinct to specialize a waiting emotion on the first fit thing that came to hand did not, of course, suggest itself to Ella" (LLI, 11). In the same way, Boldwood falls in love with Bathsheba by way of the valentine; Bathsheba herself is initially attracted to Sergeant Troy by his scarlet uniform and gold braid;

Mrs. Charmond draws men to her by means of the false hair she has obtained from Marty South; and Jude Fawley is attracted to Arabella partly by her hair (also false).

One of the most extraordinary examples of this theme of mediated love is "The Fiddler of the Reels" (LLI, 165-185). This story is structured around a sequence of looks. Mop plays his fiddle with closed eyes, but opens one secretly and covertly watches Car'line, the girl he seduces with his playing. The climax of her fascination comes when she sees that one eye watching her, "quizzing her as he smile[s] at her emotional state" (LLI, 168-169). When she has borne him a child and is living in London married to another man she thinks she catches a glimpse of him one day at the Great Exhibition, but the glimpse is once more indirect: "While standing near a large mirror in one of the courts devoted to furniture, Car'line started, for in the glass appeared the reflection of a form exactly resembling Mop Ollamoor's — so exactly, that it seemed impossible to believe anybody but that artist in person to be the original. On passing round the objects which hemmed in Ned [her husband], her, and the child from a direct view, no Mop was to be seen" (LLI, 177). This passage stands alone in the text of the story. It is not followed up in the narrative, but remains as an emblem of the relation between Mop and Car'line. Car'line's love for Mop has never been straightforwardly oriented toward him, but has been a fascination induced by his music and by his covert glances. This indirection is perfectly symbolized by the reflection in the mirror which cannot be followed to reach the real person.

This text in "The Fiddler of the Reels" is matched by the passage in *The Return of the Native* in which Eustacia, after the death of Mrs. Yeobright, sees Clym's face in the mirror, "ashy, haggard, and terrible" (RN, 386), or by that passage in *Desperate Remedies* in which Cytherea sees Edward Springrove's inverted image reflected in a stream, and then realizes that if she can see his reflection, he can see hers (DR, 280-281), or by that scene in *A Pair of Blue Eyes* in which, a moment after Elfride has enjoyed the pleasure of "looking [Knight] full in the face," he holds her over the pool in the little river so that she can see herself adorned in the earrings he has just given her (PBE, 314, 316-317). Admiring herself in the water, she is also conscious of his admiration of her, and this doubling of looks means that she is aware of herself in part as existing in his eyes. He, on the other hand, watches her watch herself in the mirror of the water, just as Gabriel Oak watches Bathsheba, though here both persons are conscious of the interplay of direct and reflected looks.

A final such scene is that admirable passage in *The Woodlanders* in which Grace Melbury comes unawares upon the sleeping Fitzpiers, turns from him, encounters his image in a mirror and discovers that the eyes of the reflected image are open. In the mirror the seemingly secure watcher becomes the watched, but when she turns to the real man their relation is as before: "Approaching the chimney her back was to Fitzpiers, but she could see him in the glass. An indescribable thrill passed through her as she perceived that the eyes of the reflected image were open, gazing wonderingly at her. Under the curious unexpectedness of the sight she became as if spell-bound, almost powerless to turn her head and regard the original. However, by an effort she did turn, when there he lay asleep the same as before" (W, 150). This text combines the motifs of the observed sleeper[1] and the look by way of the mirror. It is another example of Hardy's genius for expressing objectively subtle aspects of the relations between one person and another. Fitzpiers and Grace are fascinated by one another, but each keeps his fascination hidden, as much as possible a matter of looking admiringly but secretly at someone who remains the unconscious object of a covert glance. A sleeping person is most vulnerable to this capture by a covetous look, least likely to look in return, least likely to betray the lover by a disdainful glance or by that particularly painful form of betrayal Hardy refers to in "Wessex Heights" and elsewhere: "As for one rare fair woman, I am now but a thought of hers, / I enter her mind and another thought succeeds me that she prefers" (CP, 301). The pangs of jealousy are caused in Hardy's characters not so much by physical betrayal as by the loved one's exercise of his power to put the lover out of his mind, to think about something else. If I have granted another person a godlike power to bring me into existence with a look, then if he turns his attention away I am annihilated. If I can catch him asleep his power to create me and destroy me will remain latent, stored up in his dreaming mind, and I can safely possess my possessor. If the sleeper awakes, then the situation is reversed in an instant, and I become subject once more to the loved one's look and to his power of not looking. Hardy

[1] This is another theme in Hardy which anticipates Proust. It occurs in *Two on a Tower* (45-46), in *The Return of the Native* (333 ff.), in *The Woodlanders* (150), and in *Jude the Obscure* (173-174): Lady Constantine watches the sleeping Swithin; Wildeve and Eustacia talk beside the sleeping Clym; Grace watches Fitzpiers sleeping; Jude watches Sue sleeping, in his clothes and in his room.

catches this alternation between dominion and slavery with great intuitive insight in the description of Grace watching the supposedly sleeping Fitzpiers and being secretly watched by him in return. The stealthy approach of one consciousness to another is perfectly expressed in the play of looks and reflections between Fitzpiers and Grace, just as the evasive relation between Cytherea and Springrove is imaged in the way each looks at the reflection of the other, or as the relation of Car'line and Mop is figured in her glimpse of a reflection which has no discoverable cause.

Often, however, loving is generated not by something which stands between the lover and the beloved, but by something beyond or beside the loved one to which he seems to be related. The love which drives Hardy's characters in ceaseless movements of longing is never simple desire for possession of another, but is always desire for something else which seem to be accessible by way of the beloved. Clym Yeobright, for example, is desirable to Eustacia Vye because of his association with Paris, that distant place which, as in the case of Emma Bovary, seems to promise her the rich life for which she longs. Eustacia's love for Clym is directed not toward him, but toward what he seems to stand for or to promise her. Hardy is explicit here about the religious dimension of love. Eustacia falls in love with Clym before she even sees him, falls in love because he promises access to that celestial place, Paris: "A young and clever man was coming into that lonely heath from, of all contrasting places in the world, Paris. It was like a man coming from heaven" (RN, 127). "I suppose," says Clym, when their relation is moving toward embittered indifference, "when you first saw me and heard about me I was wrapped in a sort of golden halo to your eyes — a man who knew glorious things, and had mixed in brilliant scenes — in short, an adorable, delightful, distracting hero?" (RN, 303-304).

In *The Well-Beloved* and in the poem of the same name which is a commentary on it (CP, 121-123), Hardy isolates the religious aspect of loving and presents it more or less in isolation from its usual social and sexual components. Jocelyn Pierston's loving is desire not for the woman herself, but for the goddess who is momentarily incarnated in her person. In the poem this goddess is explicitly identified as Venus. She appears to the lover, tells him it is not the mortal girl whom he really loves, but the divine power which temporarily inhabits her form. When he next sees his bride she seems to have lost all her radiance, "As if her soul had shrunk and died, / And left a waste within" (CP, 123).

This religious theme is not limited, however, to the oddest of Hardy's novels, plus a fanciful poem or two. A religious dimension is integral to the theme of love throughout his work. Eustacia's loving too is displaced religious desire, and the loving or admiration of other characters has the same quality. Giles Winterborne says of Grace Melbury after she has visited Mrs. Charmond: "Your face is like the face of Moses when he came down from the Mount" (W, 76), and Jude as he watches the sleeping Sue sees in her "almost a divinity" (JO, 174). Such passages suggest the way Hardy's lovers make a god or goddess of the persons they love and endow them with divine powers.

The effect of love is also like that of a religious vision. It causes a sudden transfiguration of the lover and of the world around him. A moment before the lover had been living in inner emptiness, surrounded by people without interest for him. Now in an instant he has been filled with a delightful excitement which changes his whole inner life, occupies it entirely with the swarming hopes and visions generated by his desire, as though he had been touched by a god. He now has a new self and a goal for that self. The loved one has the creative power of a deity. She is able to draw into existence a throng of hitherto latent emotions, and she is also able to structure these in a rigorous pattern of desire, as a magnet structures iron filings. She creates the self of the lover and gives that self a new order. Before, he had only a latent existence. Now he is oriented in longing toward the person he loves and organizes his whole life toward trying to possess her.

The Return of the Native provides a description of this miraculous change. Eustacia Vye has not yet seen Clym, only overheard a conversation describing the way he and she are in harmony with one another, but already her inner life is transformed:

> That five minutes of overhearing furnished Eustacia with visions enough to fill the whole blank afternoon. Such sudden alternations from mental vacuity do sometimes occur thus quietly. She could never have believed in the morning that her colourless inner world would before night become as animated as water under a microscope, and that without the arrival of a single visitor. The words of Sam and Humphrey on the harmony between the unknown and herself had on her mind the effect of

the invading Bard's prelude in the "Castle of In-
dolence," at which myriads of imprisoned shapes
arose where had previously appeared the stillness of
a void. (RN, 127)

From vacuity to the plenitude of a myriad tumultuous
emotions — this is the magical change love effects in the
inner life of the lover. The effect on the outer world is
no less startling. Before, the external world was a spectacle which the bored man watched dully from the detachment of his lassitude. Now suddenly the world has
a focus. That center has the power to radiate outward,
shedding a "glory" on the earth and transfiguring everything into a sign of its presence. Within the already
existing humanized space a new structure of dynamic
tensions is introduced which polarizes it, as moonlight
shining through random twigs of a leafless tree seemingly
arranges them in concentric circles. All things now share
in the divine glow of the loved one and have become
expressions of his godlike power. The power is divine in
the sense that it is an ability to organize nature and give
it meaning. If the loved one were absent from the world
it would become once more a fragmented collection of
valueless objects. When the loved one is there, he seems
to permeate everything with his living spirit, like an immanent deity, so that houses, furniture, clothes, the landscape — all declare the glory of his presence in the world.
Everything now has a value and a significance. Everything can be measured in relative worth according to its
proximity to the beloved.

This transformation of the world is described succinctly in a late poem called "I Was the Midmost" (CP,
630). The first stanza recalls a text from the *Life* discussed

earlier. It affirms that when the speaker was a child he was the "midmost" of his world, though only a few people "gleamed" within its "circuit." The second stanza describes his infatuation with a lady who becomes a new center, the axis around which everything else revolves:

> She was the midmost of my world
>   When I went further forth,
> And hence it was that, whether I turned
>   To south, east, west, or north,
> Beams of an all-day Polestar burned
>   From that new axe of earth.

Center, axis, polestar — the lady is all these. She has power to establish all the directions of the compass, measuring everything by its relative closeness to her or degree of association with her. Everything moves around her, and she beams forth from her central point to infuse her presence in all things.

Hardy, as I have shown, ascribes to human beings the power to imprint themselves on the objects they use, saturating houses, furniture, or musical instruments with their emotions, so that these may be released many years later, even by unknowing strangers. An important special case of this is a transformation of objects which operates only for the entranced vision of the lover. This is the reverse of the sequence of loving described in "An Imaginative Woman." There the woman falls in love with her poet by way of his poetry and the objects in his room. Here the lover's attention is directed first to the loved person and then by way of him to the objects around him which seem to have become impregnated with his presence. This process is described repeatedly in the poems. If Hardy's world is everywhere pervaded by the presence of other people, one of the most poignant versions of this is the way a house or a landscape seems to a lover to be permeated with the personality of the woman he loves and to express her presence even after her death.

While the lady was alive she "shed her life's sheen" around her on the place where she lived ("A Dream or No," CP, 328). In her absence or after her death the landscape becomes "Her Haunting-Ground" (CP, 770). The place "wherein she made such worthy show" is "deep lined" "high and low" with her presence, inscribed with the survivor's memory of her, and the landscape has become, even more than her tombstone, "Sacred to [her] Memory" (CP, 634-635).[2] A house and its surroundings have no value in themselves for a lover, but when they become associated with the woman he loves they form the "background" for her "figure," and the lady becomes "the sight that richen[s] these" ("The Background and the Figure," CP, 426), or, as Hardy puts it in "The Figure in the Scene," the lady, even though "the place now knows her no more," is nevertheless "the Genius still of the spot" (CP, 447). Poem after poem returns with moving eloquence to this experience of the way a dwelling or a scene can speak for the lady when she is invisible, absent, or dead. The essence of the person passes into his environment and, at least to the infatuated

2 This poem is about Hardy's sister Mary, but the transformation of the landscape is the same as that in the lyrics which are love poems in the ordinary sense.

eyes of the lover, seems expressed in every line, color, and movement of the scene:

> Upon that fabric fair
>   "Here is she!"
> Seems written everywhere
>   Unto me. ("Ditty," CP, 14)

> That was once her casement,
>   And the taper nigh,
> Shining from within there,
>   Beckoned, "Here am I!"
>   ("In the Mind's Eye," CP, 210)

> Primaeval rocks form the road's steep border,
>   And much have they faced there, first and last,
> Of the transitory in Earth's long order;
>   But what they record in colour and cast
>   Is — that we two passed.
>   ("At Castle Boterel," CP, 331)

Sometimes Hardy plays variations on this theme, as in a tenderly whimsical poem on the death of a pet cat. Even though he has done his best to efface every mark on his house and yard made by the cat, in the attempt to forget the pain of losing him, the cat's death has magically multiplied the signs of his life, according to a paradox of presence in absence of which there are many examples in the poetry. Though the house, while the cat was alive, "scarcely took / Impress from his little look," now that he is dead it "grows all eloquent of him" ("Last Words to a Dumb Friend," CP, 622). In another beautiful and characteristic poem, perhaps a covert description of the effect of moving Emma Gifford from

Cornwall to Dorsetshire, Hardy tells of a friend who thought he was bringing a girl's environment to him when he brought the girl — "The pure brine breeze, the sea, / The mews — all her old sky and space." The girl's atmosphere soon fades, however, like the aroma of a flower uprooted from its native soil, and the lover is left with less than nothing. If a person can be reached through the landscape around him, this poem says, the landscape cannot be preserved in the person and carried safely to an alien place. To change the environment is to change the person, and the girl remains magically attractive only on her native "surfy shore" ("Fetching Her," CP, 602-603).

In another poem the poet laments the fact that since the woman he loves "will never see this gate, path, or bough," the scene can hold no joy or interest for him ("The Difference," CP, 292-293), but in another curious poem he tries to make use of such a scene to escape the suffering of loss. Nothing in the new scene "bespeaks" the lady or bears, as the lover does, her "imprint through and through." By staying long enough in the new place he hopes gradually to absorb its indifference, until, as he says, "my heart shares / The spot's unconsciousness of you" ("In a Cathedral City," CP, 206).

In all these poems the presupposition is the same: milieu and person, scene and figure, interpenetrate and become one. When this has happened either may provide indirect access to the other. The scene has the power to preserve the haunting presence of the beloved in a kind of death in life or life in death. The "Poems of 1912-13," written after the death of his first wife, are Hardy's fullest expressions of this strange experience of an evanescent presence in the landscape, the presence of

an ungraspable phantom which vanishes when he reaches
out for it:

> Why do you make me leave the house
> And think for a breath it is you I see
> At the end of the alley of bending boughs
> Where so often at dusk you used to be . . .
> > ("The Going," CP, 318)

℘

The power a human being has to transform what is
around him into a sign of himself is expressed in the
poems subjectively, as an intimate personal experience.
It is testified to directly by a man who finds the woman
he loves soliciting him from every circumambient object,
driving him to cry out: "Woman much missed, how you
call to me, call to me" ("The Voice," CP, 325). This
motif is fundamental to the fiction too, but there love's
transfiguration of the world is reflected in the cool eyes
of the witnessing narrator. His disillusioned vision makes
it clear that this way of seeing the world is generated
only by the lover's fascination. The change is not visible
to an objective witness. Nevertheless, the same kind of
relation between figure and scene holds for the fiction as
for the poems. A transformation of the scene is repeatedly
described in the novels as one effect of falling in love.

Stephen Smith, in *A Pair of Blue Eyes*, early in his
acquaintance with Elfride Swancourt watches her as she
plays and sings by candlelight. Ever after he associates
her with that scene. This fact leads the narrator to a
formulation of the psychological law which operates in
all such cases: "Every woman who makes a permanent

impression on a man is usually recalled to his mind's eye as she appeared in one particular scene, which seems ordained to be her special form of manifestation throughout the pages of his memory" (PBE, 18).

As in Proust's imagination, so in Hardy's, the beloved is by the strength of the lover's emotions identified inextricably with a characteristic scene, so that the two are ever afterward associated in his mind.[3] Though she may later be encountered in many different places, she carries with her for the lover an almost palpable atmosphere or aura which is her single most appropriate background, the one which is so permeated by her presence that it seems an extension of her hidden essence, something possessing the power to make that essence visible. The lady's characteristic scene is a means of understanding her, and, far from being a mere background or neutral frame, it is a pervasively subjective milieu, the exteriorization of her otherwise hidden self.

There is no better example of this in the fiction than the text in *Tess of the d'Urbervilles* which describes the way Angel Clare's growing infatuation with Tess transforms the dairy-house at Talbothays and its surroundings until they seem to him permeated with her personality:

---

[3] Compare, for example, with the passage I have cited from *A Pair of Blue Eyes* what the narrator of *À la recherche du temps perdu* says of Gilberte: "Le plus souvent maintenant quand je pensais à elle, je la voyais devant le porche d'une cathédrale, m'expliquant la signification des statues, et, avec un sourire qui disait du bien de moi, me présentant comme son ami à Bergotte" (*Du côté de chez Swann, À la recherche du temps perdu*, éd. de la Pléiade, I [Paris: Gallimard, 1954], 100); "Most often then when I thought of her, I would see her standing before the porch of a cathedral, explaining to me the meaning of the statues, and, with a smile which spoke well of me, presenting me as her friend to Bergotte." (Translations from Proust throughout are mine.) See also Georges Poulet's discussion of Proust's use of this theme in *L'Espace proustien* (Paris: Gallimard, 1963), pp. 34-44.

"The aged and lichened brick gables breathed forth 'Stay!' The windows smiled, the door coaxed and beckoned, the creeper blushed confederacy. A personality within it was so far-reaching in her influence as to spread into and make the bricks, mortar, and whole overhanging sky throb with a burning sensibility" (Td, 198). "Throb with a burning sensibility" — the phrase is especially important. In *À la recherche du temps perdu* a scene is often associated with the sensibility of a single person and reveals that person's individuality to Marcel's vision. In the passage from *Tess of the d'Urbervilles,* the sensibility in question is neither that of Tess nor that of Angel. It is the sensibility of both in their relationship. This relation exists by way of the house and the landscape, so that Tess and Angel participate in one another's lives by means of the physical objects around them. The dairy and its landscape are imbued not so much with Tess's presence as with the "burning sensibility" which is generated between them by Angel's fascination with her. The scene embodies their relationship and throbs with the tension it has created. Tess and Angel are not self-enclosed personalities. They exist outside themselves and communicate by way of the physical objects around them.

What is true of *Tess of the d'Urbervilles* is also true of Hardy's other fiction. Love transforms both the lovers and their environment. It creates within the already humanized world of their community a new milieu polarized by their love and made over into an expression of it. A concentrated example of this change is given in a passage in *The Trumpet-Major* describing a scene in the theater and the "deadlock of awkward suspense" which takes place there between four of the characters.

Their awareness of one another stands out against the background of the audience at the play as an almost visible field of interacting forces generated by their strong emotions of love and jealousy. "Had personal prominence in the scene been at this moment proportioned to intentness of feeling," says the narrator, "the whole audience, regal and otherwise, would have faded into an indistinct mist of background, leaving as the sole emergent and telling figures Bob and Anne at one point, the trumpet-major on the left hand, and Matilda at the opposite corner of the stage" (TM, 266).

Such transformation of a social and physical world into an intensely personal world expressing the attractions and repulsions among the protagonists of the story is fundamental to Hardy's fictional art. In page after page, scene after scene, chapter after chapter, the grain or texture of his style presupposes the existence of a place which has been charged with the tensions between the characters and can be used dramatically as an incarnation of these. The geography of each novel is a subjective landscape in which every hill, road, house, or wood objectifies the relations among the main characters. This landscape forms for the reader an inner space identifying the characters with certain locations in a topography of the mind. The reader is invited to imagine the relations between the characters as tensions between centers of subjective energy reaching across the gaps between those locations. Each novel has, like any other fiction, a time special to it created by the slow dance of approach or withdrawal performed by the characters in their relations to one another. This dance takes place within an interpersonal space which embodies it. If the novel exists as a temporal movement generated by the love or hate of the chief

characters, it also exists as a landscape which is the necessary arena for that movement. Many of the novels occur
in some "self-contained place" (W, 4), like the village of
Little Hintock in *The Woodlanders.* The result of such
sequestration is that "from time to time, dramas of
a grandeur and unity truly Sophoclean are enacted in
the real, by virtue of the concentrated passions and
closely-knit interdependence of the lives therein" (W, 4-
5). Self-enclosed unity of place leads to an intensification
of the relations among the people who live in that place.
The locale objectifies these relations, and a novel about
life in such a place can in a way be summed up by a
description of its landscape.

This point could be demonstrated in any of the novels.
A good example is the topographical relationship in *Two
on a Tower* between Lady Constantine's house, the tower
with its surrounding grove, and Swithin's house in the
village. Another example is the relation between the
heath, Captain Vye's house, Mrs. Yeobright's house, Clym
Yeobright's cottage, and the reddleman's wagon in *The
Return of the Native.* Hardy's deliberate use of an
imaginary topography as he composed this novel is con-
firmed by the fact that he included a "Sketch Map of
the Scene of the Story" in the first edition. In a letter to
his publishers he asserted that making such a map was
possible because he had carefully and consciously preserved unity of place in the novel: "I enclose a sketch-
map of the supposed scene in which *The Return of the
Native* is laid, copied from the one I used in writing the
story; and my suggestion is that we place an engraving of
it as frontispiece to the first volume. Unity of place is so
seldom preserved in novels that a map of the scene of
action is as a rule quite impracticable. But since the

present story affords an opportunity of doing so I am of opinion that it would be a desirable novelty" (L, 122). Another example of such a subjectivized space is the tension between Marygreen and Christminster in *Jude the Obscure*. In the same way the houses and the landscape of Casterbridge objectify the relations of the characters in *The Mayor of Casterbridge,* and *Tess of the d'Urbervilles,* as I have said, is organized in terms of the places where Tess lives in her tragic progress toward execution.

Space for Hardy, however, is not, as for Proust or for Dickens, a discontinuous set of places, each with its characteristic quality and personage, each cut off by an all but impenetrable barrier from the other places. His space is a continuum. Every dwelling place, village, or field in his world is open to the others, and even Little Hintock is not so much a single place as a set of dwellings — Grace Melbury's house, Marty South's house, Fitzpiers' house, and so on. People in their relations to one another have the power to traverse space in real movement or in imagination and to create thereby a complex structure of interactions between one place and another. Each novel has its own given pattern of this kind. The motif of the journey or of movement across the landscape which occurs so often in the fiction and poetry indicates the unity of that intersubjective space his characters have created and inhabit together. Specific houses or spots in the landscape are located within an imaginary topography. Between the locations there are lines of force which are generated by the relations between the characters. These forces and the subjectivized landscape which incarnates them are brought into existence in a form which remains more or less definitive for the novel in question by the fateful act of falling in love. Falling in love is the origin of everything else in Hardy's stories, but it could not work out its drama to its predestined end if it did not have power to make over the physical world according to its own patterns of desire.

V

The Dance of Desire

CERTAIN TEMPORAL STRUCTURES are characteristic of the love affairs which take place in these magically charged milieus. Within the space created by the act of falling in love each love relationship moves onward through time, driven by its own energies, for nothing, in Hardy's intuition of human existence, remains static. Every human relationship keeps changing until it ends. This movement takes typical forms which recur from novel to novel.

If the spatial form of the novels is constituted by the polarization of objects according to tensions across the distances which separate the main characters, their temporal form, as it is watched retrospectively by the narrator, is created by the movement of the characters toward one another or away from one another within a world which has been impregnated with emotions. The novels focus with great intensity on the minutiae of these movements, following them step by step and moment by moment as each successive phase embodies itself in circumambient objects. This country dance of approach and withdrawal is often symbolized by the literal dances which occur so frequently in Hardy's world, for example, the dance where Angel and Tess first see one another, or the rustic festivities where Eustacia and Wildeve secretly meet and dance together by moonlight: "Eustacia floated round and round on Wildeve's arm, her face rapt and statuesque . . . The dance had come like an irresistible attack upon whatever sense of social order there was in their minds, to drive them back into old paths which were now doubly irregular" (RN, 309, 310-311).

The circulation of mutually fascinated characters around one another, in a graceful dance of crossings and exchanges, generates the temporal structure of each of the novels. In concentrating so exclusively on this movement, these novels are excellent proof that a work of fiction has a predominantly temporal existence. Fiction is a temporal art in part because its fundamental theme, the development of interpersonal relations, exists in the openness of the movement of one person toward the future fulfillment of himself by possession of another person.

Hardy's lovers, like most lovers, seek to obtain possession of the persons they desire. They want to approach closer and closer to the central figure who radiates a divine glow transfiguring the universe. To possess the beloved would be to coincide with what appears the spiritual center of the world, to enjoy directly what is visible everywhere in reflected, mediated forms, and thereby to achieve self-fulfillment. His characters, however, are special in the slowness, the reticence, the surreptitious indirection, with which they move toward those they love.

Sometimes his lovers seem to suspect that love will disappear as soon as the barriers are down. They linger in their approach, holding off the other, dwelling on all those things which keep the object of love at a distance as well as giving indirect access to it. Other lovers aim vigorously at possession, but are kept from it by a succession of obstacles, some accidental, some put there by the persons they love. The more they are thwarted from consummating their love, the more violent their desire. Sometimes a whole lifetime may be spent in a state of frustrated fascination, a tantalizing movement toward someone who always slips away or is removed behind another ambiguous veil, another windowed wall, or some other obstacle which is a means of communication as well as an impenetrable barrier.

Some lovers move in an alternation between the inflaming and cooling of desire. This variation appears wayward, proof of the intermittences of the heart, evidence of the way his characters are the victims of emotions which, like the wind, blow where they list, driving the men and women subject to them to love or to feel indifference unpredictably. In other cases the alternations between desire and indifference are directed not toward a single person, but toward a series of different persons. Such a lover moves from infatuation to distaste, is attracted anew by someone else, goes through the cycle again and then again. He moves in an ever renewed rhythm of desire and disgust in which he always turns to a new object of love as soon as he abandons the old. Such lovers love only when they do not possess what they desire, ceasing to love when they obtain what seemed to promise perpetual happiness.

Hardy shows great inventiveness in imagining in each of his stories a new version of this theme. Once the situation of desire has been established, often a tangled one involving a crisscross of mismatching loves, the form of each novel is determined by the development of these loves. The narrator, from his safe detachment, watches them through their various stages of proximity and distance, describing each stage with minute circumstantiality as the characters circle around one another in willing enslavement to some form of fascinated desire.

Henchard in *The Mayor of Casterbridge* is Hardy's fullest portrait of the man who knows "no moderation in his requests and impulses" (MC, 88). He is driven by a passionate desire for full possession of some other person. This means that his life is a sequence of relationships in which he focuses first on one person and then on another, desiring each with unlimited vehemence when she seems to promise what he wants, turning from her just as abruptly when she fails to provide it. From Susan, to Lucetta, to Farfrae, to Elizabeth-Jane, Henchard moves in exasperated desire, striving to fill the "emotional void" in himself, turning from Susan and Lucetta, one after the other, when they have yielded to him, desiring Lucetta anew when she becomes desirable to Farfrae, centering his whole life suddenly on Elizabeth-Jane after Susan's death only to discover at that very moment that she is not his daughter, so that a new barrier is created as if by magic between them, turning against Farfrae in an attempt to destroy the rival who is the mediator of his loving, determining for him without his awareness which women will be desirable to him, turning back again at last to Elizabeth-Jane and desiring her with burning possessive jealousy when Farfrae comes again between him and what he wants, to take her too from him.

The Mayor of Casterbridge is a nightmare of frustrated desire. It is structured around episodes which provide repeated opportunities for formulations of the law of love in Hardy's world. "[W]hen I was rich," says Henchard, "I didn't need what I could have, and now I be poor I can't have what I need" (MC, 269). If he has something he does not want it. When it is unavailable his desire is inflamed. Elizabeth-Jane suffers the same incongruity of desire and possession: "Continually it had happened that what she had desired had not been granted her, and that what had been granted her she had not desired" (MC, 205). When Lucetta was Henchard's mistress he felt nothing for her but "a pitying warmth" which "had been almost chilled out of him by reflection," but as soon as she begins turning toward Farfrae and so becomes "qualified with a slight inaccessibility" she becomes "the very being to make him satisfied with life" (MC, 201). Her marriage to Farfrae makes him desire her all the more: "During the whole period of his acquaintance with Lucetta he had never wished to claim her as his own so desperately as he now regretted her loss" (MC, 264). The same pattern is repeated later with Elizabeth-Jane. "Shorn one by one of all other interests," says the narrator of Henchard, "his life seemed centering on the personality of the stepdaughter whose presence but recently he could not endure" (MC, 333). This new movement of desire, like the others, produces the circumstances which will frustrate it, in this case the return of Newson, Elizabeth-Jane's real father, and the court-

ship of Elizabeth-Jane by Farfrae after Lucetta's death.
The "sudden prospect of [Elizabeth-Jane's] loss" causes
him "to speak mad lies like a child," and his affection for
her grows "more jealously strong with each new hazard
to which his claim to her [is] exposed" (MC, 338, 339).
The narrator speaks toward the end of the novel for
Henchard's indistinct awareness of the pattern of his life:
"Susan, Farfrae, Lucetta, Elizabeth — all had gone from
him, one after one, either by his fault or by his misfortune" (MC, 341).

It is both his fault and his misfortune, or rather it is
neither. It is a law of life in Hardy's world that if someone by nature seeks complete possession of another person he is doomed to be disappointed over and over,
either by his failure to obtain the woman he loves or by
his discovery that he does not have what he wants when
he possesses her. Character is indeed fate, and *The Mayor
of Casterbridge* is the story of "the life and death of a
man of character," as the subtitle says. Henchard is
destroyed neither by an external fate nor by a malign
deity, but by "the shade from his own soul upthrown,"
as the quotation from Shelley's *The Revolt of Islam* specifies (MC, 376). The context of the phrase from Shelley
sheds much light on Hardy's conception of Henchard.
The passage comes in the eighth canto of *The Revolt of
Islam*. The heroine, having been captured by some sail-
ors, explains to them that the conception of God has
arisen by projection from evil qualities in man:

> What is that Power? Some moon-struck sophist
> stood
> Watching the shade from his own soul upthrown

Fill Heaven and darken Earth, and in such mood
The Form he saw and worshipped was his own,
His likeness in the world's vast mirror shown . . .
(ll. 3244-3248)[1]

Just as in Shelley's view God is not an independently existing Power who governs heaven and earth, but is the reification of tyrannical tendencies in man's mind, so Henchard is not, as he sometimes thinks, the victim of a malign power imposing suffering on him: "The movements of his mind seemed to tend to the thought that some power was working against him" (MC, 219). Henchard's fate is determined not by a "power" external to himself, but by his own character. This has projected itself on the world around him, creating necessarily the conditions which will produce repetitions of the same pattern of failure in his relations to other people. His fate-producing character is not a psychological mechanism, not some unconscious drive to self-punishment. He is rather one of Hardy's most dramatic demonstrations of a condition of existence in his universe. However vehemently Henchard approaches another person, the shadow cast between them by his own soul will remain as an impenetrable obstacle, his consciousness forbidding union with any of the people he loves.

The impossibility of an enduring love is experienced by each protagonist in a different way. Even those novels

1 Percy Bysshe Shelley, *The Complete Poetical Works*, ed. Thomas Hutchinson (London: Oxford University Press, 1960), p. 117.

which have a happy ending contain underlying shadows which show that they belong in the same world as *The Mayor of Casterbridge* or *Tess of the d'Urbervilles*. *Under the Greenwood Tree*, for example, is the most light-hearted and idyllic of Hardy's novels, but even so the happy ending has darkly ironic undertones. The country people in this novel, with their quaint speech and customs, their full memory of the past and continuity with it, are not so much a "chorus" as a background of unselfconscious absorption in a traditional way of life. In their lack of detachment they scarcely differ from nature itself, as the title suggests. The figures of Fancy Day and Dick Dewy detach themselves momentarily from this stable background, a background as regular, undeliberate, and repetitive as the round of the seasons which gives the novel its temporal structure. The protagonists separate themselves in the sense that their relation to one another makes them self-aware and aware of one another: Dick conscious of himself as unassuaged longing and as a question, the question of what Fancy is thinking; Fancy, as her name implies, alienated by her inconstancy, her vanity, her shallowness, her betrayal of Dick, and her sense of guilt for this betrayal. Though the drama they enact, that of a man meeting and marrying a maid, is of immemorial antiquity and is performed in a milieu and in a rhythm which identify it as a natural sequence, nevertheless their marriage is founded on a deception. It has, like all Hardy's love relations, a vein of betrayal running through it — self-betrayal, betrayal of the other.

Outside these two levels of consciousness, the numb involvement in traditional life of the rustics and the relative self-consciousness of Fancy and Dick, there is the consciousness of the narrator who tells the story. He is more knowing, objective, and cynical than any of the characters. In his objectivity, the objectivity of the "loving" historian of old country ways, he undercuts what he describes. He destroys it in the act of celebrating it, according to that paradox of the historical imagination whereby the deliberate representation of a traditional way of life testifies to the historian's exclusion from it. To see life under the greenwood tree so clearly and to describe it with such optic detachment, however sympathetically, is to be separated from it, to be unable to live it unthinkingly from the inside.

In the same way, Fancy's shallowness and vacillation are suggested in her ability to sit coldly inside her window watching Dick, unwilling to bend far enough out into the rain so he may kiss her, and then thinking "how plain and sorry" a man looks wet through by the rain and without an umbrella (UGT, 180-181). According to a propensity for infidelity usual in Hardy's people it is but one step from this measure of detachment to Fancy's betrayal of Dick when she accepts Mr. Maybold's proposal. Though she finally marries Dick and will presumably live happily with him, the novel is consistent with the other novels in the way the possibility of tragedy lies just under the surface. Hardy seems to be recognizing this in his preface of 1912 when he says that "the realities out of which [the novel] was spun were material for another kind of study of this little group of church musicians than is found in the chapters here penned so lightly, even so farcically and flippantly at times" (UGT, x). Though Dick and Fancy may be presumed to be absorbed into the traditional ways of Mellstock life after their marriage (with the exception of Fancy's secret awareness of her momentary infidelity to Dick), the story of their courtship is set against the background of an historical change, the replacement of the choir in the country church by an organist. This change, though apparently trivial in itself, is part of that wider series of changes which is leading to the destruction of the traditional life, "rooted in one dear perpetual place,"[2] which Hardy so prizes in rural Wessex.

If even *Under the Greenwood Tree* does not have an unequivocally happy ending, there is greater ambiguity still in the nominally happy endings of his later novels. The marriage of Thomasin Yeobright and Diggory Venn at the end of *The Return of the Native* seems, as he admits in his postscript, a falsification of the direction of the novel and a concession to the "circumstances of serial publication" (RN, 473). Most readers find "the more consistent conclusion" preferable, the one never written in which Diggory "was to have retained his isolated and weird character to the last, and to have disappeared mysteriously from the heath, nobody knowing whither — Thomasin remaining a widow" (RN, 473).

Even in the novels where the apparently happy ending was not retracted there is always some dark strand woven into the texture of the story which renders the ending ambiguous. The marriage of Elizabeth-Jane and Farfrae at the end of *The Mayor of Casterbridge,* for example, might seem to qualify Henchard's death by suggesting that happiness is possible, but the final paragraphs show that Elizabeth-Jane, though she has been given so much, is someone who demands or expects little from life. She has long since come to believe that "a brief transit

---

2 W. B. Yeats, "A Prayer for My Daughter," 1. 48, *The Collected Poems* (New York: The Macmillan Co., 1958), p. 186.

through a sorry world" is "a doubtful honour" and happiness "but the occasional episode in a general drama of pain" (MC, 385-386). The irony here is that Elizabeth-Jane's stoic detachment, forced on her in part by the experiences of her early life, renders her unwilling or unable to take full advantage of the opportunities for happiness which she now has. Henchard in such circumstances, the reader feels, would have embraced his happiness fervently, thereby once more preparing its end.

The only happy love relationship for Hardy is one which is not union but the lovers' acceptance of the gap between them. Such a moderate and reasonable love, a love based on detachment, provides the "happy" ending of *Far from the Madding Crowd*. Bathsheba Everdene and Gabriel Oak have outlived the time when they might have sought the bliss of full union with another person. Their dispassionate self-possession keeps them apart, as Fancy's secret infidelity keeps her apart from Dick, though in both cases the degree of separation promises relative security for the marriage. Moreover, the temperate marriage of Gabriel and Bathsheba takes place against the dark background of Bathsheba's tragic relations to Farmer Boldwood and Sergeant Troy, just as *The Woodlanders* ends with Grace back in the arms of a husband who has already betrayed her with Suke Damson and Mrs. Charmond, and is likely, as her father foresees, to betray her once more before a year is out (W, 439-440). "[T]he heroine," said Hardy of Grace Melbury, "is doomed to an unhappy life with an inconstant husband" (L, 220).

Seen from this perspective, the role of Tess's sister, 'Liza-Lu, in the ending of *Tess of the d'Urbervilles,* which has seemed to some readers sentimental, reveals itself to be perhaps the saddest touch of all in the novel. Read in the context of the whole work the ending suggests that the cycle just fulfilled in Tess's execution is about to begin its inevitable round again in the relation of Angel and 'Liza-Lu, just as Elfride Swancourt's abortive elopement with Stephen Smith in *A Pair of Blue Eyes* ironically repeats the life of her grandmother, Elfride, who also ran away with her lover. The doomed repetition of the sequence of earlier lives which Tess has so feared and hated has not been brought to an end by the expiatory act of her acceptance of death, but must, so it seems, be endured again and again by those who come after her for as long as the human race continues. If *The Mayor of Casterbridge* demonstrates the impossibility of escaping from the past, *Tess of the d'Urbervilles* has an even darker theme: the impossibility of avoiding not so much the effects of the past as its repetition. The past has embodied itself in the persons of the present as well as in their surroundings. This embodiment forces people against their will to re-enact the patterns of the past. It is as if they were caught up in a great wind of history which whirls them into the rigid forms of a predetermined dance. This dance moves them toward other people or away from them in ways they do not choose.

The only permanent and (ironically) happy love relationships are those which are not union at all, but for one reason or another prolong indefinitely the time before possession. This is dramatized in an odd story called "The Waiting Supper" (CM, 27-83), in which a pair of lovers scrupulously postpone their union because the woman's husband may be still alive. They put off their marriage from year to year even when it becomes legally permissible, enduring "Time's ceaseless scour over themselves, wearing them away without uniting them" (CM, 81). "The dim shape of that third one stood continually between them; they could not displace it; neither, on the other hand, could it effectually part them. They were in close communion, yet not indissolubly united; lovers, yet never growing cured of love" (CM, 79-80). An admirable expression of the paradoxical happiness open to Hardy's lovers! They can be happy only if their relationship is articially fixed by an obstacle which maintains love while preventing its fulfillment. As is so often the case in his work, the lovers are joined by what separates them. What stands between them prevents their love from dying by preventing also its consummation.

The notion that the real happiness of love lies in unfulfilled hope is argued even more openly in a poem called "The Minute Before Meeting" (CP, 219). The speaker in this poem tells his lady that he would "detain / The few clock-beats that part us," so that he might "live in close expectance never closed / In change for far expectance closed at last." This may seem an echo of Robert Browning's "The Last Ride Together," but in fact it is very different. Browning wants to prolong forever the last time of a kind of possession. Hardy wants to prolong forever the moment before possession, as the play on "close" and "never closed" suggests. Like some of the more perceptive lovers in his fiction, Lady Constantine in *Two on a Tower*, for example, the speaker in this poem knows that as the interval between himself and the woman he loves gradually vanishes, he is moving nearer not only to the brief moment of union, but also to its inevitable aftermath, the time when it "will all *have been*" (CP, 219), and love will be over.

Most of Hardy's lovers do not have the prescience of the speaker in "The Minute Before Meeting." As the flame draws the moth, they are drawn to the persons they love. Their desire for union is only increased by the obstacles forbidding possession. Hardy has an inexhaustible power to invent new situations which dramatize a condition of proximity without union, the barrier to possession inflaming love and providing a means of indirect access as well as forbidding contact.

Sometimes an accident separates the lovers, some ill-luck like the drowning of the wrong woman which in "Fellow-Townsmen" (WT, 111-173) keeps Barnet still unhappily married, still deprived of the woman he loves. This story is an excellent example of Hardy's obsession with the theme of unlucky obstacles which prevent the fulfillment of love. Repeatedly Barnet misses possession of his Lucy, "either by his fault or by his misfortune." The story is, like *The Mayor of Casterbridge*, a nightmare of frustration, though Barnet, unlike Henchard, never reaches even momentary union with the girl he loves. Unlike Henchard again, he remains fascinated by desire for a single person.

Often, as in "Fellow-Townsmen" and many other stories, the obstacle forbidding union is the prior marriage of one of the lovers. Sometimes they are separated by barriers of class, as are Elfride and Stephen in *A Pair of Blue Eyes* or as are Gabriel and Bathsheba in *Far from the Madding Crowd*. Sometimes it is the fastidiousness or scrupulosity of one of the lovers, like Angel Clare's conventional distaste for "fallen women" which makes Tess's honeymoon a grotesque mockery combining proximity and distance in agonizing intensity. In other cases it is a matter not of marriages which are unconsummated, but of unions which are not real marriages, either because their secrecy keeps them from social recognition or because one of the partners is still unwittingly married to someone else, as in the case of Lady Constantine and Swithin St. Cleeve in *Two on a Tower*. Sometimes, as in the elopement of Elfride and Stephen in *A Pair of Blue Eyes*, one lover steps back at the last moment so that though the lovers are compromised in the eyes of the world they are not actually married. In presenting all these variations on the theme of a proximity which is communion without union Hardy shows great skill in imagining scenes which will dramatize concretely some form of obstructed relationship. An example is the communication across windows, doors, streams, or by letter which runs as a connected series of motifs through the poems and fiction. Another is the scene in *Jude the Obscure* in which Jude has Sue Bridehead actually sleeping in his room, dressed in his own clothes, and yet is forbidden to possess her.

The most important and pervasive barrier between Hardy's lovers, however, is neither accident nor physical obstacle nor social convention, but the presence of a third person. His fiction might be defined as an exploration of the varieties of mediated love. The third

person standing between most inflames love and most
successfully prevents the lover from reaching his goal.

Eustacia Vye is the clearest example in Hardy's fiction
of that submission to the law of mediated desire which
is so important in his work, as well as in the work of
Proust and of so many novelists.[3] Eustacia's fluctuations
of love for Wildeve and indifference toward him provide the occasion for statements which are of capital
importance as formulations of the pattern of loving in
all his fiction. Just as Festus, in *The Trumpet-Major*,
is turned away from his love for Anne Garland by the
way John Loveday's supposed desire for Matilda makes
Matilda desirable to Festus too, and just as Lady Car-
oline in "The Marchioness of Stonehenge" "perversely
and passionately centre[s] her affection on quite a plain-
looking young man of humble birth and no position at
all" because she is "stimulated in this passion by the
discovery that a young girl of the village already loved
the young man fondly" (GND, 95-96), so Eustacia ceases
to love the man who is not loved by others and loves
him again when he becomes desirable to another person.
Her relation to Wildeve is mediated by way of his relation to Thomasin. When Eustacia has Wildeve to herself she soon tires of him, but as soon as he turns from
her to Thomasin he becomes desirable again: "The man
who had begun by being merely her amusement, and

3 For a discussion of this concept see René Girard, *Mensonge romantique et vérité romanesque* (Paris: Grasset, 1961).

would never have been more than her hobby but for his skill in deserting her at the right moments, was now again her desire. Cessation in his love-making had revivified her love. Such feeling as Eustacia had idly given to Wildeve was damned into a flood by Thomasin" (RN, 109). As soon as she learns that Thomasin no longer wants Wildeve and that she can have him wholly to herself again, he is magically drained of his attractions for her. She becomes once more indifferent:

> What curious feeling was this coming over her? Was it really possible that her interest in Wildeve had been so entirely the result of antagonism that the glory and the dream departed from the man with the first sound that he was no longer coveted by her rival? She was, then, secure of him at last. Thomasin no longer required him. What a humiliating victory! He loved her best, she thought; and yet — dared she to murmur such treacherous criticism ever so softly? — what was the man worth whom a woman inferior to herself did not value? The sentiment which lurks more or less in all animate nature — that of not desiring the undesired of others — was lively as a passion in the supersubtle, epicurean heart of Eustacia. (RN, 116-117)

The self-deception peculiar to mediated loving appears with great clarity in this text. Eustacia has felt that she has loved Wildeve directly for himself. She has believed that the glory and the dream he radiates are evidence of powers in him, his numinous glow making him so different from other people as to be almost like a god in his superiority. Now through her rival's indifference she discovers in a moment that her love has gone by way of that rival. The divine radiance which seems intrinsic to Wildeve is a subjective mirage cast on Eustacia's vision of him by the fact that Thomasin loves him. Eustacia has been doubly deceived and has fallen into a double inauthenticity. Having become unwittingly a victim to the rival she thinks she despises, she has been led to attribute spiritual qualities to Wildeve which he does not possess. This humiliating phenomenon of mediated love whereby only the desired of others is desirable is the hidden motivating force of most loving in Hardy's work. It takes forms which are appropriate to his own special imaginative world.

In identifying these forms Hardy's own image of the country dance can again guide the interpretation. Along with this figure goes a related image of the circulation of planets around one another in cycle and epicycle. The subjective space of each of the novels has transformed the preexistent physical and social space. This space is created and re-created in the constant changes of relation among the main characters. The interpersonal space is not generated exclusively by the fascination of one character for another, a tension between two persons like the growing love of Angel Clare for Tess which makes all Talbothays seem to breathe of her presence. Nor is it often only three persons — the lover, the beloved, and the third who stands between as mediator and obstacle. Hardy sometimes limits himself to three persons, as in the relation of Swithin St. Cleeve, Lady Constantine, and her absent husband, or as in the relation of husband, wife, and lover in "The Waiting Supper,"

or as in the relation of Fancy, Dick, and Mr. Maybold in *Under the Greenwood Tree*, or, more subtly, as in the relation of Angel, Alec, and Tess in *Tess of the d'Urbervilles*. More often, however, the kaleidoscopic motion within the subjective space of a novel is generated not by the changing relations among two or three persons only, but by the arrangements and rearrangements of a whole group of characters, at least four or more. They circulate around one another in constantly altering configurations determined by complex relations of attraction, repulsion, or neutrality. These complicated movements, in their ironic crisscrossings, contradictions, and incongruities, constitute the temporal dimension of the novels. A novel by Hardy is usually not a pas de deux, nor even a three-cornered dance. It most often develops from the changes through time of desire, hatred, or indifference by a whole group of characters who are fascinated with one another in various ways. Like a darting goldfish in a bowl, like a planet in its course, like a dancer in a reel, each character is driven to circle erratically not by his relation to one other person, but in response to the varying pulls of several, as "the dance whizze[s] on with cumulative fury, the performers moving in their planet-like courses, direct and retrograde, from apogee to perigee" (WT, 7).

I have suggested that the temporal structure of *The Mayor of Casterbridge* is made of the sequence of Henchard's loves, as he moves from one love to another, going from desire to dissatisfaction to estrangement and back to desire once more. In fact, it would be better to think of the novel in terms of the revolutions around one another of a group of characters, Henchard, Farfrae, Newson, Susan, Elizabeth-Jane, Lucetta. Each of these has his own specific nature, the heat of Henchard as against the cold detachment of Elizabeth-Jane, or the butterfly inconstancy of Lucetta which is both like and unlike the insouciance of Farfrae.[4] Each character may be thought of as having his own particular emotional charge, a charge which remains more or less fixed throughout. The movements of the characters toward one another and away are governed not by direct desire or indifference, but by attractions which are always mediated by way of intervening characters. So Lucetta becomes desirable to Henchard again when she turns to Farfrae, just as in *Under the Greenwood Tree* Fancy's love for Dick Dewy is inflamed by her father's objections, so that she "love[s] him more for the opposition than she would have otherwise dreamt of doing" (UGT, 166).

The Woodlanders, even more obviously than *The Mayor of Casterbridge*, has no central character, though one character or another may momentarily be chosen as a focus or as a point of view from which to see the others. The novel consists rather of the modulations of multiple relationship among the five principle characters: Marty South, Dr. Fitzpiers, Giles Winterborne, Mrs. Charmond, and Grace Melbury. Each is determined in his relations to any one of the others not by direct longing or hatred, but by a complex feeling which depends on a reaction to several characters at once. There is much looking from afar in this novel, as in all Hardy's fiction. As Grace watches Fitzpiers, so Winterborne watches Grace, Marty watches Winterborne, and Fitzpiers watches over Grace at the end of the novel. The novel is like a slow minuet

---

[4] For a discussion of the pattern of variations in character among Hardy's protagonists, see Richard Beckman, "A Character Typology for Hardy's Novels," *ELH*, XXX (March 1963), 70-87.

in which the characters one by one are shown making obeisance at a distance to other characters. When one person is watching another, that person is scarcely conscious of the existence of the devoted watcher, but is focusing all his attention on a third character, and so on. The love of Winterborne for Grace or of Marty for Winterborne is more or less static only because it is made hopeless by the interposition of a successful rival, but the loving of the philandering Fitzpiers and even of the milder and more conventional Grace wavers like a weathervane in a fitful breeze depending on whether the loved person is accessible or is hidden behind some barrier. Just as Mrs. Charmond, "a woman of perversities, delighting in piquant contrasts" (W, 234), is attracted to her former lover Fitzpiers partly because of his new relation to Grace, so Fitzpiers is a "man whom Grace's matrimonial fidelity [cannot] keep faithful," but who is "stung into passionate throbs of interest concerning her by her avowal of the contrary" (W, 400). Grace herself feels little interest in Winterborne when she is engaged to him, but returns his love when she can no longer have him: "There could not be the least doubt that gentle Grace was warming to more sympathy with, and interest in, Winterborne than ever she had done while he was her promised lover"; "she loved Winterborne now that she had lost him more than she had ever done when she was comparatively free to choose him" (W, 129-130, 265).

The same law of loving operates in *Far from the Madding Crowd*, in *A Pair of Blue Eyes*, in *The Return of the Native*, in *Jude the Obscure*, in *The Well-Beloved* — in fact throughout Hardy's work. All his novels are variations on the tragicomedy of crossed fidelities. Each novel describes the relations not of a single pair of lovers, but of a group in their tangle of conflicting desires. *The Return of the Native,* to give another example, does not focus exclusively on Eustacia Vye, but is made up of the changing relations of Thomasin and Clym Yeobright, Wildeve, Diggory Venn, Eustacia, and Mrs. Yeobright. If Eustacia moves from Wildeve to Clym and, having "love[d] too hotly to love long and well" (RN, 245), back to Wildeve, according to the permutations of mediated desire, Diggory echoes Gabriel Oak in his static fidelity, as well as in the reasons for it, while Wildeve is driven by the same inexorable law which governs Eustacia's loving: "The old longing for Eustacia had reappeared in his soul: and it was mainly because he had discovered that it was another man's intention to possess her" (RN, 253); "Obstacles were a ripening sun to his love, and he was at this moment in a delirium of exquisite misery. To clasp as his for five minutes what was another man's through all the rest of the year was a kind of thing he of all men could appreciate. He had long since begun to sigh again for Eustacia; indeed, it may be asserted that signing the marriage register with Thomasin was the natural signal to his heart to return to its first quarters, and that the extra complication of Eustacia's marriage was the one addition required to make that return compulsory" (RN, 310-311).

"Compulsory" — the word suggests a psychological law, a law which governs the desires of all men and women with implacable coercion. The rigors of this law are the central theme once more in *Jude the Obscure.* This story concentrates more than any other of the novels not on a single character or group of characters, but on the relation between two lovers. Just as Jude's relation to Sue is the center of his life, so Sue, as Arabella says at the end of the novel, after Jude's death, has "never found peace since she left his arms, and never will again till she's as he is now!" (JO, 494). Though their love is consummated in physical union, it is prolonged beyond union (an unusual occurrence in Hardy's work) by the instinctive reticence and scrupulous reserve of both lovers. This persists even beyond their union. Sue, who has caused the death of one of her earlier lovers by "holding out against him so long at such close quarters" (JO, 177), resists Jude's advances coolly when they are together and then writes tender little notes to him when they are separated. The unchanging fixity of their relation is suggested by the frequency with which they communicate by letters or through windows or across some other physical, psychological, or social barrier. There always remains some obstacle between them, usually one created or maintained by Sue. It is as if she suspects that their love will end as soon as all the barriers are down, just as in *The Well-Beloved* Jocelyn Pierston has "seldom ventured on a close acquaintance with any woman, in fear of prematurely driving away the dear one in her," that is, the goddess she incarnates (WB, 38).

Though *Jude the Obscure* concentrates so exclusively, so poignantly, and so intensely on a relation between two lovers, even here the mediators who stand between play an important role. Like the other major novels, it dramatizes the complex tensions among a number of protagonists. Phillotson and Arabella have somewhat the same functions here as Farfrae and Lucetta in *The Mayor of Casterbridge*, or as Giles and Mrs. Charmond in *The Woodlanders*. Hardy's novels repeat not only external situation, theme, and motif, but also the deeper organizing principles which give an inner structure to each story. Phillotson's role as the mediator of Jude's longing to win a place for himself at Christminster makes it appropriate that he should marry Sue and establish himself as the permanent obstacle forbidding Jude's full possession of her, just as it is almost inevitable that Farfrae should deprive Henchard of Lucetta and Elizabeth-Jane. Jude's rapid disgust with Arabella, after his brief yielding to fleshly love, suggests that Sue is right not to give herself to Jude if she wants him to go on loving her. As another obstacle between Jude and Sue, Arabella keeps warmth in Sue's dog-in-the-manger desire to fascinate Jude without submitting herself to him. From proximity to distance and back to proximity without ever yielding to the lure of unmediated closeness, Jude and Sue perform their version of the dance of desire. All Hardy's lovers must move in this dance, and their approach or withdrawal is motivated as much by the presence of other people as by the natural rhythm of their love.

Even a relatively simple early novel like *A Pair of Blue Eyes* dramatizes this theme. Elfride Swancourt, the charming but dangerously inconstant heroine of this novel, is another example of the waywardness of love and of the inevitability of betrayal. She is "a girl whose emotions [lie] very near the surface" (PBE, 1). Powerfully but superficially attracted to the men she has glimpsed at a distance or has heard of indirectly, she loves the man who has a "private mystery" (PBE, 74), but who has not yet yielded to her charms. She quickly becomes coy again when she has him in her power. She moves through life from betrayal to betrayal. One man has already died for love of her before the novel begins. Later she leaves

Stephen Smith to turn to Henry Knight, attractive to her because Smith so much admires him. Then she betrays Knight to marry Lord Luxellian. A woman loving three men in sequence, Elfride, as Proust saw, reverses the pattern of Jocelyn's life in *The Well-Beloved*.[5] Hardy may have had this in mind when he said in his preface of 1912 that *A Pair of Blue Eyes* "exhibits the romantic stage of an idea which was further developed in a later book" (PBE, viii), though perhaps he may rather have been remembering the sequence of Bathsheba's loves or of Eustacia's tumultuous passions and betrayals. A similar pattern of love is exemplified in all four cases. Whether his lovers have the butterfly vanity of Elfride or the deeper desires of Eustacia Vye, the course of their loving is the same.

The complex tangle of incongruous loves in *Far from the Madding Crowd* will provide a final example of this. Gabriel Oak remains a faithful lover at a distance not only because his love is unfulfilled, but because the succession of men in Bathsheba's life keeps his love undimmed. To Bathsheba, on the other hand, Gabriel is of little interest when he makes a direct offer of his love, but Farmer Boldwood piques her vanity by his reserve, though he becomes distasteful when her imprudent valentine transforms him into a passionate lover, while Sergeant Troy attracts her by the way he appears mysteriously from a distance. Troy, however, tires of Bathsheba when he has married her, just as he tired of Fanny Robin when she yielded to him. He returns to passionate devotion to Fanny after her death has interposed the

---

5 See Chapter VII for a discussion of Marcel's analysis of Hardy's work in *À la recherche du temps perdu*.

most impenetrable barrier of all. Once more the circling dance of a group of lovers structures the dramatic action of the novel as the characters revolve in complicated patterns of approach and withdrawal.

The power of death to renew love, so important in *Far from the Madding Crowd*, is also one of the most pervasive motifs in the lyrics, for example in the poems Hardy wrote about his first wife after her death. It is also the fundamental theme of *The Well-Beloved*. As death puts an infinite distance between lover and beloved, so it raises love to a measureless intensity of longing. Just as Sergeant Troy centers his whole life on his regret for Fanny after her death, just as Hardy brooded over his past life with his wife when she died and wrote poem after poem about her, and just as *The Woodlanders* ends with the irony of Marty South's claim that she possesses Giles Winterborne completely and exclusively only when he is dead, so Jocelyn Pierston in *The Well-Beloved* is the most self-conscious, theoretical, and intense of Hardy's lovers because his loving is mediated not by the presence of a rival, but by the infinite distance of death. Most of the lovers are too unreflectively absorbed in their pursuit of the well-beloved to see their love with any perspective. In Jocelyn Pierston's loving the usual structure of desire in the novels has been transposed by the strange conditions of Jocelyn's life to a more "metaphysical" level, but the same pattern of love exists in *The Well-Beloved* as in the other novels.

The "antirealistic" texture of *The Well-Beloved*, penultimate novel by Hardy, presents some of the idiosyncratic qualities of his imagination in a purer form than they take in the more conventional novels. It is also valuable as an implicit commentary on the design of loving in his other fiction. Love goes through the same movements in all his novels and poetry. These patterns are, in his view, "more or less common to all men" (WB, vii), but in *The Well-Beloved* the gestures of desire are brought explicitly to the surface of the protagonist's consciousness as well as to the surface of the narrator's mind. As a result, their constant patterns and the laws which determine these patterns may be more clearly seen. *The Well-Beloved* is certainly given to abstract formulations, as the poems sometimes are and as *The Dynasts* is, but it is also like the poems in being more "frankly imaginative" (WB, viii), more intense, more legible in its governing matrix, and closer to the motivating center of Hardy's imagination.[6]

A distinction must be made here, however. To Jocelyn it seems that the person he loves is the incarnation of a goddess, "one shape of many names" in the phrase from Shelley's *The Revolt of Islam*[7] Hardy used as an epigraph for the novel. A divine essence, he thinks, embodies herself successively in the various women he loves, leaving each incarnation when she abandons it a "mournful emptied shape," "like the nest of some beautiful bird

[6] The first version of *The Well-Beloved* was entitled *The Pursuit of the Well-Beloved*. It was published weekly in serial form from October to December of 1892 in *The Illustrated London News*. The revised text was published in volume form only in 1897, two years after the first publication of Hardy's last written novel, *Jude the Obscure*. The ending of the first version of *The Well-Beloved* differs considerably from the version of 1897 in thematic statement, in atmosphere, and in dramatic event.

[7] The phrase appears twice in *The Revolt of Islam*, canto I, l. 363, and canto VIII, l. 3276 (Shelley, *Complete Poetical Works*, pp. 46, 118).

from which the inhabitant has departed and left it to fill with snow" (WB, 38). "As flesh she dies daily," says Jocelyn, "like the Apostle's corporeal self; because when I grapple with the reality she's no longer in it, so that I cannot stick to one incarnation if I would" (WB, 52). If the protagonist is caught until almost the end of his life in this Platonic or Shelleyan dream, the narrator sees through the deception and recognizes that Jocelyn's loving is, like Fitzpiers' love for Grace or like desire throughout Hardy's work, "a subjective phenomenon" (WB, 11). Shelley's "one shape of many names" is "Power" or God, that is, the same concept of a malign force originating in man's subjectivity but seeming to be an external evil as is described in the text from *The Revolt of Islam* quoted toward the end of *The Mayor of Casterbridge* and discussed earlier in this chapter. In fact the two phrases come within a few lines of each other in Shelley's poem. If Henchard's sufferings are projected outward from his character, Jocelyn Pierston's "one shape of many names," his elusive well-beloved, is no less a distortion or shade in his own character which he casts outward and gives a seeming objectivity in the external world. Jocelyn's self-consciousness, his power to analyze his emotions and to offer a theoretical explanation for them, is doubled in a further analysis by the narrator which reveals that Jocelyn's explanation is false. The narrator replaces metaphysics by psychology as the true subject matter of the novel. Further confirmation of this is given by a note of 1926 cited in the *Life*. "It appears," says Hardy, "that the theory exhibited in *The Well-Beloved* in 1892 has been since developed by Proust still further: 'Peu de personnes comprennent le caractère purement subjectif du phénomène qu'est l'amour, et la

sorte de création que c'est d'une personne supplémen-
taire, distincte de celle qui porte le même nom dans le
monde, et dont la plupart des éléments sont tirés de nous-
mêmes' " (L, 432).[8]

When *The Well-Beloved* is seen to be based, like
Proust's novel, on a subjective theory of love it shows
itself not only to be consistent with Hardy's other novels,
but to be a revealing variation on them. Just as Henchard tires of Susan, Lucetta, and Elizabeth-Jane after he
has them at his disposal, so Jocelyn moves from one
woman to another, desiring them from afar when they
seem to embody the deity of love, turning from them in
an instant when a close approach shows the woman to
be only a woman after all. Repeatedly, like the young
Hardy himself, he falls in love with a girl he glimpses
"in the distance — at the end of a street, on the far sands
of a shore, in a window, in a meadow, at the opposite
side of a railway station," but "mostly, when at close
quarters," he is "disappointed for his pains" (WB, 49,
50). In one place he formulates succinctly the rhythmic
law of his loving. He has, he says, "been always following a phantom whom I saw in woman after woman while
she was at a distance, but vanishing away on close approach" (WB, 110).

When he meets Avice Caro, however, the situation
changes. Though at first he thinks the goddess has incarnated herself in Avice, he decides, after all, that she has
not, "because," as he says, "I retain so great a respect for

8 *À l'ombre des jeunes filles en fleurs, À la recherche du temps perdu,*
éd. de la Pléiade, I, 468: "Few people understand the purely subjective
character of the phenomenon of love, and the sort of creation which it
is of a supplementary person, distinct from the one who carries the same
name in the world, and a large part of whose elements are drawn from
ourselves."

her still" (WB, 37). The true test of an incarnation of
the Well-Beloved is the evanescence of Jocelyn's infatuation, and so Avice is proved to be "the only woman he
had *never* loved of those who had loved him" (WB, 73).
When after Avice's death he meets the second Avice,
daughter of the first, then he falls in love with the only
lasting passion of his life. He is plunged into the most
extraordinary experience of mediated loving in Hardy's
work. He loves not the second Avice and not the memory
of the first Avice, but the first Avice as reincarnated in
the second, for "the lost and the found Avice [seem] es-
sentially the same person" (WB, 86). He now loves by
mediation as he never could love directly. He desires the
first Avice by way of the second. This is quite different
from his loves so far. These have been an attempt to find
the ideal permanently incarnated, without equivocation
and without distance, in a living person. The second
Avice is the "double" or the "daps" of the first, and in
her "the past shines in the present" (WB, 83, 89, 93).
The first Avice lives in the present with an intense combination of presence and absence which guarantees that
Jocelyn's love will never change. It will never change
because, like Sergeant Troy after Fanny's death or like
Hardy after his wife's death, he is separated from the object of his desire by an impenetrable barrier and so can
never consummate his love. At the same time, unlike
Troy or Hardy he has before him constantly the second
Avice. She is "the living representative of the dead"
(WB, 101). In her the "phantom of Avice" has "grown to
be warm flesh and blood," "[holding] his mind" not on
herself, but "afar" on the absent Avice whom she represents with an irresistibly fascinating combination of
tangible flesh and intangible spirit (WB, 85). Avice is

untouchable forever beyond the borders of death, yet she "surround[s] him like a firmament" (WB, 73) in the person of the second Avice: "He loved the woman dead and inaccessible as he had never loved her in life . . . [N]ow the times of youthful friendship with her, in which he had learnt every note of her innocent nature, flamed up into a yearning and passionate attachment, embittered by regret beyond words" (WB, 74). In this superimposition of two women, the dead and her living daughter, the elusive goddess of love, "that Protean dream-creature, who had never seen fit to irradiate the mother's image till it became a mere memory after dissolution" (WB, 90), is incarnated anew, but this time in a way more permanent and more painful than any other appearance she has made. He was tormented before by the disappearance of the goddess when he made a close approach to any woman. "[N]ow the terrible thing is," he says, "that the phantom does *not* vanish, but stays to tantalize me even when I am near enough to see what it is!" (WB, 110).

The accidents and obstacles which prevent the physical consummation of Jocelyn's love for the second Avice are oblique evidence that his love is really for the first Avice, with whom union is impossible. That Jocelyn should fall in love with a third Avice, granddaughter of the first, after the death of the second Avice, confirms once more the fact that his love is that strange form of mediation which is the repetition of one person in another. This is a widespread theme in romantic and post-romantic literature. It appears, for example, in the work of Gérard de Nerval, of W. M. Thackeray, and of Proust. Hardy's version must be interpreted, however, in the context of his other work, and it would be a mistake to impose on it, for example, the romantic idealism of Nerval. The narrator of *The Well-Beloved* understands that it is not a supernatural goddess whom Jocelyn loves. Jocelyn, he sees, is the victim of a displaced religious desire which focuses itself on one woman after another. The theme of repetition in *The Well-Beloved* is the fullest exploration of that law of mediated desire in Hardy's work which dictates that love will be inflamed by whatever separates the lover from his goal while at the same time providing him indirect access to her.

In the second and third Avices, Jocelyn finds an intense version of the presence in absence which tantalizes Hardy's other lovers too. His love is therefore exemplary for the desire they all experience as they are driven hither and thither in the ever-renewed dance of love, circling around one another in stylized patterns of distance and proximity which repeat in one way or another the universal form of love. The temporal structure of each of Hardy's novels is a variation of this form. As his lovers approach one another or separate the novel changes like a field of forces in dynamic motion. Each character is a node of energy in the field, and the movement of the novel is determined by the waxing and waning of a group of mediated loves. As long as there is distance, desire is exacerbated. Some third thing or person must always stand between two lovers to sustain their love, and the closer they move to one another without union, the greater their desire.

VI

"The End of the Episode"

THE LAW WHICH GOVERNS the ending of love in Hardy's world is stated with admirable brevity in a notebook entry of 1889: "Love lives on propinquity, but dies of contact" (L, 220). Love vanishes as soon as the goal of love is obtained. It exists only so long as that goal is close enough to be seen, but has not yet been reached. Sexual union is the goal of desire for most of Hardy's lovers. Though it is rarely treated so openly as in the scene of Tess's deflowering, it remains the silent and unspoken center of his love stories, either as the consummation which his lovers seek, or as an undescribed interlude after which the reader encounters characters whose relationship has radically changed. Since physical union is the closest approach his characters can make to one another, it has the greatest power to change suddenly the quality of their relation. When proximity becomes at last "contact," the lover is returned almost instantaneously to his dissatisfaction, his indifference, his boredom. With contact love dies. The world which until a moment before had been polarized around the object of love, dynamized ever more intensely by the presence of the well-beloved, now becomes flat and dull once again. It becomes once more a collection of disconnected objects unorganized by any permeating spiritual power.

Hardy, like Proust, is fascinated by the experience of falling out of love as much as by the changes produced by falling into love. In the note of 1926 on the similarities between *The Well-Beloved* and *À la recherche du temps perdu* Hardy quotes a passage from *À l'ombre des jeunes filles en fleurs* which describes succinctly the progress of love in his own work: "Le désir s'élève, se satisfait, disparaît — et c'est tout. Ainsi, la jeune fille qu'on épouse n'est pas celle dont on est tombé amoureux" (L, 432).[1] Falling out of love, like falling into it, changes everything within the lover and without. A text in *The Return of the Native* identifies the curious moment when this change is taking place. Eustacia is no longer completely infatuated by Wildeve nor has she yet returned completely to her senses. She is halfway between, neither asleep nor awake, neither beguiled nor disillusioned, in an odd state like that of a man who is dreaming and yet knows that he is dreaming, or like that

---

[1] "Desire appears, satisfies itself, disappears — and that's all. Thus, the girl one marries is not the girl with whom one fell in love." The page reference to the second volume of the 1922 edition of Proust's *À l'ombre des jeunes filles en fleur* given in the *Life* is incorrect, and I have so far failed to locate this needle in that haystack of words, *À la recherche du temps perdu*. Among the many other texts in Proust's novel which apply well to Hardy's sense of love the following seems especially apposite: "Every loved person, even to a certain extent every person is to us like Janus, presenting to us the face that pleases us if that person leaves us, the dreary face if we know him to be perpetually at our disposal" (*La Prisonnière*, *À la recherche du temps perdu*, éd. de la Pléiade, III, 181: "Tout être aimé, même, dans une certaine mesure, tout être est pour nous comme Janus, nous présentant le front qui nous plaît si cet être nous quitte, le front morne si nous le savons à notre perpétuelle disposition.").

of the light when night has not yet fled, but dawn is unmistakably approaching. This is "that peculiar state of misery which is not exactly grief, and which especially attends the dawnings of reason in the latter days of an ill-judged, transient love. To be conscious that the end of the dream is approaching, and yet has not absolutely come, is one of the most wearisome as well as the most curious stages along the course between the beginning of a passion and its end" (RN, 118).

This stage, when a person is half in love and half out of it, is extremely unstable. Once a passion has begun to fade it quickly ends. Dawn comes, and the lover is returned to the common light of day. Then the magic glow of the beloved disappears. Like Henchard when the reader first meets him stalking along beside Susan, with "a dogged and cynical indifference" (MC, 1), like Jude after he has been lured into sexual submission by Arabella, like all Hardy's lovers when they have obtained the goal of their desire and "fitful friendship" (LLI, 12) or the "atmosphere of stale familiarity" (MC, 3) peculiar to marriage has replaced the ardors of courtship and flirtation, Eustacia soon tires of her conquests. Wildeve becomes "no longer to her an exciting man whom many women strove for, and herself could only retain by striving with them. He was a superfluity" (RN, 118). In the same way, the solitude in which she and Clym Yeobright live after their marriage, isolated in their lonely house on the heath, has "the disadvantage of consuming their mutual affections at a fearfully prodigal rate" (RN, 284). The narrator can later say, "The glory which had encircled him as her lover was departed now" (RN, 416).

A poem called significantly "At Waking" (CP, 208-209) describes, in terms which are valid for all Hardy's

characters who fall out of love, the instantaneous transformation, in an unhappy moment of insight, of the person seemingly endowed with a supernatural charm into
the "bare / Hard lines" of a woman who is "but a sam-
ple / Of earth's poor average kind":

> Yea, in a moment,
> An insight that would not die
> Killed her old endowment
> Of charm that had capped all nigh,
> Which vanished to none
> Like the gilt of a cloud,
> And showed her but one
> Of the common crowd. (CP, 208)

Lois Deacon and Terry Coleman argue in *Providence
and Mr. Hardy*[2] that this poem, which is identified in the
Collected Poems as having been written at Weymouth in
1869, describes a crucial moment in Hardy's relationship
to Tryphena Sparks. If this is so, it suggests that the most
important stage in his love affair with Tryphena was not
the original fascination, but the experience of falling out
of love. The girl who had seemed encircled with a golden
glow suddenly becomes deprived of her radiance. She is
transformed into an ordinary human being like the
others, a woman without special interest or significance.
Hardy's betrayal of Tryphena, if betrayal there was, may
have been not so much a willful act as a spontaneous
transformation of his feelings for her, a change of attitude which represented the most irremediable act of
faithlessness. In any case, a devastating disillusionment

[2] Pp. 77-78.

and the infidelity it causes occur repeatedly as fundamental motifs in the poems and fiction.

If the glory departs from the loved one, like gilt from a cloud, it also departs from the world she has transfigured. When I possess the woman I love the distance between us disappears. I then stand in the same place as she, in that spot which has seemed the spiritual center of the world, with a magic power to transfigure everything, myself included. As soon as I reach this place the ordering radiance my lady has shed on the world vanishes in an instant. I find myself back again in a universe infinitely wide in space and time, a universe I view again with detached objectivity. No field of force orients this desolate expanse as to high and low, great or small, good or bad. Now I can see clearly that the world is a chaotic mass of objects and people driven in random motion by the impulsions of a blind energy working within them. The words "blank" or "blankness" echo through the poems as terms for this "vision appalling" ("At Waking," CP, 209). The words describe the dizzying emptiness, the barrenness and neutrality, of the landscape when the woman once loved is lost or dead, or when the lover has ceased loving her. What was once a plenitude everywhere shining with the presence of the beloved becomes a wilderness, an abyss:

> . . . it cannot be
> That the prize I drew
> Is a blank to me!
>
> ("At Waking," CP, 209)

> There shall remain no trace
> Of what so closely tied us,

And blank as ere love eyed us
  Will be our meeting-place.
      ("The End of the Episode," CP, 211)

  Till in darkening dankness
  The yawning blankness
Of the perspective sickens me!
      ("The Going," CP, 318)

I am laughing by the brook with her,
  Splashed in its tumbling stir;
And then it is a blankness looms . . .
      ("The Dream is — Which?" CP, 615)

Many poems describe the juxtaposition, in the awak-
ened lover's mind, of the old illuminated world and the
new barren one. Once the dream has vanished, it can
never be recaptured. The disillusioned lover can do no
more than swear to stick to his "clear views and certain"
("He Abjures Love," CP, 221). He swears never to allow
himself to be again bewildered by the fantasies of love.
Now he can set the recollection of those fantasies against
the dreary reality which has been there all along but
which has been invisible to his infatuated eye:

  No more will now rate I
    The common rare,
  The midnight drizzle dew,
    The gray hour golden,
  The wind a yearning cry,
    The faulty fair,
Things dreamt, of comelier hue
    Than things beholden! . . .
      ("He Abjures Love," CP, 220-221)

Midnight drizzle, a gray vista, a wind which expresses no human meaning — Hardy's characteristically drab landscape is here, as well as the low-keyed note of re-signed but clearheaded despair with which his spokesmen habitually behold and describe it.

The same experience of disillusionment ends "I was the Midmost." It will be remembered that the first stanza of that poem describes childhood, when the speaker was the safe center of his own world, while the second stanza describes the transfiguration of everything after love has made the lady seem the axis and radiant polestar of the world. The third stanza, in a reversal characteristic of the movement of Hardy's poems (as of his fiction), takes the protagonist beyond love into a clear-eyed vision of reality. The disillusioned lover encounters once more the "scene that lours" (CP, 221) of "He Abjures Love," but here the emphasis is not on the dreariness of the scene but on its disorder. The lady was not really the center of the world. In fact it has no center. The some-time lover now hears only a confused babble of voices located randomly here and there. These voices solicit his attention with cries of hopeless longing from every direction:

> No midmost shows it here, or there,
>   When wistful voices call
> "We are fain! We are fain!" from everywhere
>   On Earth's bewildering ball! (CP, 630)

The catastrophic experience of falling out of love is proof that in Hardy's world no person can play the role

of God for another. His work is a prolonged exploration
of the fact that in a world without God no attempt to
replace God by another person will succeed. For men
who believe in God love for another human being can
be an authentic religious experience, as Dante's love for
Beatrice is a means of salvation, or as Donne can take
more than half seriously the metaphors transferring divine powers to the lady, or as Gérard de Nerval's search
for the evasive spirit who incarnates herself first in one
woman and then in another is a religious quest led on by
glimpses of a power from beyond the world, or as sexual
love and religious experience are inextricably mixed for
W. B. Yeats, since "natural and supernatural with the
self-same ring are wed," and even heaven itself is a realm
of erotic energy where "Godhead on Godhead in sexual
spasm [begets] / Godhead."[3] In all these cases some supernatural power makes possible the transfiguration of
natural love. Lacking this belief, Hardy sees in love only
a subjective infatuation, but his characters are possessed
of a longing for God or for something like a God to give
order and meaning to themselves and to their world.
When they fall in love they think they have found in the
loved one a power of this sort. Their disillusion when
they obtain possession of what they have so intensely desired is a negative religious experience. If Hardy's lovers,
like the good lovers in Meredith's novels or in George
Eliot's, were able to accept the fact that the persons they
love are fallible human beings like themselves, then a
happy and enduring love might be possible. Henchard,
Eustacia, or Jude would not be satisfied with this sort of

---

3 W. B. Yeats, "Ribh Denounces Patrick" and "Ribh in Ecstasy,"
Collected Poems, pp. 283, 284.

love. Their love is a covert religious quest, and each must sooner or later discover that the person he or she has loved is no god, that there is in fact no godlike presence anywhere, no spiritual power radiating order and value on the lover and on his surroundings.

Each of Hardy's protagonists has, like Henchard, the sense of a void within. This inner emptiness is the absence of any absolute ground for the self. These characters seek escape from their ontological insufficiency by way of relations to other people, in a yearning movement of one subjectivity toward another which generates the dramatic action of Hardy's fiction as of the fiction of so many other novelists. In his world, however, the gap always remains, that pain of loss or sense of hollowness which the permutations of the game of love can never more than momentarily ease. His characters, in a world without a center, a world without any supernatural foundation, seek unsuccessfully to locate a center and a foundation.

When I win the woman I have loved, all the mediators and barriers vanish. I discover that she is a human being like myself and that as such she has no more right than I do to be called the center of the world. Worse yet, when I win her my perspective coincides with hers, and I discover that her extraordinary power comes only from me and has existed only in my own eyes. "Brides are not what they seem," says Venus in "The Well-Beloved," "Thou lovest what thou dreamest her" (CP, 122). My lady's seeming "glory" ("Quid Hic Agis?," CP, 415) has come only from myself. I have been the source of her power and have endowed her with the divine aura she seems to have.

Each man lives in a world of his own. Of this world he is the center, and from this center he casts a subjective glow outward on the world. "A world of [his] own has each one underneath," and this means that each man is "severed" from his fellows by "many a mile" ("The Ballet," CP, 463). Each man can say, "Life is a wheeling show, with *me* / At its pivot of interest constantly" ("Lady Vi," CP, 760). Hardy's habitual image for this is the "halo" or "nimbus" which each person unwittingly radiates around himself, changing the aspect of everything he sees into something private and illusory. In one poem the speaker once "hied" "gaily gallantly on" encircled by a "halo" which is both "beauty and dream" ("Just the Same," CP, 649). In another a "faded woman" boasts that when she was young "an iris" "ringed [her] with living light" ("Her Apotheosis," CP, 634). "The Youth Who Carried a Light" (CP, 451-452), in another poem, is surrounded by "the radiance of a purpose rare," an "inner" light, "giving out rays," which "displac[es] the gray of the morning air." In the same way Henchard and Susan carry their indifference to one another like a "nimbus" enclosing them in their own somber worlds (MC, 3), while Tess's young friends have each "a private little sun for her soul to bask in; some dream, some affection, some hobby, at least some remote and distant hope" (Td, 12). This image is echoed with fine symbolic and ironic effect in the description of the drunken party going home by moonlight on the night Tess is seduced: "and as they went there moved onward with them, around the shadow of each one's head, a circle of opalized light, formed by the moon's rays upon the glistening sheet of dew. Each pedestrian could see no halo but his or her own, which never deserted the head-shadow, whatever its vulgar unsteadiness might be; but adhered to it, and persistently beautified it; till the erratic motions seemed an inherent part of the irradiation, and the fumes of their breathing a component of the night's mist; and the spirit of the scene, and of the moonlight, and of Nature, seemed harmoniously to mingle with the spirit of wine" (Td, 84). Each man lives imprisoned in a private world, but this world is so inextricably mixed with the solid and objective exterior world, like breath with mist, that the man imprisoned in his subjective vision of things, like a man bewildered by drink, has no power to distinguish what comes from himself from what is objectively there. Surrounded by a halo cast out from his own subjectivity, he lives self-inebriated, imprisoned in the dreams his drunkenness generates.

Falling out of love brings sobriety. It is the experience of a double awakening. It means finding that there is, after all, no source of meaning exterior to the self, and it means finding that I have been unwittingly the origin of what seemed to be an objective structuring of the world. Far from escaping the dangerous situation of being myself the power which creates order and value in a world without them, I find that I have myself all along been casting out from myself the radiance which seemed to come from the lady. This is just the situation I have been trying to avoid, and so I am returned, at "The End of the Episode" (CP, 211), back to a world moved only by the incessant impulsions of the Immanent Will. The world is just as stale and uninteresting as ever, in fact more so, for the one hope for an escape from boredom has failed.

Sooner or later, for Hardy's most important characters, there comes a moment when they recognize once and for all how they have been duped by love and resolve to be duped no more. This recognition brings, most often, a spontaneous detachment which so closely coincides with the character's recognition of the futility of love that no relationship of priority may be established. At one moment the character is still wholly oriented toward the person he loves, striving with all his heart to possess her. When possession is attained he discovers that it is not what he expected. This discovery is immediately followed by a withdrawal of the lover's consciousness into lucid detachment. It might be better to say that the lover discovers he has always been separated. No strategy of involvement, he comes to see, will close the gap which keeps him isolated from what is outside himself, the prisoner of his consciousness. Now that he has been disabused of his illusions he becomes a disinterested spectator of life. From a situation of cool uninvolvement he watches everything, the woman he once loved, the world around him, the triumphant rival, even himself as a half-comic actor in the closing scenes of the vile drama of life. This movement of disengagement appears repeatedly at the climax of Hardy's stories.

Henchard at the end of his life, for example, gives up all attempts to involve himself with other people. He wanders off alone, "an outcast, an encumberer of the ground, wanted by nobody, and despised by all." In this forlorn state he "live[s] on against his will" and has "no wish to make an arena a second time of a world that [has] become a mere painted scene to him" (MC, 369). The concluding phrase here is significant. Henchard, most warmly engaged, most emotive and "choleric" of all Hardy's heroes, becomes in the end so separated from life that the world appears as an artificial backdrop without depth or substance, something against which no authentic drama of existence can be enacted.

In the same way the unwritten ending of *The Return of the Native,* in which Diggory Venn was "to have disappeared mysteriously from the heath" (RN, 473), would have been a final ratification of Diggory's watching detachment throughout the novel and of the association of this separation with the heath. Disappearing from the heath, Diggory would have seemed to have been reabsorbed into it and to have become again a part of its "watchful intentness." Though this ending remained unwritten, existing only as a ghostly footnote on the last page, there is a climactic moment when Eustacia herself, the person in the novel most heroically determined to fulfill an ideal love, reaches a "state . . . so hopeless that she [can] play with it" (RN, 403). Her playing takes the form of dividing herself into two persons, one who is an actor and sufferer in life and one who is a detached watcher of that suffering. "[L]ike other people at such a stage," says the narrator, she can "take a standing-point outside herself, observe herself as a disinterested spectator" (RN, 403).

The same division of the self into an actor and a spectator of the action is expressed in a strangely moving poem called "He Follows Himself" (CP, 610-611). In this poem the speaker remembers being "in a heavy time" the detached consciousness which watched the other half of the self, "dogging" it, haunting it like a ghost, and reproaching it for all its foolish involvements in life. In the end past tense becomes present tense. Both parts of the self then join to become ghosts together and to haunt the grave of a dead friend:

> And I seemed to go; yet still was there,
> And am, and there haunt we
> Thus bootlessly.

More often, however, the movement of detachment is not a division of the self into two persons, but is a separation from life in which the character becomes completely changed into an uninvolved witness of all that once had lured him to longing and suffering. At the end of *The Hand of Ethelberta,* Christopher Julian, who has received a "perpetual snubbing" from Ethelberta ever since he has known her, stands back just out of sight to watch her sweep by in her fine carriage: "He stood a long time thinking; but he did not wish her his" (HE, 454). Near the end of "Fellow-Townsmen" Barnet abandons his ever-renewed, ever-frustrated pursuit of Lucy and wishes only to wait outside the church to watch her marriage to his rival, Downe. "I'll stand back," he says, "and see you pass out, and observe the effect of the spectacle upon myself as one of the public" (WT, 159). In the same way, Jocelyn Pierston is in the end cured by an illness of his infatuation with his evasive well-beloved. Having now "no love to give" (WB, 216), he makes a marriage of convenience and ends his life advancing plans for the hygienic improvement of his native town. Among them, significantly enough, is "a scheme for the closing of the old natural fountains in the Street of Wells" (WB, 217). Now Jocelyn is willing to live all on the surface, seeking no longer to join his secret depths to the depths outside himself. A final example of this motif is the scene at the end of *The Mayor of Casterbridge* in which Henchard watches as an unseen spectator the dance celebrating Elizabeth-Jane's marriage to Farfrae. The rival is once more triumphant, or rather the two rivals triumph, for Newson, Elizabeth-Jane's real father, has also "supplanted" Henchard and dances with the bride (MC, 374-376). In each of these cases Hardy has provided a striking gesture or scene which serves as an emblem of the final separation of the character from what had drawn him to engagement in life. He is transformed into a watching lucidity of consciousness.

This change would seem to be the end point of Hardy's exploration of human existence. It will be remembered that a spontaneous withdrawal of the mind into onlooking separation is the beginning of his own adventure in life. Frightened by the glare and garish rattle around him, he moves to the periphery and watches quietly from a safe position of disengagement. This disengagement seems to lie behind Hardy's choice of a career as a writer. It also determines the voice and stance of his narrators, that cold detachment and wide vision of all events in time and space which is present from the first words of each novel in the objectivity of the narrative language. His writing, I have argued, is undertaken as a safe means of exploring various kinds of involvement, especially that fascinated pursuit of another person which is his concept of love. Writing is a secure way of gambling with life, a way in which it appears that he cannot lose, whichever side of the coin falls uppermost. In a note of January 1, 1902, Hardy writes what he calls "a Pessimist's apology": "Pessimism (or rather what is called such) is, in brief, playing the sure game. You cannot lose at it; you may gain. It is the only view of life in which you can never be disappointed. Having reckoned what to do in the worst possible circumstances, when better arise, as they may, life becomes child's play" (L, 311). Writing is a way of taking the pessimist's view and of playing the sure game. If the search through writing for some plausible satisfaction in love turns out to be unsuccessful, no damage has been done, for he has involved himself only vicariously. He remains immobile and protected, watching his narrator watch the adventures of imaginary characters who each seek union with those they love. If success in love is proved possible by this indirect exploration of it, then there is nothing to prevent him from coming out of his seclusion and yielding in the real world to the lure of one or another of those women who appear so beguiling when glimpsed at a distance.

The outcome of this circumspect exploration of life might have been predicted in advance. It might have been guessed that Hardy would be most interested in those lovers who ask more from love than it can possibly give in a world constructed as his is. Given such a world, Henchard, Eustacia, Jude, and Jocelyn are doomed from the start, as the narrator knows well enough, though it is hidden from the characters.

Hardy's relations to Tryphena Sparks, to his first wife, and to the other women who attracted him more or less fleetingly at various times in his life match strikingly the pattern of the love stories in his fiction and poetry. He was not always able to remain detached, investigating indirectly the promises of love. He was recurrently driven to enact in his own life a drama like that in his fiction and poems. Life seems to have imitated art here as much as art life. The pattern followed by the course of love was established early in Hardy's experience and in his earliest writing. Both his art and his life were ever-deepening variations on this pattern. Just as in a backward view the reader can see that Hardy's fictional lovers were destined to be disappointed, so one is not surprised to find that his marriage to Emma Gifford, the central event of his life, led eventually to "deep division" and "dark undying pain" ("Had You Wept," CP, 358). There came to be, as he said, a "thwart thing betwixt us twain, / Which nothing cleaves or clears" ("The Division," CP, 205). One may imagine, knowing Hardy, that part of him remained coolly separate, watching the antics of himself as lover even in the midst of his first infatuation with his wife-to-be, not to speak of the time after their marriage, when his ardors had cooled with possession of what he had desired, just as the passions of Henchard, or Jude, or Eustacia eventually cooled.

Certainly the reticence, the distance, the impersonality of the published letters to his wife[4] confirm the notion of a passive estrangement. Hardy seems to have returned after his marriage to his habitual position of witnessing detachment, as the slender evidence of the *Life* suggests. There is, for example, his comment on a somber little poem called "A January Night (1879)." In that poem "The rain smites more and more, / The east wind snarls and sneezes," and "There is some hid dread afoot / That we cannot trace" (CP, 438). The poem, he explains in

---

[4] See the letters collected in *Dearest Emmie* (London: Macmillan, 1963), and see also Carl J. Weber, *Hardy of Wessex,* 2nd ed. (New York: Columbia University Press; London: Routledge and Kegan Paul, 1965), chapter XVII, "Deep Division," pp. 211-218, for a discussion of further evidence for Hardy's marital unhappiness in the nineties.

the *Life*, describes an incident after he and his wife had taken a house at Tooting, on the Surrey side of the Thames. There, he says, "they seemed to begin to feel that 'there had past away a glory from the earth.' And it was in this house that their troubles began" (L, 124). What the "troubles" were, he does not specify, but they appear to have involved marital estrangement. The echo from Wordsworth recalls strikingly his similar use of it to describe Eustacia's disillusionment with Clym Yeobright: "The glory which had encircled him as her lover was departed now." Hardy seems to have lived in his own life several dramas of fascination and disillusionment like those of his fictional lovers. He may in fact have been less wholeheartedly abandoned to his loves even at their height than Henchard or Eustacia, and probably he had more prescience of their end. This very prescience may have entered as a cause of the end of love and may even offer some justification for Tryphena's betrayal of him, if she did indeed betray him, or for Emma's coolness toward her husband. Who can wholeheartedly love a man who keeps so much of himself in reserve? Such speculations about Hardy's life will always remain guesses because of the incompleteness of the evidence. The poems, however, are apparently often direct expressions of one or another of his experiences or moods, in spite of his claim that they are dramatic monologues. The lyrics throughout, like the novels, are spoken by a man who cannot desire the fulfillment of love without at the same moment foreseeing its end.

This foresight is justified by the event. Hardy's lovers are led fatefully one by one to that moment when they perform the act of separating themselves from the world with which he himself began. They become what the narrator of their stories has been all along: onlookers, watchers from a distance. Abandoning all hope of achieving what they have sought in life, they separate themselves resolutely and look from the outside at everything, even at themselves. The structure of Hardy's works of fiction may therefore be defined as an ultimate convergence of the protagonists' point of view with the narrator's point of view. This final agreement in stance of hero and storyteller is exactly the opposite of that approach of author and hero which René Girard sees as fundamental in fictional form.[5] For Girard, when Flaubert says, "Madame Bovary, c'est moi," he is performing an act of humility made possible by the writing of the novel. This self-abasement is the author's acceptance of his incarnation, his acceptance of the fact that he is a limited human being like any other, not a superior judge able in proud arrogance to look down on his poor characters and condemn them for their blindness and narrowness. In Hardy's case the movement is the reverse. The character moves toward that superior position the narrator has occupied from the beginning. Looking down on himself he judges himself in the same way the narrator does. This final coincidence of the narrator and the protagonist justifies the narrator in his detachment. It demonstrates conclusively that Hardy was right to suspect that it is far better to remain separate from life, immobile, untouched, never to involve oneself with other people, never to "perambulate" this "afar-noised World." His fiction seems to be a triumphant vindication of the attitude toward life which has been natural and instinc-

---

5 See *Mensonge romantique et vérité romanesque*, pp. 298-299.

tive for him from the beginning. It proves what he wants it to prove, that it is best to live "in quiet, screened, unknown," "Shut from the noise of the world without, / Hearing but dimly its rush and rout" ("A Private Man on Public Men," CP, 885).

VII

"I'd Have My Life Unbe"

THOUGH THIS COINCIDENCE of the protagonist's point of view with that of his witness may be the recurrent climax of Hardy's writing, it is not the last stage in his spiritual adventure, nor is it even the last stage in the adventures of his characters. After the convergence of the protagonist and the narrator, they diverge again. In this divergence the justification of Hardy's art may be found. The divergence begins with the kind of insight detachment from life brings his characters. It is increased still more by the reaction of the characters to this insight.

The spontaneous withdrawal from life which forms the denouement of so many of Hardy's stories causes simultaneously a number of further movements of the mind. There is a change in orientation from future to present and then to past. As long as my infatuation continues, as long as my love is unsatisfied, I focus my life in absorbed attention toward the future, spending my time in a continual attempt to move closer to the woman I love. I am caught up in the dream of a transfiguration of my existence when I shall come to possess her. This change remains in the future, and the momentum of my life is a perpetual advance toward a goal which always recedes further, like the rainbow. When I reach my beloved, discover my folly, and am freed from my enchantment, this movement stops. At first, after my involuntary stepping back from my foolish pursuit of happiness, I look from above, in an immobile insight, at my present self and at my present situation. This insight then spreads backward in time to illuminate my past and to reveal the pattern it has formed. Until now I have been so absorbed in the present and in its yearning movement toward the future that I have had no perspective on my life or on the connection its moments have had to one another. The detachment given by falling out of love gives me enough distance from my life so that I can see it as a whole and see the connections between its parts. Having moved forward in complete absorption, seeking to join myself to someone who is a center of energy and value always ahead and outside, I am now free to turn back to see the hitherto hidden pattern my life makes and to see also the inevitability of that pattern.

To say "pattern" is to use a spatial term, a term fully justified by this alteration of perspective in Hardy's characters. The change from infatuated movement forward to a detached seeing of the past is also a change from time to space. Detachment spatializes time, freezes it into a fixed shape. As the perspective of the characters approaches that of the narrator it approaches also his wide view of all moments in time as simultaneously present, juxtaposed side by side in a spatial design. The movement in orientation from future to past is a transformation of time as it is lived from moment to moment into the spatialized time of a permanent destiny. An example is the incident in court in which the old furmity-woman makes public Henchard's "mad freak," so many years before, of selling his wife. This is spoken of as "the edge or turn in the incline of Henchard's fortunes" (MC, 251) — as if his life were a spatial movement which could be graphed as a line. When Henchard has gone bankrupt the narrator comments that now his "whole career was pictured distinctly to his neighbours" (MC, 254). Pictured as a design which may be grasped in a single glance by his neighbors, it is also ultimately pictured so for Henchard himself. At the end of his life he looks back to see how all those he has loved have gone from him one by one. As the characters reach the narrator's "long vision," they reach also his ability to see life as a fixed pattern.

This change in relation to life from existential temporality to spatialized time is dramatized in a poem called "Self-Unconscious" (CP, 311-312). The poem describes someone who once walked "watching shapes that reveries limn," so absorbed in his dream that "seldom he / Had eyes to see / The moment that encompassed him." He is entirely caught up in his dream of the future. It would have been better, the poem says, if he had taken more notice of what was around him and of himself in the midst of those surroundings. This then slips into something a little different. What the man most needed, the speaker of the poem says, was enough perspective on his life to see it as a single pattern: "O it would have been good / Could he then have stood / At a clear-eyed distance, and conned the whole." To separate oneself from direct involvement in life is to substitute clear vision for that clouded state of mind which is so blindly preoccupied, so emotionally involved, that it is both "self-unconscious" and unconscious of what is immediately before the senses. It is to substitute for absorption in a narrow part of life a view of the parts as they fit together to make a whole.

As is always the case in Hardy, such wide vision is impossible when it would be helpful, that is, when a man is so wrapped up in "projects" and "specious plans" that he can see nothing else. These projects are leading him ineluctably to the moment when he will be granted, too late, a view of the whole, granted it at a time when "such vision / Is mere derision, / Nor soothes his body nor saves his soul" (CP, 312). This postponement of insight until the wisdom born of it can no longer be put into practice is a constant law in Hardy's universe, so that a recurrent refrain of his fiction and poems is the lament born of a delayed insight: "If I had only known what I know now." One never knows at the time. The experience is too close when it is happening, too isolated from what comes before and after and gives it its true meaning, to be understood. Only when it is part of the irremediable past may an encounter with another person, a decision to marry or to part from someone, an act of betrayal or of allegiance, be comprehended. As a consequence, "Life offers — to deny!" ("Yell'ham-Wood's Story," CP, 280). Existence is "A senseless school, where we must give / Our lives that we may learn to live!" The "lessons" of life take up all our days and "leave no time for prizes" ("A Young Man's Epigram on Existence," CP, 281). There is an "ingenious machinery contrived by the Gods for reducing human possibilities of amelioration to a minimum — which arranges that wisdom to do shall come *pari passu* with the departure of zest for doing" (MC, 369). An insight into this law leads the narrator of *Tess of the d'Urbervilles* to make a sour comment on

Roger Ascham's aphorism about learning by experience. "By experience," said Ascham, "we find out a short way by a long wandering." "Not seldom," says the narrator, thinking of Tess's seduction, "that long wandering unfits us for further travel, and of what use is our experience to us then?" (Td, 124). When Hardy's people reach a clear-eyed distance and con the whole, it is already too late for this vision to help them live their lives happily. Even so, this recognition of the pattern their lives make is something at least gained from life. All the most important characters sooner or later reach a point in which they see their past lives clearly, see them "as a vain pantomime" ("On One Who Lived and Died Where He Was Born," CP, 624).

To see time as a pattern in space is to see it as determined to follow just the sequence it does follow. Space fatalizes. From the perspective of any moment in time chosen as the present, the past and future seem to exist still and already. Everything which happens appears to be inevitable, all events existing on the same plane of irrevocability. To represent time as a movement through space is already implicitly to be a fatalist. Hardy is not exempt from the almost irresistible power of this habit of mind. His constant practice, in the poems, in the fiction, and in *The Dynasts,* of presenting temporal passage, whether historical or personal, as movement across the landscape is an expressive form of more strength than any theoretical statement in persuading the reader to accept a vision of life as determined. Often the motif which organizes a novel or poem, the motif which most concentrates the meaning of a character's life and which remains in the reader's mind as an emblem of it, is the image of travel across the land. As he goes from one place toward another place the character is in the middle of the journey of his life. He is moving not just from one place to another, but from the completed past toward a future which has not yet come into existence. To express the temporality of human life in this way is to suggest covertly that the future already virtually exists, just as the past cannot fade from existence. The town I have just left is still there as tangibly and solidly as when I was in it, and the town I travel toward is already present, containing as concretely as the stones of its houses the possibility or rather the certainty of the experiences I shall have there.

This is strongly expressed in many of the poems which use the motif of travel, for example, "The Wind's Prophecy" (CP, 464-465). This poem may describe Hardy's involuntary betrayal of Tryphena Sparks when he met and fell in love with Emma Lavinia Gifford, his first wife.[1] The poem is spoken in the present tense by someone who is moving as the poem progresses across a desolately stormy landscape near steep cliffs and the sea, a landscape like that of northern Cornwall, where Hardy first met Emma Gifford. Though the speaker continues to swear allegiance to the black-haired girl from whom he has just parted, the wind foresees his betrayal of her and his new allegiance to a girl with "tresses flashing fair." The image of a journey reinforces the reader's premonition of the speaker's infidelity. He travels fatefully across the land

[1] As Lois Deacon and Terry Coleman suggest in *Providence and Mr. Hardy*, pp. 84-85.

toward an encounter which can no more be avoided than the steady flow of time itself, or than the fact that one girl is in the place he has abandoned, the other girl in the place toward which he moves. His betrayal is not something for which he can be held responsible, but happens as inevitably as the passage of time and as irrevocably as the law of space which says that if I am in one place I am separated from all the other places.

The image of a journey is used repeatedly to the same effect in the novels. *The Mayor of Casterbridge,* for example, may be summed up as Henchard's passage through life, from the opening scene when he walks toward the fateful wife-selling at the Weydon-Priors Fair to his final wanderings and death in a ruined cottage twenty miles from Casterbridge. In the same way, Jude Fawley's life is contained in that moment when, having walked two or three miles from home, he stands on the ladder by the "Brown House" near the intersection of the public highway and the old Roman road, Icknield Street. Marygreen and his early childhood are behind him, and before him is Christminster, the "heavenly Jerusalem" (JO, 18) toward which he longs to go. Tess's life, as I have suggested, is contained in her movements from Blackmoor Vale to Trantridge, to Froom Vale, to Flintcomb-Ash, to the final wanderings with Angel Clare which reach their end at Stonehenge and lead to the scaffold at Wintoncester. The spatial design of the novel diagrams its temporal structure. Tess travels a determined course through life toward her fated end. This course, as the method of narration powerfully suggests, pre-exists its actualization in the same way as the stations of her life are already there before she reaches them. This form of determinism adds its weight to the notion that Tess's life repeats the lives of those who preceded her to confirm even more strongly the fatalistic "It was to be" (TD, 91) with which her neighbors encounter life.

Hardy's concept of fate is neither that of some all-powerful transcendent force, malign or benign, consciously manipulating the lives of its puppets, nor is it like Faulkner's notion of some single catastrophic event after which a life is doomed to follow a certain sequence to its end. Each man for Hardy remains free until his death, but when the moment of retrospective illumination comes he sees that he has all along been the victim of an unconscious power which has used his free acts as part of the irresistible forward movement which hurries him on, keeping him from fulfilling his intentions and from attaining any desirable life. His life has at no point been determined once and for all by some cataclysmic event. Even Tess's seduction, for example, might have been followed by a happy life if Angel Clare had been willing to accept her as his wife after his discovery of her past, or if her letter of confession had not miscarried, or if Tess had been more adroit in appealing to his sympathy after their marriage. While Hardy's characters are alive they remain open toward the future, still potentially capable of exchanging sorrow for happiness. When they look back on those lives from a point near death they can see that they have been victimized by a whole sequence of small causes, each natural in itself, none shattering enough to produce a definitive revelation about the nature of existence, but constituting in sum a complex sequence of contiguous events, each closely interwoven with the next, so that there never was any possibility of escape from the series, and all adding together when seen in retrospect to make the remorselessly inevitable pattern of a life, like those dots in the child's puzzle which, when joined together with lines, are turned magically into the picture of a lion or a rabbit.

Like most people in his epoch, Hardy accepts without question a universal principle of causality. Every event, every choice, every experience has its appointed physical cause. His notion of causality is not the Aristotelean or Christian one of an original or final cause. Nor is it the secular version of the Protestant notion of responsibility which appears in George Eliot's early work: the idea of a single act which starts an irremediable chain of effects. Nor is it that more sophisticated notion in *Middlemarch* of a complex web of causes interacting simultaneously. Hardy's image of the total working of the Immanent Will may be of the latter sort, but his image of a single human life is simpler. A life is a chain of small causes, each effect becoming a cause in its turn, or being effected anew by a single cause entering from the outside. The whole forms a linear sequence which is the course of a life. A phrase in *The Mayor of Casterbridge* defines this image of existence succinctly. Human lives are "concatenations of phenomena wherein each is known to have its accounting cause" (MC, 235).

When a person gets enough distance from his life to look back on the multiplicity of events which has made up its detail he sees that those events, taken together, have the tight-fitting pattern made, for example, by stones cemented closely together to form a building. The Immanent Will works in its unconscious fabrications as though it were a good craftsman in that profession of architecture which was once Hardy's own, or in that profession of master-builder in stone and wood which was his fa-

ther's, or in that craft of stonemasonry which he gives
to Jude Fawley. The close neatness of effect wrought
by a sleeping craftsman is an important part of the irony
of his world, or of "the pity of it," as the narrator says
of Tess's seduction. Every event in a man's life, every
place he has lived in or visited, every choice, every emotion, every person he has known — all can be seen to
fit closely together, when viewed in retrospect, to form
the fated structure of his life. The craftsmanship of
Hardy's novels is a fabrication of the structure of the
lives of the protagonists, the chapters or scenes fitting
closely together in blocks of self-contained narrative to
construct solidly the edifice of a group of interlocking
destinies.

❦

If the pattern of a man's life is in closeness of fit like
a stone house or church, it is also like a building in its
symmetry. Marcel Proust first made this comparison. In
a brilliant passage in *À la recherche du temps perdu*
Proust's narrator tells Albertine that architectural balance of design is a salient quality of Hardy's imagination.
Marcel has been explaining how each artist has special
hallmarks which are his personal signature, a certain
pattern of notes for a composer, a certain interior or
quality of light for a painter, a certain scene or situation for a novelist. This means, he says, that "the great
writers have never written more than a single work, or
rather, they have refracted across diverse milieus that
unique beauty which they bring into the world." He sees
that in Hardy's case one such signature is the architec-

tural parallelism of his plots, that "stone-mason's geometry in [his] novels."[2] Hardy's stories, when viewed from a distance, as a spatialized form, reveal themselves to be constructed like a well-designed building. They are organized around symmetrical recurrences of theme and event, each prominent motif balancing a similar one in another part of the book, a pillar, gable, or window here to match a pillar, gable, or window there. It is just the sort of structural habit one might expect to find in a man who was trained as an architect in stone:

> ". . . I returned to the stonecutters of Thomas Hardy," says Marcel. "You will remember them in *Jude the Obscure*, have you seen in *The Well-Beloved*, the blocks of stone which the father takes from the island coming by boat to be piled up in the studio of the son where they become statues; in *A Pair of Blue Eyes*, the parallelism of tombs, and also the parallel line of the ship, and the contiguous railroad cars in which ride the two lovers and the dead beloved; the parallelism between *The Well-Beloved* where the man loves three women, *A Pair of Blue Eyes* where the woman loves three men, etc., and finally all those novels which may be superimposed one on top of the other, like the houses [in *The Well-Beloved*] vertically stacked on high upon the rocky soil of the island."[3]

2 *La Prisonnière, À la recherche du temps perdu,* éd. de la Pléiade, III, 376: "les grands littérateurs n'ont jamais fait qu'une seule oeuvre, ou plutôt réfracté à travers des milieux divers une même beauté qu'ils apportent au monde"; "cette géométrie du tailleur de pierre dans [ses] romans."

3 *Ibid.,* III, 377: "je revins aux tailleurs de pierre de Thomas Hardy. Vous vous rappelez assez dans *Jude l'obscur*, avez-vous vu dans la *Bien-Aimée*, les blocs de pierres que le père extrait de l'île venant par bateaux

Proust has here specified with great insight the characteristic pattern of Hardy's novels. The examples he gives might be multiplied, for example by reference to the way Henchard, in *The Mayor of Casterbridge,* repeats throughout his life the same rhythm of possession and rejection, or to the way Jude's relation to Arabella, in *Jude the Obscure,* is ironically mirrored in reverse in Sue's relation to Phillotson, or to the way *The Trumpet-Major* is structured around the symmetries of Anne Garland's love first for one and then for another of two brothers. Hardy's stories almost always have an elegant balance of artificial design, and the parallelisms within each novel are doubled by the parallelisms between one novel and another. All his novels are like variations on the same architectural plan and may be, as Proust's metaphor suggests, superimposed in the mind like buildings following one after another in echoing similarity up a steep hill. He could have said of himself what William Faulkner said of his own work in a letter of 1944 to Malcolm Cowley, that he kept "telling the same story over and over to [him]self and to the world."[4]

The most important aspect of this formal symmetry, however, is the complex irony it embodies. This irony is wrought into the intimate fabric of Hardy's representation of life. As his characters live their lives they

---

s'entasser dans l'atelier du fils où elles deviennent statues; dans *les Yeux bleus,* le parallélisme des tombes, et aussi la ligne parallèle du bateau, et les wagons contigus où sont les deux amoureux, et la morte; le parallélisme entre *la Bien-Aimée* où l'homme aime trois femmes, *les Yeux bleus* où la femme aime trois hommes, etc., et enfin tous ces romans superposables les uns aux autres, comme les maisons verticalement entassées en hauteur sur le sol pierreux de l'île."

4 Malcolm Cowley, *The Faulkner-Cowley File: Letters and Memories, 1944-1962* (New York: The Viking Press, 1966), pp. 14-15.

strive to impose on them a pattern which will conform to a desire to win the persons they love and to find happiness in this possession. A wish to have lives which are logical and consistent, each part conforming to the others and fulfilling a rational plan, is characteristic of his people. The guilt they feel when they betray themselves and others is partly an exasperation about their failure to hold their lives to a preconceived pattern. "See now how it's ourselves that are ruled by the Powers above us!" says Farfrae when he finds that he is to be the new mayor of Casterbridge. "We plan this, but we do that" (MC, 280). However earnestly they work to accomplish their intentions, "the thing unplanned" comes into existence nevertheless: "against what I willed worked the surging sublime / Of the thing that I did" ("The Thing Unplanned," CP, 750). The thing that I willed is powerless to oppose itself against the irresistible energy of the thing I am fated to do. No voluntary design, however earnestly pursued, is ever brought into existence, or if it is, as in the exceptional case of that strange novel, *The Hand of Ethelberta,* the successful schemer possesses an almost demonic strength of will.

The characters who most interest Hardy are not so strong in character as Ethelberta. Their susceptibility to feeling and to the fascination others exert destroys their plans. When failure gives them farsighted clearness of mind each can look back on his life and see that after all it forms a beautifully symmetrical design, structured around harmonious repetitions and neatly patterned convergences. This abstractly beautiful shape has led each man step by step to unhappiness and the frustration of all his hopes. Moreover, the pattern of his life has not been intended or recognized by him. Its beauty has until now remained hidden. It has all along been completing its own perfection according to a secret plan of its own, a plan as undeliberate as the growth of trees or as the formation of crystals, in sublime indifference to his desires and intentions. It has rigidly coerced him to an abstract pattern of fitness. The final irony is that this perfect pattern is not even the result of the conscious design of some malign transcendent power. It is the accidental outcome of random movements of the blind force which drives all things.

Sexual passion is the chief way in which Hardy's characters participate in the impulsions of this force. When they fall in love they are seized as though by a giant hand and whirled into the pattern of a dance. Though what they do is compatible with their natures (the choleric act impulsively, the cold remain withdrawn), still their passion puts them beside themselves. The reader is appalled to see them so much in the grip of something which bends them to designs they have not chosen. Boldwood, in *Far from the Madding Crowd,* is an extreme example of this destroying power of passion, but the theme is exemplified in many other characters too.

Only when Hardy's people have fallen out of love can they look back and see how they have been victims. It is not so much that their characters are distorted as that they are driven to act in ways determined by forces beyond their control or knowledge, forces which make use of their wills and emotions to create more examples of the universal pattern of love's futility. The reader can see this pattern gradually taking place out of the apparently independent movements of the characters. He finds something pathetic or even horrifying in the alienation of the characters from themselves. Ultimately they too attain an insight into the way they have been the sport of an irresistible puppet-master, a puppet-master who is not even aware of the ironic symmetries of the play he is directing.

Many critics have found Hardy's neatly balanced plots offensively artificial, evidence of the concocting mind of the novelist at work in abstraction from the reality of life. To interpret this aspect of his work in such a way is to miss its meaning and to deny him the right to his own peculiar sense of life and of the relation of art to life. Proust was right here. The notion that life is full of unexpected parallelisms, parallelisms which happen spontaneously rather than being the expression of any conscious plan, is a fundamental aspect of Hardy's vision of existence. His carefully proportioned plots express his notion of the ironic incompatibility between a man's conscious intentions, the pattern he wants to give to his life, and the actual design which is surreptitiously being created all the time by a hidden power which even makes use of a man's free acts to construct its chaste symmetries. These symmetries are not something the novelist has imposed on life, but something he has observed there. So in "The Wind's Prophecy" the speaker thinks his journey is preserving his fidelity to his black-haired love, but the irresistible will beyond him is preparing the harmonious juxtaposition of a black-haired girl and a blonde, side by side in a sequence of mirroring loves.

Here may be identified the significance of that theme of convergence which occurs so often in Hardy's work. This theme exists in the background of "The Wind's Prophecy," but is made more explicit in "The Convergence of the Twain" (CP, 288-289). Though a man is intent on his own goals, moving through life toward their attainment, there may be preparing for him a stealthy convergence with another person or thing which will change his life in unexpected ways. This convergence is happening in a perfectly explicable way, according to psychological or physical laws which are known to all, and yet it is completely unforeseen and will destroy the man's carefully prepared plans or even end his life. The *Titanic* was designed for a long service carrying passengers in luxury across the Atlantic. No one could know that a "sinister mate" was preparing for the ship, nor that the two "were bent / By paths coincident / On being anon twin halves of one august event" (CP, 289). The same pattern is created by the convergent paths of two persons in "The Destined Pair" (CP, 867-868). Though they were ignorant of one another's existence, they were "drifting / Each one to the other," for "the tracks of their feet /Were arcs that would meet" (CP, 867). Such unanticipated convergences also often occur in the fiction and are described in the same terms, as in that meeting between Darton and Helena in the story called "Interlopers at the Knap." This meeting "practically settled the point toward which these long-severed persons were converging" (WT, 202). Another example is the chance return of the furmity-woman which is the "edge or turn in the incline of Henchard's fortunes."

When the ironic convergences prepared by an unintentional fate are brought into the open at last, then Hardy's characters recognize that they have been unknowingly the instruments of "the Immanent Will that stirs and urges everything" ("The Convergence of the Twain," CP, 289). Their lives have had meaning not in relation to the willed design they have tried to impose on it, but in relation to a "blind force persisting" ("A Philosophical Fantasy," CP, 854), a force working within their lives which alienates them from themselves. Each life reveals itself to a backward "Surview" (CP, 660) to have an admirably delineated shape and meaning, but these are ironically indifferent to any humanly willed design and to any human standards of morality and justice. The meaning of each human life is its meaninglessness in relation to human concepts of value, for each is the expression not of conscious intent but the effect of that "mindless" will which moves in "purposeless propension" "along lines of least resistance" ("A Philosophical Fantasy," CP, 856).

When Hardy's characters see this, their insight moves in orientation spontaneously from past to future. When they turn toward the future they see that the "unsensed persistence" ("A Philosophical Fantasy," CP, 856) which has brought them where they are now has also put them on a line which is leading them inevitably toward an ignominious death. They see not only the "vain pantomime" of the past, but also "Life's tending, its ending, / The worth of its fame" ("On One Who Lived and Died Where He Was Born," CP, 624). The failure of love first cures a man of his infatuation so that he can see his present situation clearly. Then it allows him a retrospective view of the entire course of his life so he can see how he has been unknowingly manipulated by the inhuman energy which keeps everything in motion. Finally his detachment allows him to see that he is even now moving rapidly toward the end which awaits everyone, death, each man's "normal condition" (DR, 438).

Many of the characters are led to the moment when they have, with varying degrees of clarity, this triple illumination of present, past, and future. "If I had only got her with me," says Henchard of Elizabeth-Jane, "if I only had! . . . But that was not to be. I — Cain — go alone as I deserve — an outcast and a vagabond" (MC, 361). "O, the cruelty of putting me into this ill-conceived world!" cries Eustacia near the end of her life. "I was capable of much; but I have been injured and blighted and crushed by things beyond my control! O, how hard it is of Heaven to devise such tortures for me, who have done no harm to Heaven at all!" (RN, 422). "As for Sue and me when we were at our own best," says Jude as he lies dying, "long ago — when our minds were clear, and our love of truth fearless — the time was not ripe for us! Our ideas were fifty years too soon to be any good to us. And so the resistance they met with brought reaction in her, and recklessness and ruin on me!" (JO, 484).

In these cases the insight is only partial. Though the characters now understand themselves far better than they did when they still hoped for happiness, the reader is aware of some ironic incongruity between the protagonist's understanding of his life and the superior insight of the narrator. Henchard is wrong to think he would be happy if Elizabeth-Jane were his. Eustacia is wrong to think a conscious deity has made a sport of her. Jude is wrong to place all the blame on the incongruity between society and the advanced ideas he has shared with Sue. Nevertheless, these ultimate self-judgments show some power in Henchard, Eustacia, and Jude to see in a backward vision the whole pattern of their lives. They have some insight into the fact that the cause of their suffering has been external to their conscious intent.

A possible explanation for Hardy's ceasing to write novels may be found in the progressive increase in the clarity of the final illumination his protagonists attain. His fiction depends on the distinction between the wide, disillusioned vision of the narrator and the narrow, infatuated vision of the characters. Each novel moves toward the partial convergence of the protagonist's point of view and the narrator's point of view. In the novels this convergence is never complete, but the understanding of Jude just before his death more nearly approaches the narrator's understanding than does the understanding of earlier heroes like Eustacia or Henchard.

The two versions of *The Well-Beloved* support this notion of a development in Hardy's fiction. In the first version, that published in *The Illustrated London News* in 1892, Jocelyn is never fully emancipated from his slavery to his well-beloved. He resigns the third Avice to a lover more nearly her age, attempts suicide unsuccessfully, and is joined again by his wife Marcia, now "a wrinkled crone, with a pointed chin, her figure bowed, her hair as white as snow." The novel ends with Jocelyn's hysterical laughter as he contemplates the discrepancy between his memory of the young and beautiful Marcia and of the Avice whom he still loves, on the one hand, and the ugly wife whom he actually possesses: "The Juno of that day was the Witch of Endor of this. . . . His wife passed by the mantelpiece, over which hung an enlarged photograph of Avice, that he had brought thither when he left the other house, as the single object which he cared to bring. The contrast of the ancient Marcia's aspect, both with this portrait and with her own fine former self, brought into his brain a sudden sense of the grotesqueness of things. His wife was — not Avice, but that parchment-covered skull moving about his room. An irresistible fit of laughter, so violent as to be an agony, seized upon him, and started in him with such momentum that he could not stop it. He laughed and laughed, till he was almost too weak to draw breath."[5]

The new version of the ending of *The Well-Beloved* written after the publication of *Jude the Obscure* ends with a much more complete self-recognition on the part of the protagonist. The illness which cures him of his pursuit of a phantom goddess leads him to a disillusioned perspective on life which corresponds closely to the one the narrator has possessed from the beginning of the novel: "Yes. Thank Heaven I am old at last," he says. "The curse is removed" (WB, 213). After writing this new ending for *The Well-Beloved* Hardy's composition of fiction ceased, with the exception of his writing of three short stories, "The Grave by the Handpost," presumably written in 1897, and "A Changed Man" and "Enter a Dragoon," written in 1899.[6] The change in the ending of *The Well-Beloved* may be taken as an emblem of this farewell to fiction. It seems as if the cycle of novels undertaken to seek vicariously for a happy love comes to an end when the characters reach the same understanding of the futility of the search which the narrator possesses. The earlier heroes, even Jude, never understand their situations quite as well as the narrator. When the convergence is complete, as it seems to be in the second version of *The Well-Beloved*, then Hardy's kind of fiction, in which there always remains a distance between

5 *The Pursuit of the Well-Beloved, The Illustrated London News*, CI, no. 2800 (December 17, 1892), 775.

6 See Richard Little Purdy, *Thomas Hardy: A Bibliographical Study* (London: Oxford University Press, 1954), pp. 152, 153, 156.

narrator and protagonist, becomes impossible. The writing of lyric poetry remained possible. It had of course been going on more or less continuously at the same time as the writing of the fiction. Many of the poems put within one person at different times of his life the double vision of life divided between hero and protagonist in the fiction. The poems presuppose from the beginning that coincidence of two points of view which only gradually becomes completely attainable in the fiction.

The Dynasts, written in the decade after the renunciation of fiction, combines the two modes. Often lyric in expression, it nevertheless takes a dramatic form like that of the novels: the gradual recognition by the protagonist that happiness is impossible in this life, that all men are victims of the Immanent Will. Last of the long line of such heroes in his fiction, Napoleon is also the most clearheaded and wide-seeing of all Hardy's heroes. As *The Dynasts* presents the most elaborately articulated version of his picture of human life, so its central figure achieves the most lucid awareness of his plight. Though Napoleon has this insight he is still in the power of the omnipotent force sweeping through history, but, as the Spirit of the Years perceives, he is "of the few in Europe who discern / The working of the Will" (D, 179). His victory is not an escape from the impersonal energy making use of him. No one can escape. His triumph is rather in the fact that he has "ever known / That such a Will I passively obeyed!" (D, 519). He knows, as he says, that "History makes use of me to weave her web / To her long while aforetime-figured mesh / And contemplated charactery" (D, 330). His fullest expression of this recog-

nition will serve as a summary statement of the deepest
insight into the meaning of human existence possible to
Hardy's characters while they are alive:

> We are but thistle-globes on Heaven's high gales,
> And whither blown, or when, or how, or why,
> Can choose us not at all! . . . (D, 204)

🌱

Hardy's protagonists respond in various ways to their
culminating insights. Eustacia's defiant reproaches directed against heaven's injustice are unusual in his
characters, as is her mistaken sense that there is a conscious power aligned against her whom it is rational to
defy. More typical is Henchard's resigned acceptance and
stoic fortitude, with its ironic out-Caining of Cain: "But
my punishment is *not* greater than I can bear!" (MC,
361; see Genesis 4:13). When the characters are freed of
their illusions and can see present, past, and future
clearly, each recognizes the inevitability of his fate and
even its impersonality. Understanding that happiness is
"but the occasional episode in a general drama of pain,"
and seeing that in an unjust universe no "human being
deserved less than was given," they see also that no
strategy of action or attitude will avoid suffering and
the doom assigned. There is a kind of relief in this full
look at the worst. At least I shall no longer be beguiled
by false hopes. There is even a bitter joy in saying: "so
it must be" (MC, 386, 385, 384). Now that the scales
have fallen from my eyes I can see the whole course of
my life from its beginning to its fast approaching end.

I also see that there is a kind of appropriateness or congruence in the sequence and even in my unjust suffering and in the ignominious death after the defeat of all my plans which I now confront. At least it has not been my fault, and at least it can be said that all the stages of my life have fitted neatly together to form a destiny demonstrating conclusively that all is for the worst in this worst of all possible worlds. I can take a certain masochistic pleasure in this and can feel, now that the truth is out, more secure than in my brief moments of happiness, for even when I was happy I had a premonition that this happiness would have to be paid for dearly. So I accept my fate in a curious mood combining resignation, defiance, and a desire to demonstrate that I am strong enough to take whatever suffering is allotted to me. I yield to the ineluctability of what has happened and also admire its symmetrical appropriateness. The punishment has fitted the crime. To "justify" something, for example a line of type, is to make its parts fit according to a predetermined pattern or measure, and in this sense "justice" *is* done to Tess and to Hardy's other protagonists.

When I understand that my life is justified I can even accept the death which I see ahead as the inescapable goal of the track I have been following. Or rather I choose death as the only fitting end to such a life as mine. Without the ignominy of death in failure the pattern of my life would not be complete, and as victim desires the knife, so I find myself yielding to the movement which leads to my death and even cooperating in that movement. Many of the characters come at the end of their lives, even if they do not actually commit suicide, to a suicidal passivity, a self-destructive will not to will which is the exact opposite of Nietzsche's will to power and which brings Hardy, as previous critics have noted, close to Schopenhauer. So dies Aeneas Manston, in *Desperate Remedies*; he does literally kill himself. So dies Giles Winterbourne, in *The Woodlanders*. So die Henchard, Jude, and Tess.

The mood in which, having lost all their illusions, Hardy's characters face death and even go eagerly to meet it is admirably expressed in a poem called, significantly, "He Fears His Good Fortune" (CP, 479). The speaker remembers a time of happiness when he felt that his joy was "too rare, too rapturous, rash" to last. "I've no claim . . . to be thus crowned," he said; "I am not worthy this." His sense of unworthiness made him sure that sooner or later all would go "amiss," with a "crash." This premonition, however, brought not anxiety, but, curiously enough, a kind of tranquillity, in which he could say: "Well . . . let the end foreseen / Come duly! — I am serene." And sure enough, "it came." This odd serenity, in which a man is sure of disaster and yet calmed by that certainty into a mild, resigned happiness, is characteristic of the mood in which Hardy's people go to meet death. This mood, it appears, is the last stage in his drama of existence and the last consequence of the insight his characters gain when they lose the illusions which have bewildered their sight. There is no more moving expression of this mood than Tess's last speech, when she wakes on the Stone of Sacrifice at Stonehenge and sees that her captors have found her: " 'It is as it should be,' she murmured. 'Angel, I am almost glad — yes, glad! This happiness could not have lasted. It was too much. I have had enough; and now I shall not live for you to despise me!' " (Td, 505).

❧

This emergence, beyond disaster, in the brief time before death, into a region of calm gladness, a region where good fortune can no longer be sought or feared, where all is at last as it should be, is not, however, the last step taken by Hardy's characters. There is one final movement of the spirit for them, one last gesture before the soft embrace of death.

His heroes sometimes choose death because it is inevitable in any case, or because it is the fitting end for the lives they have led, or because they hope to escape in death from the pain of consciousness, that lucidity of insight or "fret of thinking" ("Freed the Fret of Thinking," CP, 715) which is an unnatural accident of nature and makes human suffering necessary. The desire for a return to "normal unawareness" ("The Aërolite," CP, 732) is expressed, for example, in the poem called "A Wish for Unconsciousness" (CP, 800). I should have "no cross to bear," says the speaker of that poem, "If I could but abide / As a tablet on a wall, / Or a hillock daisy-pied, / Or a picture in a hall, / And as nothing else at all."

This desire to return to the insentience of inanimate matter is not the deepest cause for the death-wish of Hardy's characters. They have a stronger and more extravagant motive. They choose death not solely as escape from consciousness, but also as a means to obtain the obliteration of their lives. They want not only to forget, but to be forgotten. Only the absolute erasure from memory of lives which have been committed to suffering and are a perfect testimony to the alienating omnipotence of the Immanent Will can suffice as atonement for the crime of being born. The drama of the lives of Hardy's most important characters ends with a detachment from life and insight into its meaning which approaches the perspective of the narrator and justifies that perspective. This insight leads to a fervent wish to be forgotten wholly. They will be satisfied only if they sink without a trace back into the unconscious heavings of the impersonal force that stirs and urges everything. This unconscious absorption into the general life is that "normal condition" of man of which Aeneas Manston speaks in *Desperate Remedies,* but the happiness of this condition will not be complete unless every evidence or memorial of a man's temporary condition as a conscious being is annihilated along with that consciousness itself.

The strange wish for this ultimate form of vanishing appears frequently enough in Hardy to justify calling it a characteristic desire of his protagonists when they face death. The anxious earnestness with which they plead to be forgotten utterly forms a last wish which is moving and yet somehow ominous, an uneasy promise of something worse to come. It is as though the characters suspect that unless they can be forgotten completely they may not, after all, escape from suffering when they die. Henchard's last desire in the litany of self-annihilation which makes up his will is: "& that no man remember me" (MC, 384). Jude as he lies dying murmurs those terrifying words from Job's curse of himself: "Let the day perish wherein I was born, and the night in which it was said, There is a man child conceived. . . . Let that day be darkness" (JO, 488; Job 3:3-4). In "Tess's Lament" (CP, 161-162), a poem written as it were in the margin of *Tess of the d'Urbervilles* and as a commentary on it, Tess, like Jude and Henchard, asks that all record of her life be expunged. "I would that folk forgot me quite," she says, and moves through a sequence of vivid memories from her life to a conclusion of intense self-loathing and desire for obliteration which goes beyond any other version of this motif in Hardy's writing. Tess's bitter invocation of annihilation may be taken as the strongest expression of the final gesture before death of his remorselessly victimized characters:

> I cannot bear my fate as writ,
>   I'd have my life unbe;
> Would turn my memory to a blot,
> Make every relic of me rot,
> My doings be as they were not,
>   And gone all trace of me!

At first it appears that Tess's wish is granted. Death for her and for everyone else seems precisely that oblivious reabsorption into the general life of things which she and Hardy's other characters desire. In a number of poems he shows how all living things, men and women included, lose after death their individualities and join again in that sequence of natural transformations from which they temporarily stood aloof while they were alive. This year's finches, nightingales, and thrushes were a few months ago "only particles of grain, / And earth, and air, and rain" ("Proud Songsters," CP, 798). A few months hence they will be dust again. In the same way all men after death will sink back into the obscurity and indistinction of earth's particles, driven in incessant changes by the Immanent Will. Hardy is fascinated not only by death, but by the material state of the dead and by their surroundings. He likes to think what it will be like to lie in the dark earth enclosed by those six boards which await somewhere even now a final unforeseen convergence and are destined to form the coffin in which he will lie "remote / From mundane hurt" ("The Six Boards," CP, 781). His imagination is stirred by churchyards, gravestones, funerals, coffins, passing-bells, ghosts, skeletons. No motifs recur more vividly in his poems than these, or so bring out the brooding lyric intensity which is his special note as a singer.

What most appeals to Hardy about the dead is their liberty, their lilting insouciance, their carefree irresponsibility. It is as if a great weight has been lifted from their shoulders, as indeed it has, the weight of life, of consciousness, of individuality, the weight of time. He achieves the fine comic effect of some of his best poems from the ironic contrast between the earnest and always unsuccessful striving of the living and the gay detachment of the dead. In their last narrow rooms they find not imprisonment, but, paradoxically, an unchained freedom and airy openness. In such poems the dead speak from their safe unconsciousness (a further wry incongruity), and the tradition of the tombstone verse spoken as if by the dead is renewed in richly somber poems which express as well as anything he ever wrote the special quality of his imagination. Sometimes, as in "Friends Beyond" (CP, 52-54), the dead speak "with very gods' composure" of their happy detachment from everything which most concerned them when they were alive. "William Dewy, Tranter Reuben, Farmer Ledlow late at plough, / Robert's kin, and John's, and Ned's, / And the Squire, and Lady Susan, lie in Mellstock churchyard now," but though they are gone they whisper in "muted, measured note" to the man who can be quiet enough to listen:

> We have triumphed: this achievement turns the
> bane to antidote,
> Unsuccesses to success,
> Many thought-worn eves and morrows to a morrow
> free of thought.
>
> No more need we corn and clothing, feel of old ter-
> restrial stress;
> Chill detraction stirs no sigh;
> Fear of death has even bygone us: death gave all
> that we possess.

Then each of the dead speaks in turn of his indifference even to what was his ruling passion when alive. William Dewy: "Ye mid burn the old bass-viol that I set such value by"; the Squire: "You may hold the manse in fee, / You may wed my spouse, may let my children's memory of me die"; the farmer's wife: "If ye break my best blue china, children, I shan't care or ho," and so on. One is tempted to quote all of this admirable poem, in which the melodic sway of the lines, their rhythm as of "a ripple under archways," embodies the equable composure of the dead.

Sometimes, however, Hardy's dead folk lament wistfully the fact that all their experience, everything they saw or thought or did, is buried with them. Each person while he lives makes a unique interpretation of the

world and sees, for example, "far-off views, / That nobody else discern[s] outspread." When he dies all this
dies "unrecorded" with him and lies compressed in
secrecy with him in his coffin:

> Not only I
> Am doomed awhile to lie
> In this close bin with earthen sides;
> But the things I thought, and the songs I sang,
> And the hopes I had, and the passioned pang
> For people I knew . . . ("Not Only I," CP, 744)

If everything a man ever experienced while alive is
interred with his bones, then it is "lost to the world and
disregarded," and the man has achieved his goal of being forgotten by all. Sometimes, however, the dead speak
not of this successful obliteration of their lives, but, for
example in "Voices from Things Growing in a Churchyard" (CP, 590-591), of their metamorphosis into new
forms of life. They escape even that mode of persistence
involved in remaining enclosed in their coffins. They
vanish altogether into the flowers, trees, and ivy which
grow from their graves. The dead here speak not from
their coffins or tombstones, but from the freedom they
have achieved through their dispersal in new forms taken
by the Immanent Will. The irony of a speech of the
speechless, a consciousness of the unconscious, underlies
this poem as it does "Friends Beyond," and there is the
same triumphant lilt in the "murmurous accents" of the
dead:

> — The Lady Gertrude, proud, high-bred,
> Sir or Madam,

> Am I — this laurel that shades your head;
> Into its veins I have stilly sped,
> And made them of me . . .

In this transmigration not of souls but of the impersonal life energy which once inhabited those souls, Hardy's characters seem to achieve that annihilation they desire. Though neither matter nor the anonymous force which traverses it can die, consciousness can die with the death of the form that accidentally generated it. With the death of consciousness, if a man is lucky, all memory of the sad course it traced through time may vanish also. Over all such characters might be spoken that requiem which Hardy imagines an attendant spirit addressing to his friend Frederic Treves, when Treves lies once more in the "chalky bed" whence he has drawn his substance: "Enough. You have returned. And all is well" ("In the Evening," CP, 781).

What is the meaning of the fact that the dead do after all speak in such poems? There are so many poems in which dead men speak that it must be defined as a normal occurrence in this poetic universe. Is this no more than a paradoxical ascription of consciousness to the unconscious, a conventional power of speech granted to those who are beyond speech or hearing, deaf and mute forever? Is it no more than an "as if" or poetic license which allows the dead to express vividly not their own awareness but the poet's sense of their safe escape from the pains of life? He ascribes to them, it may be, an awareness and power of articulation which are only his own.

There is more to the talkativeness of the dead than such a convention. Though a man may escape from the sufferings of his life in death, though he may no longer be troubled by the vain longings which so pained him when he lived in time, nevertheless he does not achieve that unconsciousness for which he longed. A belief that consciousness persists into the grave justifies all those poems in which the ghosts of the departed turn back on their past lives, view them dispassionately, and dismiss them as no longer of concern. The dead are not only still conscious, but they have a more unclouded and far-seeing vision than they ever had when alive. In death they complete the imperfect illumination which came in the moments before death and made their consciousness approach that of the poet or narrator but not quite coincide with it. In death this coincidence becomes perfect, and the character attains at last the writer's detachment, lucidity, and power to view each event in the perspective of a vision of life as wide as all time and space. Though she has vanished from the world, says Hardy of one of the dead, though she is "lost to each meadow, each hill-top, each tree around," she has now "largened sight" which allows her to "see around" "the whole truth." "Can she, then," he asks, "know how men's fatings befall?" The answer returns in a strong echo: "Yea indeed, may know well; even know thereof all" ("Paradox," CP, 766). In death Hardy's people, even those who were not particularly wise or farseeing while alive, reach that perfection of human consciousness, that "spacious vision" ("Midnight on the Great Western," CP, 483), possessed by the choruses of spirits in The Dynasts, but only by exceptional human beings during life. Now at last the dead can do as they could never do perfectly when they were alive, however disillusioned they were. They can stand "at a clear-eyed distance, and [con] the whole." Freed from limitation, freed from anxiety, freed from all narrowness and blindness, they are nevertheless not freed from consciousness.

This is a bad enough disappointment of the characters' wish to forget and to be forgotten, but the situation is even worse. In the *Life* Hardy tells us that on that evening when Leslie Stephen unexpectedly called him to his house to ask Hardy to witness his resignation from holy orders, that act of honest disassociation so symbolic of the Victorian crisis of belief, he and Stephen then stayed up far into the night discussing "theologies decayed and defunct, the origin of things, the constitution of matter, the unreality of time" (L, 105). The "unreality of time"! What can this mean? Can a man so preoccupied in his poems and fiction with "slow effacement" ("The Ageing House," CP, 461), with the remorseless passage of time, and with the distance between present and past, have seriously entertained such an idea? Two late poems, "The Absolute Explains" and "So, Time" (CP, 716-719), provide an answer.

The explanation is so strongly reinforced by other texts among the poems that it must be accepted as a motif integral to Hardy's sense of the world. "The Absolute Explains" is based on that image of time as a journey which appears so frequently in his work, but here wider implications of this image are revealed. A man living his life from moment to moment, says the Absolute, is so absorbed in what is immediately before him that he is like a man "upon a dark highway, / Plodding by lantern-light." Such a man "Finds but the reach of its frail ray / Uncovered to his sight." He can see only the local area around the single spot on the road where he is at the moment. His "Now" is "just a gleam, a glide / Across [his] gazing sense." His life is not so much a sequence of discontinuous glimpses as a fluid continuity of partial insights flickering evanescently athwart the world. Each moment flows into the next, and at no moment can he see beyond the restricted circle cast by the feeble beams of his lantern. The road, however, is there all the time. It "lies all its length the same, / Forwardly as at rear." The Absolute is not tied to time and sees all the road at once. He extracts from his vision of the whole the fact that all the past and future, together with the present, exist simultaneously in a single realm outside time, all with the same mode of immediate actuality. Time is therefore unreal, since "All things are shaped to be / Eternally," and "outside what you 'Present' name, / Future and Past stand sheer, / Cognate and clear."

"Cognate and clear" — the spatialization of time means the destruction of time and its replacement by an all-embracing fixed realm of eternity. In this trans-temporal region each thing which has happened, is happening, or will happen stands side by side with all the others, each like the others in kind, all in permanently clarified juxtaposition forever. All things which ever were or will be, says Hardy in a striking phrase, *"lie their length,* with the throbbing things / Akin them, down the Void, / Live, unalloyed" (my italics). There is no possibility of "transience" in such a world. All things exist in their original vibrating actuality in the spacious bosom of the Void. Within this infinitely capacious "Vast" all remain as "beings continuous, / In dateless dure abiding." Though there is movement within the void, the movement appropriate to the things when they were alive, and, beyond that, a drifting of events within the infinite according to their original momentum, like stars or comets moving in astronomical space, still this is an atemporal movement, a movement in place which never exhausts itself or frees any event from the endless repetition of itself, over and over again forever. Far from forgetting themselves or being forgotten by dying, Hardy's characters enter in death a realm in which every occurrence is doomed to re-enact itself eternally, in an endless failure to escape from itself. Every song, every laugh, every moon, every flower, now "fadeless, fixed," "remaining still in blow," all "wild love-makings," every fleeting event or emotion, every failure in love, every pang of suffering or betrayal, all remain forever, "Coiled like a precious parchment fell, / Illumined page by page, / Unhurt by age."

This spatialization of past, present, and future in a single, "cognate" realm of immediacy is Hardy's objectivized version of that tradition of "presence" or παρουσία which is fundamental to Occidental concepts of time from Plato's *Timaeus* through the eleventh book of St. Augustine's *Confessions* down to Edmund Husserl's *Phänomenologie des inneren Zeitbewusstseins* in our own century. For Hardy, as for these writers, the essential quality of that which exists is its immediate proximity to some apprehending mind, divine or human. Memory and anticipation are conceived not as what brings absence or emptiness into the present, but as voluminous expansions of the closeness and actuality which characterize experience in the "now." In such a concept of time, a concept profoundly traditional and influenced only in its external form by nineteenth-century scientific ideas, nothing can ever be lost because every-

thing exists eternally in the closed circuit of its presence
to itself and in its presence to an all-embracing cosmic
mind.

Hardy's apprehension of existence therefore leads him
to affirm a new version of the theme of the eternal return, a theme which often recurs in the writing of his
epoch, for example in Thomas De Quincey, in Matthew
Arnold, in Friedrich Nietzsche, or in W. B. Yeats. His
idea of recurrence is not like the vision of cyclic repetition in Arnold or Nietzsche, the notion that each event
of history eventually repeats itself, bringing in its time
a new recurrence of something which has already happened innumerable times before. His idea of repetition
is closer to De Quincey's image of the palimpsest of
memory, or to Yeats's notion of the Anima Mundi, the
great memory or memory of the world. Having once
happened each event cannot cease to go on happening
in inexhaustible repetition of itself. Or rather, all things
have always been happening. They enter time for a
moment and actualize themselves there, then return to
their normal condition, which is an eternal re-enactment
of themselves in the Void. Just as in De Quincey's vision
of life every thought, every experience, every emotion a
man has had remains in layers with the others indelibly
recorded on the palimpsest of his brain, ready to be resurrected in certain privileged moments, so for Hardy a
man's life has always been written out from all time and
remains even after his death recorded on the coiled
parchment which inscribes his fate down to the last detail. To perform an act, feel an emotion, or glimpse a
landscape is only to bring into temporal existence something which has always already been fated and which
will continue to exist forever in eternity, for "Nor God

nor Demon can undo the done, / Unsight the seen" ("To Meet, or Otherwise," CP, 292).[7]

§

In the numerous poems which describe this irremediable persistence of all events the image which always underlies Hardy's language is that of an enormous container or sphere, vast enough to hold everything and yet still be almost empty. This receptacle is clearly modeled on the vacancy of interstellar space as it was seen by the popular astronomy of his time. For him, however, this realm is beyond ordinary time and space. It is a fixed region of eternity. When an event has happened on earth it enters this extraterrestrial reservoir by the force of its own momentum, and like light traveling forever in the line of its direction or like a physical object moving eternally at the same speed if it encounters no obstacle or new field of force, so each event, in Hardy's vision of eternity, advances onward forever side by side with the drift of other things.

Sometimes, to vary the metaphor, these images from celestial mechanics are accompanied by a musical image. Each event is like a single note which takes its place in

---

[7] The idea that nothing dies, that everything which happens has happened before and will continue to remain inscribed indestructibly in a realm of eternal repetition, is a widespread motif in nineteenth-century literature, which echoes in its turn the tradition coming down from Plato and the Church Fathers. Hardy's special version of this idea has antecedents in the English romantic poets, especially in Coleridge, and also in Gautier, in Nerval, in Baudelaire, as well as in De Quincey and others. For a discussion of this theme in its variations among these writers and in its relation to the motif of affective memory see Georges Poulet, "Les romantiques anglais," *Mesure de l'instant* (Paris: Plon, 1968), pp. 157-192.

the full melody of existence. A brief meeting of the poet with the girl he loves, for example, will supply "one note, / Small and untraced" to the "long-sweeping symphony / From times remote / Till now, of human tenderness," but this musical metaphor is completed by the astronomical one. Their brief moment of tenderness "will ever be / Somewhere afloat / Amid the spheres" ("To Meet, or Otherwise," CP, 292). Another poem combines the two metaphors even more closely in a description of the way the call of a fossil bird long dead and the song of a woman heard a few hours before will persist forever in the Vast, harmoniously mixed together:

> Such a dream is Time that the coo of this ancient
>   bird
> Has perished not, but is blent, or will be blending
> Mid visionless wilds of space with the voice that I
>   heard,
> In the full-fugued song of the universe unending.
> ("In a Museum," CP, 404)

Sometimes the image is of a moment of brightness in the poet's spirit. Though the moment passed and the clouds again covered the sun, the light still exists beyond its "occultation," and this the poet takes as evidence that his "late irradiate soul" must still "live on somewhere" ("The Occultation," CP, 434). In another case the figure is once more of the subjective glow of a soul, but now it is imagined still to be traveling on, by a strange species of metempsychosis, "to be a new young dreamer's freight, / And thence on infinitely," passing from one dreamer to another without ever being extinguished ("The Youth Who Carried a Light," CP, 452). Sometimes it is the notion that a person "when dead" is more himself than when he was alive, for in death he will "resume [his] old and right / Place in the Vast" ("When Dead," CP, 683-684). Or sometimes, to give a final example, it is the charming notion that a kiss does not die with the moment of its enactment. That brief touch starts a sound which like everything else in Hardy's world leaves time and enters magically, by an unperceived transition, into that eternity in which it will be preserved in its fragile intensity forever. Again there appears the characteristic image of a continuous motion within a space which is wide enough to give room to all motions without interference or perturbation:

> It cannot have died; that know we well.
> Somewhere it pursues its flight,
> One of a long procession of sounds
>   Travelling aethereal rounds
>   Far from earth's bounds
>   In the infinite. ("A Kiss," CP, 438)

To Tess, Jude, or Henchard, however, this eternal persistence of every evanescent event or feeling would not seem charming at all. It would seem the defeat of their last hope. The ultimate poignancy or bitterness of their wish to be forgotten is the fact that it cannot be satisfied. Nothing dies. This includes all moments of shame or pain as well as times of tenderness or joy. Every experience endures forever in a state which is a horrifying parody of immortality and constitutes the worst alienation of all for Hardy's characters. The Immanent Will has blindly and unintentionally brought Tess, Henchard, and the rest into existence. Having done so, and having unwittingly imposed suffering on them until they die, it is also powerless to free them from existence and from the suffering existence entails. Somewhere every one of their moments of pain or ignominious defeat still continues moving forever, re-enacting itself interminably, traveling without pattern or redemption along with everything else in a universe incapable of freeing itself from even the least part of itself. Having occurred once in time, each moment enters again that universal space of simultaneity where those things which once having been, can never cease to be, move endlessly in chaotic drifting. In that all-embracing spatialized time of the void, each song, each kiss, each flower, but also each moment of despair or unassuaged longing, is destined to repeat itself forever in a horrifying inability to escape from itself. Tess can never be forgotten or have her life "unbe," for all things which have ever happened continue to exist forever.

This existence takes an odd form which makes it even more frightening to imagine. Each kiss, each parting, each moment of betrayal continues to exist in an obscure movement of disconnected bits of experience, detached fragments of consciousness of which no one in particular is conscious. After their deaths the individual minds of Tess, Jude, and Henchard disappear and in this sense they are freed from the burden of life. This disappearance is not, however, the obliteration of consciousness, but rather its perfection. What disappears is the local, personal awareness of Tess, her absorption in a particular moment of her life with its sensations and hopes, its longings for happiness. This awareness does not simply disappear at death. It expands to embrace in clarity and breadth of scope the whole universe at once in an anonymous awareness which is simultaneously aware of everything and of the relative insignificance of each part of that everything. Consciousness after death becomes identical in clarity and inclusiveness with the space of eternity which Hardy describes in terms of the vacancy of astronomical space. The mind of each limited individual loses its limitation and melts into a universal consciousness in which there is no longer any Jude, Tess, or Henchard, but only the co-presence of every moment of their lives in an encompassing awareness, each moment detached from the others and taking place without the possibility of cessation in its own moving spot in the void. With death the individual will, which kept each character focused on a single aim in life, relaxes and gives place to a lack of will which must passively witness the inexorable repetition of the drama of existence, like those bad dreams which compress an eternity of experience in an instant.

Hardy's vision of human life seems to end not with death but with a glimpse of the fact that it may be impossible to die. In this his work anticipates the darker apprehensions of the novels of Samuel Beckett or of a story by Franz Kafka like "Der Jäger Gracchus." From the perspective of a vision of immortality something like Beckett's or Kafka's the dead in Hardy's poems speak of their resigned indifference to everything they most cared for in life. To be indifferent is still to remember, and his dead are unable to forget, much less able to escape from that embracing anonymous wakefulness which surrounds them and keeps everything alive for them in a memory as wide as the whole expanse of time and space.

VIII

Literature as Safeguarding of the Dead

HUMAN EXISTENCE FOR HARDY seems to end in the anguish of a futile desire for obliteration. By no strategy can he or his characters forget or be forgotten. Everything is destined to persist forever, unredeemed and unredeemable, in a terrifying space which swallows everything in its vacancy, like that ghastly deep black void around and beyond the stars which Swithin St. Cleeve sees through his telescope. Here, however, the importance of the divergence between Hardy and his characters can be seen. This divergence is presupposed in his conception of the function of literature.

Near the end of their lives the characters reach a moment when they see with approximate clarity that they have been deluded puppets of an alienating force. They choose death as the only escape from this alienation, but death, it turns out, is no escape, and so they seem doomed to remain eternally victims, powerless to free themselves from themselves. Hardy, on the other hand, reaches long before death the clarity, detachment, and wide scope of vision which allows him to coincide with the empty space which surrounds all things and contains them. He has full recognition of the nature of existence while he is still alive and while he still possesses or is possessed by that part of the universal will which is his own individuality. He has not been in the same way as Tess or as Henchard a victim of the Immanent Will, caught up in some illusory pursuit of happiness. He has made from the beginning that withdrawal to the periphery of life which allows him to live as a spectator watching the sufferings of others.

One may wonder why this insight did not lead Hardy to the same desire for oblivion his characters experience. His view of human existence seems to imply a conviction that life is not worth living. Sometimes he does express a wish for death, as in "The Prospect," a poem of December 1912. Here, in the anguish of remembering that his wife was still alive in the last July, he longs to join her in death: "But well, well do I know / Whither I would go!" (CP, 732). Nevertheless, he rarely expresses a wish for death in his own person, and he did not commit suicide. He lived out a long life writing indefatigably to the end, first completing the admirable achievement of the fiction and then the equally admirable abundance of poems. Though he lived far into the twentieth century he remained a Victorian in his prolific creativity.

Writing is exactly the opposite response to existence from that of the characters in the fiction. If they have sought happiness, lost it, and die cursing their lives with a certain masochistic joy, Hardy himself, from the perspective of that detachment which foresees the end of every involvement, turns back on the lives of his people after they are dead and broods over them with fascinated attention. His characters seek death in order to forget and to be forgotten. He chooses to be a writer instead. Hardy's writing is remembrance of things past and a permanent record of that remembrance. Far from granting his characters the oblivion they desire, his writing cooperates with the impersonal mind of the Void by keeping their fugitive moments of experience alive in the new form his words give them. His writing gives his people that immortality they flee.

This would seem wholly undesirable. Why did not Hardy choose from the beginning the silence he elects in his last poem? This would be at least a refusal to participate in the process which gives all lives an unwanted permanence. Is his writing the sign of a sadistic streak in him, a cruelty which takes pleasure in sharing the implacable refusal of the Void to grant people the oblivion they desire?

The narrators of Hardy's novels and the characteristic speakers of his poems coincide in objectivity, clarity, and inclusiveness with the eternal space embracing all things. Their possession of such "long vision" ("Wessex Heights," CP, 301) means that they contain within themselves all the swarming multiplicity of past events in simultaneous juxtaposition. A number of the poems describe the writer in this way. He is a man who enjoys "something of ecstasy" in the "companionship" of "the ghost of the past." In his mind the past is renewed in every moment "just as it was" ("The Ghost of the Past,"

CP, 290), as "A Procession of Dead Days" (CP, 609). "The House of Silence" (CP, 445), the most explicit of such texts, defines the poet as possessing "the visioning powers of souls who dare / To pierce the material screen." Though the poet seems to live quietly in his "house in the trees with the shady lawn," this solitude and silence hide a spinning brain through which "figures dance" continually. The experiences of all the men and women of history are there concentrated in a single mind and in a single hour. All time and space and their contents are contained within the narrow bounds of the poet's imagination:

> It is a poet's bower,
> Through which there pass, in fleet arrays,
> Long teams of all the years and days,
> Of joys and sorrows, of earth and heaven,
> That meet mankind in its ages seven,
> An aion in an hour.

"An aion in an hour" — the contraction of space is matched by a contraction in time, so that everything which has happened during all the years is compressed into a brief space of time in the poet's bower. In another poem ("Could I But Will," CP, 603-604), Hardy makes a connection between the recovery of the past, the resurrection of the dead, the concentration of what has been dispersed in space, and a power of willing the past into renewed existence which is expressly defined as godlike. "Could I but will, / Will to my bent," says the speaker of this poem, "I'd have afar ones near me still." This power of willing is labeled divine by the parallel construction in the next stanza: "Could I be head, / Head-god . . ." If the immanent energy that stirs and urges everything is, as in the thought of Schopenhauer, Nietzsche, and Heidegger, defined by Hardy as a power of volition, his definition of man's aim also parallels Nietzsche's speculations. Man's instinctive goal for him is the achievement of a sovereign force of will, a will strong enough to control things omnipotently. In his conception this will aims not at that transfiguration of the fated into the free which Nietzsche describes, but rather at a transformation of distance into proximity which will be a victory over time and a resurrection of the dead. To "have afar ones near me still" is to transcend both time and space, to compress their vast boundaries into the closeness of an eternal moment. This moment would return the dead to perpetual life in a paradisiacal community "Mid which old friends and I would walk / With weightless feet and magic talk / Uncounted eves."

In "Could I But Will" this godlike power is expressed conditionally. It is something desired rather than something possessed. "The House of Silence," however, ascribes to the poet as an actual power that gift of resurrection so coveted in "Could I But Will." What one poem longs for, the other poem shows the poet possessing as an inalienable attribute of his nature. The poet so perfectly overlaps with the eternal consciousness which things enter after death that he is able to give the dead a new life in his writing. He can gather together there all the people who dwell apart within the space of the universal consciousness.

This is affirmed once more in the beautiful poem, "In Front of the Landscape" (CP, 285-287). The poem opens the section called "Lyrics and Reveries" in *Satires of*

Circumstance. It has a rolling magnificence of rhetoric, like the sway of the sea, which goes beyond Hardy's usual reserved and stately melody. One of the realities which the poem superimposes in a three-leveled structure is in fact the sweeping ocean swell. The rise and fall of the sea gives the poem its rhythm. The sea also functions as an image for the reborn figures from the past who stand between the poet and the "customed landscape" of Wessex, blotting "to feeble mist" "the coomb and the upland / Coppice-crowned, / Ancient chalk-pit, milestone, rills in the grass-flat / Stroked by the light." The poet walks on in a landscape thinned to "a ghost-like gauze" by the presences from the past which flow over him like "waste waters / Stretching around." He advances, as he says in the splendid phrase which opens the poem, "plunging and labouring on in a tide of visions." The visions are those people and those "scenes, miscalled of the bygone," he once knew in the past and slighted then, "caring not for their purport." They return in "revisiting manifestations" "before the intenser / Stare of the mind" to plead with the poet to recognize them now and to commemorate them. This invocation endows them with their wavelike power to sweep the poet into their ebb and flow of speechless longing for the form of redemption only literature can give:

> — Yea, as the rhyme
> Sung by the sea-swell, so in their pleading dumbness
> Captured me these.

Captured by this mute pleading, the poet accepts his vocation, which is to give the dead their due. Hardy's writing can be defined as a response to this call. Life for him must pass into the realm of death before it can be rescued in art. The great outpouring of poems about his first wife, for example, came after her death, as a magical release of feeling and speech which was possible only when she had died. The theme of the revivification of the past runs all through his poems and relates his work to that of Wordsworth, Mallarmé, or Proust. His fiction too brings the dead to life, and the poetry can from one perspective be seen as a musing exploration of the implications of form in his fiction. The novels, like the poems, are an exercise of the historical imagination, bringing the past back to life. Hardy is the man who sees ghosts and remembers what everyone else has forgotten. To him things "That nobody else's mind calls back, / Have a savour that scenes in being lack, / And a presence more than the actual brings" ("Places," CP, 332). From a time far after the events he turns back not only to watch and remember, but to record what has happened in a poem or story. This record gives the dead a permanent existence in an art which is memory embodied.

The contents of time and space exist in the poet's mind as a given condition of his privileged state. They exist, however, in a chaotic form. The passages cited above describing the poet's passive reveries show him invaded and occupied by a vast throng of people, of moments, of visions, each existing as it did when it first occurred, all crowded together in an eager movement without order or pattern. Each still has the emotional intensity and the obscurity characteristic of immediate experience. Moreover the whole collection of moments is thrown pell-mell together into the vast receptacle which contains them, each pursuing its eternal motion without coherent relation to the others. Intensity, obscurity, multiplicity, disorder — these are predominate characteristics of the tide of visions which flows through the poet, engulfing him in its multitudinous motion, forcing him to participate in its alien sway, as if he were carried away by a great wave of the sea.

The poet's job is to turn these qualities into the clarity, simplicity, and patterned repose proper to a work of art. In accomplishing this transformation he redeems the world, insofar as it may be redeemed. He saves the events he describes from that sad persistence in an eternal repetition of their first occurrence to which they seem fated.

A contrast between each past moment and the present memory of it occurs so persistently in Hardy's verse that it may be said to constitute the fundamental structure of his lyric form. When an experience is first lived, even by the poet himself, it is lived blindly. Each man is too preoccupied with his own emotions, too much focused on the immediate future, to visualize what is happening to him in the perspective of the other moments of his life. He cannot see that the values he finds in other people and in things are projected by the mind outward rather than part of the real structure of the world. He forgets that everything passes away into death. Nevertheless, his emotions are so intense that he is without his knowledge transfiguring the objects around him. He is storing his feelings up in houses, in furniture, in musical instruments, in a certain glade by a stream, or in a given spot by the seacliffs. In emotion, event and place become one.

Only after these events have died into the past can they be seen clearly for what they were. The poet has this clear sight. He is separated from unthinking involvement in any moment and sees all moments from the perspective of a "larger vision" ("Often When Warring," CP, 513). This means first an annihilation of the illusions of the past. Then the act of turning back on past events frees old emotions from their imprisonment in the objects which contain them. It brings them back to life in a new form which allows an understanding of them impossible when they were happening. The figures from the past exist as impalpable presences hovering around the places where they first came into existence. These ghosts are expressions of the visionary possession by the brooding poet of all the events and feelings of the past. They objectify the fact that these things did in fact take place and that Hardy preserves them in his memory in a form different from that fleeting and uncomprehended existence they had when they first occurred. The poems resurrect in language these "Presences from aforetime" ("The Two Houses," CP, 564), and the characters of the novels too are ghosts brought back to life in the words of the narrator.

This pattern is pervasive in the poems. Even when the most important time of a man's life is taking place, the significance and value of this "best thing of things" is invisible: " 'Nought' it was called, / Even by ourselves," "scrawled / Dully on days that go past," "rated as nought / Save as the prelude to plays / Soon to come" ("A Two-Years' Idyll," CP, 594, 595). "While he was here with breath and bone, / To speak to and to see," says the poet of a dead friend, "Would I had known — more clearly known — / What that man did for me" ("The Casual Acquaintance," CP, 647), but this knowledge is possible only when the man is dead. The speaker in another poem laments that he "did not know / That life would show, / However it might flower, no finer glow" ("Best Times," CP, 646), and another poem describes a woman who "saw inside, when the form in the flesh had gone, / As a vision what she had missed when the real beholding" ("She Who Saw Not," CP, 626). Another woman is said to have "possessed [her lover] in absence / More than if there" ("In the Marquee," CP, 836), and another poem memorializes a brave sailor in the same terms:

> More really now we view him,
> More really lives he, moves with men,
> Than while on earth we knew him . . .
> ("The Sea Fight," CP, 765)

In all these poems the psychological and metaphysical law is the same. Only when the event is past can its value be appreciated. Hardy is therefore an idle spectator of the present. He lacks a normal interest in the present as valuable in itself or as a means of attaining a future goal. Though "The world has no use for one to-day / Who eyes things thus — no aim pursuing!" ("Old Furniture," CP, 456), his vision is focused on things of the present only as they reveal the past. In this way alone can he see the way the "hands of the generations" still hover over "each shiny familiar thing," or glimpse airy fingers dancing over an old viol playing the music of the dead (*ibid.*). He is then like his Grandmother Hardy, of whom he says, "Past things retold were to her as things existent, / Things present but as a tale" ("One We Knew," CP, 258). Like her, the poet can say: "The tones around me that I hear, / The aspects, meanings, shapes I see, / Are those far back ones missed when near" ("The Rambler," CP, 253). Indifferent to the present, he keeps alive in his mind the phantoms of the past, for example that "ghost-girl-rider," his wife when he first met her. Carrying in his mind her visionary form, he "sees as an instant thing / More clear than to-day, / A sweet soft scene / That was once in play / By that briny green." He keeps lost time in being as something "warm, real, and keen" ("The Phantom Horsewoman," CP, 333).

"With how strange aspect," the poet exclaims, "would there creep / The dawn, the night, the daytime, / If memory were not what it is" ("Conjecture," CP, 448). Without memory experience would be a sequence of inexplicable sensations. Memory gives familiarity and meaning to a man's surroundings by liberating what they contain and signify: the past. The power of memory is a ubiquitous theme of the poems, but for Hardy it is his dead wife who functions most importantly as the mediator of that recollection which releases the past from captivity. "She opens the door of the Past to me," he says, "Its magic lights, / Its heavenly heights, / When forward little is to see!" ("She Opened the Door," CP, 735). His brooding reminiscences of Emma give him the occasion for his most moving poems about the way memory recovers the past as a tantalizing presence in absence of the dead. "Slip back, Time!" he cries in "St. Launce's Revisited" (CP, 335-336). The poem goes on to tell how a return to the place where he first met his wife makes him feel sure that she and her family must certainly still be there, just as they were: "If again / Towards the Atlantic sea there / I should speed, they'd be there / Surely now as then?" This poem ends negatively ("Why waste thought, / When I know them vanished / Under earth . . ."), and yet the effect of the poem is not negative. If the dead can never be encountered in the flesh, they can be encountered in memory and in the words of poems which, like this one, commemorate the dead and bring them to life anew.

The sequence of "Poems of 1912-13" which Hardy wrote after Emma's death is his most elaborate treatment of this theme of poetic memory. The twenty-one poems he chose for the series are not a random collection but are strategically placed in a dramatic sequence. This is suggested both by the fact that some poems written at the time about Emma are omitted from the series and by the fact that the poems included are not placed exactly in the chronological order of their composition.[1] The epigraph for the whole group of poems is *Veteris vestigia flammae*: "ashes of an old fire." The phrase comes from *The Aeneid* (IV, 23), where it is part of Dido's statement that the love she once felt for her now dead husband is about to renew itself for Aeneas. Her love for Aeneas is of course doomed to end in separation and leads to her suicide. There is a complex relation between Hardy's poems about his dead wife and Vergil's story of Dido's betrayal by Aeneas. The analogy involves not only Dido's feelings for her dead husband, Sychaeus, but also the relation of Aeneas to Dido after her death. As Aeneas confronts in Book VI of *The Aeneid* the mute unforgiving

---

[1] "The Voice" is dated "*December* 1912," and comes several poems after "Rain on a Grave," which is dated "*Jan. 31, 1913.*"

ghost of Dido, so Hardy in the poems glimpses the "voiceless" ("After a Journey," CP, 328) ghost of his dead wife. The rhythm of the "Poems of 1912-13" is like that rise and fall of the ocean waves which moves within the lines of "In Front of the Landscape." In the series, however, the movement is within groups of poems, each poem playing its part by way of its careful placement in relation to the others. Each group of poems rises toward a climactic recovery of the dead wife's presence, only to fall back again to loss, only to rise once more in the next group, and then fall again, in an unpredictable rhythm which brings back the past only to lose it. This wavelike pulsation of recovery and loss is brilliantly structured around changes in person and tense. The poet moves from speaking of his dead wife as "her" to speaking to her as "you," or he moves from speaking of their past life in the past tense to direct address in the present to his wife as a ghost, to recovery of the past as a present. The interweaving of these linguistic signs of presence and absence is extremely complex, and the juxtaposition of poem and poem often gives rise to striking dramatic effects. "Lament" (CP, 323-324), for example, speaks of Emma as "Wholly possessed / By an infinite rest," as "dead / To all done and said / In her yew-arched bed." This poem is followed with fine suddenness by "The Haunter" (CP, 324-325), in which the ghost of Emma, invisible and inaudible to the poet, speaks of her constant companionship of her husband and pleads for some communication with him: "What a good haunter I am, O tell him!" "The Haunter" is followed in turn by "The Voice" (CP, 325-326). In this poem the poet is shown thinking he hears, mixed with the listless breeze, the voice of his wife calling to him across the mead as he moves forward through an autumn landscape:

> Thus I; faltering forward,
> Leaves around me falling,
> Wind oozing thin through the thorn from norward,
> And the woman calling.

This kind of suggestive juxtaposition is characteristic of "Poems of 1912-13." The group is an organic whole in which each poem plays its irreplaceable part. The more famous poems of the sequence, so often anthologized and discussed, take their full meaning only in the context of the entire series as it moves from anguished memory of the past as irremediably past to the climax of recovery in "After a Journey" (CP, 328-329). In this poem the poet returns to the Cornish coast where he met and courted Emma in 1870. He returns also back through time to his past life and to his past self. The ghost becomes visible at last, though still "voiceless," and leads him back to the spots they once "haunted"[2] together. Finally, in a moving cry of allegiance negating all the time of estrangement which followed their early happiness, the poet can say that he has not changed. He is still the same man, and she too is the same:

> Trust me, I mind not, though Life lours,
> The bringing me here; nay, bring me here again!

---

[2] The subtle irony of this word is characteristic of these poems in their interrelation. The word of course recalls the earlier poem in the series, "The Haunter." Haunting the spot when they were live young lovers in the past, they haunt it once more now that she is a ghost and he a frail old man following that ghost.

> I am just the same as when
> Our days were a joy, and our paths through flowers.

After this climax of recovery, the series moves, with many hesitations and partial returns, like a wave slowly subsiding, back to a present of loss in the final poem, "Where the Picnic Was" (CP, 336). It moves by way of the poet's gradual recognition, recorded explicitly in "At Castle Boterel" (CP, 330-331) and in "The Phantom Horsewoman" (CP, 332-333), that Emma exists not as an objective ghost which any man might see, but in the poet's mind. Though the "primaeval rocks" by a certain roadside record in their color and shape the fact that he and his lady passed there one March night long ago, this imprint of the transitory on the permanent is visible only "to one mind," the mind of the poet in whose vision "one phantom figure / Remains on the slope," though time, "in mindless rote," has long since obliterated the reality. "The Phantom Horsewoman" makes a strikingly subtle use of the variation in grammatical persons which structures these poems. Here Hardy distinguishes himself from himself. The speaker of the poem who lives in the same time-worn present as the reader and has lost his wife speaks as an "I" of that "he" who is his inner poetical self, the self who dwells beyond time and possesses Emma unchanged in all her youth and beauty forever:

> Time touches her not,
> But she still rides gaily
> In his rapt thought
> On that shagged and shaly

Atlantic spot,
And as when first eyed
Draws rein and sings to the swing of the tide.[3]

❦

If the "Poems of 1912-13" are Hardy's fullest expression of the power of poetry to resurrect dead time, many poems not about Emma Gifford dramatize the same theme. It is a universal law of his imagination, not just a motif generated by a particular experience. The irony of the presence in absence of the past is expressed, for example, in "Molly Gone" (CP, 467-468). This poem reiterates the speaker's loss of his Molly and his inability ever to do again the things he used to do with her ("No more summer for Molly and me"; "No more planting by Molly and me"; "No more jauntings by Molly and me"; "No more singing by Molly to me"), but in the act of describing all he has lost the speaker brings it back again in the words of the poem, enshrining it there in the remembering immortality of words.

Another such poem is "At Middle-Field Gate in February" (CP, 451). Here the poet on a dreary day in February remembers not the preceding summer, but a summer day long ago when a group of farm girls now long dead flourished in their youth and beauty:

How dry it was on a far-back day
    When straws hung the hedge and around,
    When amid the sheaves in amorous play

---

[3] I am indebted in this discussion of the "Poems of 1912-13" to an admirable unpublished study of them by Miss Rona Cohen.

> In curtained bonnets and light array
> Bloomed a bevy now underground!

An entry in the *Life* extends this poem by providing a litany of the names of the girls whom Hardy was memorializing in this poem. It is as if he feels he can preserve them in existence by repeating their names, names now existing only in his memory or as half-effaced inscriptions on tombstones in some country churchyard: "On the present writer's[4] once asking Hardy the names of those he calls the 'bevy now underground,' he said they were Unity Sargent, Susan Chamberlain, Esther Oliver, Emma Shipton, Anna Barrett, Ann West, Elizabeth Hurden, Eliza Trevis, and others, who had been young women about twenty when he was a child" (L, 223).

The power which a poetry of memory has to bring back the dead is affirmed once more in a charming poem called "Louie" (CP, 734-735). Here the poet takes upon himself an almost divine responsibility, as he does in "Her Immortality" (CP, 48-50), a poem possibly about Tryphena Sparks.[5] In "Her Immortality" the speaker wishes to go on living because his dead love is kept immortal only in his memory of her. "When I surcease," he says, "Through whom alone lives she, / Her spirit ends its living lease, / Never again to be!" (CP, 50). The same thing is affirmed less solemnly in "Louie." Though the poet cares most about keeping his dead wife alive in his memory, it comes to him suddenly that unless he remembers all the other women too, they will pass out of

---

4 Florence Emily Hardy, as the nominal authoress of the *Life*.
5 As Lois Deacon and Terry Coleman suggest in *Providence and Mr. Hardy*, pp. 69-73.

existence. So he takes it upon himself to go on remembering Louie, though she meant little to him when she was alive. It is so easy to invoke ghosts that the poet can afford to sport with his power and raise whole hosts of spirits to accompany the central figure of his wife. The poem expresses a curiously lighthearted awareness of a sovereign power of revivification, as if the poet were snapping his fingers and saying, "Why, I almost failed to remember Louie, and where would she be if I had?"

> I am forgetting Louie the buoyant;
> Why not raise her phantom, too . . . ?

If the poet does not give Louie a posthumous existence, no one else will. Though each moment of her life remains along with everything else in the spacious reaches of eternity, its existence there is in the form of errant fragments of consciousness of which no one is aware, no one, that is, but the poet. Though Louie may be imagined to have had at the end of her life, like most people, some insight into the meaning of her existence, that insight vanished from this world when she died. Even if it had not died it was presumably only a partial clarification, as is the self-knowledge of Tess or that of Henchard. The poet is in the unique position of coinciding with the totality of existence while he is still alive. This gives him a privileged detachment allowing him to see each event clearly and without subjective deformation, exactly as it is in the eye of eternity, for the poet's eye and the eye of eternity are one.

If the poet's resurrection of the past changes what was originally blurred by emotion into something clearly seen, the element of design is still lacking. Hardy's characters at the end of their lives are able to look back and see the shapes in time those lives make, but each has only a single life to view. The writer is in a different situation. He is overwhelmed by the presence of all the moments of all the lives, an enormous tide of visions. He is engulfed in an inextricable tangle made up of every experience of every man and woman. There seems no way to order this multitude, unless the poet is willing to define art as the imposition of order on what is without order in itself. Hardy is not willing to define art in this way, and yet he wants to believe that intelligible pattern is a fundamental property both of existence and of art. His solution to this problem completes his theory of art.

Reality itself is without order. It is an amorphous mass in random movement, like those descriptions in *The Dynasts* of the wormlike crawlings across the landscape of Europe's armies, or like that similar description in the *Life* of a view of the Lord Mayor's show from an upper window on Ludgate Hill: "as the crowd grows denser it loses its character of an aggregate of countless units, and becomes an organic whole, a molluscous black creature having nothing in common with humanity, that takes the shape of the streets along which it has lain itself, and throws out horrid excrescences and limbs into neighbouring alleys; a creature whose voice exudes from its scaly coat, and who has an eye in every pore of its body. The balconies, stands, and railway-bridge are occupied by small detached shapes of the same tissue, but of gentler motion, as if they were the spawn of the monster in their midst" (L, 131).

If this shapeless and unwholesome monster is the form taken by humanity in the aggregate, then, as Hardy recognizes in an essay of 1891 called "The Science of Fiction," an art of scrupulous realism is a contradiction in terms. This is so because a complete representation of the chaotic multiplicity of the real would be a total disorder, not art at all. The aim of a scientific realism in fiction founders on the reef of "the impossibility of reproducing in its entirety the phantasmagoria of experience with infinite and atomic truth, without shadow, relevancy, or subordination."[6] Art is therefore "science with an addition," the science being a clear view of "things as they really are," the addition being the act of selection which even the most objective artist necessarily makes. "The most devoted apostle of realism," says Hardy, "the sheerest naturalist, cannot escape, any more than the withered old gossip over her fire, the exercise of Art in his labour or pleasure of telling a tale. Not until he becomes an automatic reproducer of all impressions whatsoever can he be called purely scientific, or even a manufacturer on scientific principles. If in the exercise of his reason he select or omit, with an eye to being more truthful than truth (the just aim of Art), he transforms himself into a technicist at a move."[7]

---

[6] *Life and Art*, ed. Brennecke, p. 87. All unidentified quotations in this and the following paragraph are from Brennecke, pp. 85-87. "The Science of Fiction," along with almost all of Hardy's prefaces and other prose writings, is also to be found in *Thomas Hardy's Personal Writings*, ed. Harold Orel (Lawrence, Kansas: University of Kansas Press, 1966), pp. 134-138.

[7] In the opinion of Claude Lévi-Strauss any historian or anthropologist

Art cannot be the objective mirroring of things as they are. No artist can avoid "the exercise of the Dæ-dalian faculty for selection and cunning manipulation." Some "sweet pattern" (L, 114) is essential to art. The artist must find a way to select his material without imposing a pattern which is not objectively there. Hardy is merciless in his condemnation of such a distortion of reality, as when he asks, "Is not the present quasi-scientific system of writing history mere charlatanism? Events and tendencies are traced as if they were rivers of voluntary activity, and courses reasoned out from the circumstances in which natures, religions, or what-not, have found themselves. But are they not in the main the outcome of *passivity* — acted upon by unconscious propensity?" (L, 168). He would level the same reproach at a novelist who shows a human life as a series of conscious intentions acted upon rationally. When he condemns orthodox historians for making a false sense out of history, he is not only objecting to the way historians treat history as if it were a sequence of voluntary

---

is caught in this dilemma. His formulation is strikingly similar to Hardy's, though of course Hardy did not continue his considerations exactly along the lines of Lévi-Strauss's sophisticated neo-Kantianism or Comteanism in historical methodology. "What is true of the constitution of historical facts," says Lévi-Strauss, "is no less so of their selection. From this point of view, the historian and the agent of history choose, sever, and carve them up, for a truly total history would confront them with chaos. Every corner of space conceals a multitude of individuals each of whom totalizes the trend of history in a manner which cannot be compared to the others; for any one of these individuals, each moment of time is inexhaustibly rich in physical and psychical incidents which all play their part in his totalization. Even history which claims to be universal is still only a juxtaposition of a few local histories within which (and between which) very much more is left out than is put in. . . . A truly total history would cancel itself out—its product would be nought" (*The Savage Mind* [Chicago: University of Chicago Press, 1966], p. 257; for the original text see *La Pensée sauvage* [Paris: Plon, 1962], pp. 340-341).

actions, but also rejecting their assumption that history must in one way or another make an intelligible pattern. Any event is caused, but it is caused by such an impossibly complex set of interacting energies that no human mind could hold them in a single coordinating grasp. History, like reality, is both intelligible and unintelligible, orderly and disorderly. The laws which cause things to happen are universal. They can be comprehended by man and are the underlying meaning or explanation of every event. These laws, however, are those of the random impulsions of the unimaginably diversified forces of the Immanent Will. As such they render each event part of so complicated a system that each is, from any human point of view, unintelligible and disorderly. If this is the case, then true art is impossible, since art must have an intelligible design, and any intelligible design is a subjective fabrication, a piece of charlatanism.

The escape from this impasse is recorded in a crucial text in the *Life*. This passage provides a definition of Hardy's form of subjective realism: "As, in looking at a carpet, by following one colour a certain pattern is suggested, by following another colour, another; so in life the seer should watch that pattern among general things which his idiosyncrasy moves him to observe, and describe that alone. This is, quite accurately, a going to Nature; yet the result is no mere photograph, but purely the product of the writer's own mind" (L, 153).

Such an art is objective and subjective at the same

time, a realistic mirroring of reality which nevertheless contains the formal beauty necessary to art. Intelligible pattern can be seen by the human consciousness alone. It is the fundamental characteristic of that highest human creation, a work of art. Art is determined by the sensibility of the artist. It is the arbitrary picking out of one thread in the web and a following of that thread to its end. "Differing natures," says Hardy in the "General Preface" to his works, "find their tongue in the presence of differing spectacles," and therefore "to whichever of these aspects of life a writer's instinct for expression the more readily responds, to that he should allow it to respond" (Td, xii). A work of art is a subjective creation in the sense that the formal beauty of the single thread in its meanderings appears only by a detaching of the thread from the rest of the web of life. A work of art is objective in the sense that the thread has existed all along in the confused tangle of reality, just as the stonemason's carving lies hidden in the shapeless darkness of the stone.

This justification of the constructive imagination of the artist confirms the notion discussed earlier that Hardy's writing, like the stonemason's art, is a craft of juxtaposition, a solid setting side by side of the parts which make up a life. The reader will remember that concern he felt "when measuring and drawing old Norman and other early buildings" for the "shortcoming of the most ancient architecture by comparison with geology" (L, 93-94). Hardy's plots, I have said, are characterized by balance and symmetry. The most unlikely coincidences are assimilated into a pattern which, when the novel is over and the reader can draw back to see the whole, reveal themselves to have the artificiality of a chastely designed building. There is a multiple irony in this rigidity of construction.

Though the narrator of the novels is a recording spectator rather than a shaper of what he sees, nevertheless he is a builder in one sense at least. He has decided to focus on one part of time and space rather than another, on one group of people out of all the possible ones, on one sequence of events detached from the interweaving of circumstances and action which makes up the workings of the Immanent Will. Even *The Dynasts* follows but several strands in the web of history. In Hardy's view this web is woven by the random movement of things as they are driven by Will. To call the motive energy of this senseless process a "will" is to suggest that the voluntary actions of men and women are as much the puppet-work of the Immanent Will as the blowing of the wind or as the growth of heather on the heath. As desiring, acting, willing persons, all men are instruments of the Immanent Will. For this reason, the revelation of a pattern of meaning in the web is an act of creation rather than an act of discovery. What really exists is the shapeless and ageless marble of the hills. The imposition of a pattern on the marble by the builders and carvers of the Norman churches is only the superficial laying on of an evanescent and artificial design. The shape of a novel by Hardy is no less artificial. The rigidity of its pattern is a revelation of that fact. Any coherent sequence of events, even the most "realistic" or "psychologically plausible," is an arbitrary construction, a selection from the multitudinous turmoil of life. The novels in the schematic neatness of their design presuppose a theory of art as the will to power, in spite of the detached objectivity of their narrators. As Georg Lukács observes in *The Theory of the Novel*, the passive recording, without commentary, of a sequence of events which makes a story is a sophisticated artistic act. To mirror events in representative language, with however little reshaping, is already to endow them with a clarity and coherence they do not have in reality.[8] Even so, the pattern of art is not something imposed in the sense of being created by distortion of the facts of human life. The most surprising coincidences and accidents do occur. The form of Hardy's novels is a mirage, a fiction, but it is a fiction created by selection, not by distortion, just as the carvings of a Norman arch are detached by the craftsman from the surrounding stone. He can therefore insist that the events in his novels are realistic. By freeing a certain shape from the rock, or, to return to the alternative metaphor, by following certain strands in the total web, he has revealed a previously hidden design in life. Hardy's novels are

8 See *Die Theorie des Romans* (Darmstadt: Luchterhand, 1965), p. 47. Lukács' analysis has a provocative relevance to Hardy's work: "In the form which isolates the surprising and problematical aspects of life, that is, in the novel, this lyricism must still entirely hide itself behind the sharp lines of a given case detached and chiseled out by the writer: lyricism is here pure selection: the shocking arbitrariness of the chance which brings happiness and annihilates, which always descends without reason, can only be balanced by its clear, purely objective apprehension, without commentary. The novel is the purest artistic form: the ultimate meaning of all artistic forms is expressed by it as a mood or resonance, as the inherent meaning of form itself, even if it is also therefore expressed abstractly. Precisely because meaninglessness is glimpsed in unveiled, unadorned nakedness, the overwhelming force of a vision without fear and without hope grants this lack of meaning the consecration of form: meaninglessness as meaninglessness comes to form: it becomes eternal; it is affirmed, transcended, and redeemed by the form" (my translation).

thus what he often calls them, "seemings," "shows," "fantasies," "dreams," the outcome of a personal way of seeing things. "Art," he says in a note of 1890, "consists in so depicting the common events of life as to bring out the features which illustrate the author's idiosyncratic mode of regard; making old incidents and things seem as new" (L, 225).

The pattern which he habitually picks out of the web is one which in the incongruity of its ironic accidents, crossed intentions, misplaced fidelities, and frustrated desires reveals precisely that futility of existence which justifies the narrator and the characters in withdrawing altogether from active engagement in life. This futility, he would argue, is the universal meaning objectively present in things as they are. Hardy's form of realism combines subjectivity and objectivity in a contradictory balance which is the basis of his art.

Only this mode of art, in a universe like Hardy's, can be a redemption of things from their eternal recurrence in the void. Such an art is a resolute confrontation of reality and its injustice. This revelation of the truth of things is the poet's contribution to the universe. His patient registering of the facts is a defiance of the Will, but in its proof that things do always turn out for the worst, his art is, paradoxically, a happy one. It demonstrates the eternal fitness of things. Each man gets what the prescient expect and even what the knowing want. Moreover, Hardy's recording of the fated course of a life, his following of one strand in the web through to its happily unhappy end, turns numb suffering into the symmetry of art, that high form of art which is objective recording of the way things are. Writing *Tess of the d'Urbervilles* or *The Mayor of Casterbridge,* like singing Watts's "And now another day is gone" in the face of the red wall at sunset, transforms the fated into art and therefore transcends the power of the Immanent Will.

Such an art finds value and meaning in a world previously without them. If time is a sequence of moments which are born and die, so that each instant, with all its experiences, is swallowed up by the vastness of eternity as soon as it occurs, only the consciousness of the poet with its breadth and clarity of vision can hold the moments of time together. The pattern time makes is uncovered through art, and art is therefore a victory of consciousness over suffering. It is a sly and evasive victory, surely, for the poet only stands back and watches, recording what he sees from his distance, but it is an authentic victory nevertheless. The poet's mind is the world turned inside out, transformed into words, all existence concentrated in one place and time, an aeon in an hour. Hardy's writings are the verbal embodiment of a cosmic memory, or, one might better say, this memory is generated and maintained in being by the words he writes. When things have happened and have fallen into the past they are resurrected into that space of continual repetition which is the poet's mind. Tess's wish to have her life "unbe" can never be fulfilled as long as there remains a copy of *Tess of the d'Urbervilles* to keep her sad story from oblivion by means of the inexhaustible recurrence which goes on within the covers of a book, and Hardy's lyric poems constitute a model in miniature of his universe. Gathered together in *The*

Collected Poems a multitude of human experiences are preserved in words to go on re-enacting themselves side by side indefinitely. They re-enact themselves as existences whose present actuality consists in the fact that they have always already happened. This new form given to the lives of Hardy's characters may be said to oppose not enslavement to time and escape from it, but inauthentic and authentic experiences of temporality. In place of the characters' time, which seems an inevitable sequence of sufferings and betrayals, there is the poet's time, the time he calls in the last line of "Wessex Heights" "some liberty" (CP, 301). This liberty is a free assumption of the burden of the past. With such freedom goes an openness toward a future which will be a never-ending repetition of the events of the past. Here the importance of the word "seem" in the fourth line of "Wessex Heights" appears. When the poet goes up on the heights in Wessex, the reader will remember, he "seem[s] where [he] was before [his] birth, and after death may be" (CP, 300). The perspective on life attained on the heights is a perfect emblem of the safe distance from reality possessed by Hardy's narrators. The poem defines this distance as an escape into the atemporal realm which exists before birth and after death, the realm from which Tess and her fellow sufferers came and the realm to which they now have returned. The speaker of "Wessex Heights," however, only *seems* to have reached a place before and after time. If he were to describe himself as out of time altogether he would be claiming to have obtained a release from time which is impossible for a man while he is still alive. The speaker of "Wessex Heights" is still involved in time, still open toward a future which will be the re-enactment of episodes from the past, in an always unsuccessful attempt to free himself from them completely, so turning "some liberty" into complete freedom. This perpetual present of repetition is one version of authentic human temporality. Time, as long as a man is alive, is movement toward a future which will be, but never yet is, the perfected assumption of the past. The men and women of Hardy's poems and novels dwell not in a fixed region of eternity but in a realm of time characterized by repetition, the repetition which happens within a work of literature. The life of this recurrence is the never-ceasing attempt to reduce the distance between the verbal imitation of things and the things themselves, as if they might in some final repetition coincide.

The energy which creates the patterns of the stories and poems is the Will itself as it is embodied in the poet. The Will writes itself by means of the poet, using the poet as its pen or stylus. In Hardy's writing the Will comes to consciousness and makes the models of itself or representations of itself which are works of literature. In one sense his novels and poems are different from the real world, set over against it as mirroring image, as fiction. They describe in words and in the past tense something which is assumed within the fiction of the work to have once happened in the present and in material reality. In another sense, since the words which embody the poet's mind are expressions of the Immanent Will, originated by it, instruments of it, and since the poet's mind contains all the years, the words of his writings are literally (in both senses of the word) the place where the universal workings of the Immanent Will come to consciousness and to order.

The work of the Immanent Will in nature and in history is itself, according to a metaphor Hardy often uses, a kind of writing. History is the tracing of various lines which inscribe themselves through time as the destinies of all the individuals who make up mankind. History is the weaving of the "long while aforetime-figured mesh" which with its "contemplated charactery" (D, 330) transforms nature into the record of all that has happened in it. The Hintock woods in *The Woodlanders* are natural hieroglyphs. The old Roman road in *The Return of the Native* is traced as a kind of inscription across the timeless countenance of Egdon Heath. Tess's seduction is a form of writing even before it is described in words. "Why it was," says the narrator, "that upon this beautiful feminine tissue, sensitive as gossamer, and practically blank as snow as yet, there should have been traced such a coarse pattern as it was doomed to receive . . . , many thousand years of analytical philosophy have failed to explain to our sense of order" (Td, 91).

This tracing, according to another metaphor which is repeatedly used in *The Dynasts,* constructs itself within the nerve fibers of a monstrous sleeping brain. This brain is the drowsing Immanent Will. The traces of time are stored within it, as a computer stores information. The Spirit of the Pities in *The Dynasts* is granted power to watch the outstretched spectacle of the earth "endu[ed] . . . with a seeming transparency, and exhibiting as one organism the anatomy of life and movement in all humanity and vitalized matter included in the display." The Spirit sees "strange waves" "like winds grown visible, / Which bear men's forms on their innumerous coils, / Twining and serpentining round and through. / Also

retracting threads like gossamers — / Except in being irresistible — / Which complicate with some, and balance
all" (D, 6-7). These, the Spirit of the Years explains, "are
the Prime Volitions, — fibrils, veins, / Will-tissues,
nerves, and pulses of the Cause, / That heave throughout the Earth's compositure. / Their sum is like the
lobule of a Brain / Evolving always that it wots not
of; / A Brain whose whole connotes the Everywhere"
(D, 7). The poet's mind is the awaking to consciousness
of this dreaming brain. In the poet's extension into
human language of the inscribing power of the Cause
the unconscious becomes conscious and Hardy's hope
for a transformation of the cosmic energy, "Consciousness the Will informing, till It fashion all things fair!,"
is paradoxically fulfilled. It is fulfilled within the "as if"
or delegated representations of literature, which is to say,
not fulfilled in reality at all.

The representation of the design of a life in a novel
or poem is a revelation of more than that local design.
It is a revelation of the cause behind the design. This
cause first becomes safely visible through the formal patterns of art. Those who, like Napoleon, see it work in
their own lives, see it only at the moment when they
recognize that they have been driven to failure and death
by its blind "propension." Hardy's preservation in words
of the pattern of Napoleon's life, of Tess's, or of Henchard's is a vicarious and therefore less dangerous bringing
to light of the hidden cause.

Such a revelation, however, is never complete. The
Immanent Will is the unconsciousness of nature and of
all Hardy's characters. It is his own unconsciousness too.
The Will is the secret motive force behind everything
which happens, his acts of writing and all the events

about which he writes. The symmetrical patterns of art are nevertheless incommensurate with their source. They are symbols or metaphors of the Will, not the Will itself. The Will as it is in itself remains in reserve, unconscious, sleeping in the dark. The Will is always a matter of elsewhere or of another time, in the past or in the future, never a matter of the present or of presence. It is visible only at a distance from itself, in the signs or traces of it, for example in Hardy's writings. Its coming to consciousness exists only within the images of his work. Its actual coming to consciousness is always deferred. The Will is the principle of distance, its writing always signs of itself, not its real self. This writing constitutes that chain of postponements which keeps Hardy and his characters always unsatisfied, always seeking something more, some ultimate satisfaction of their desires, some impossible coincidence with a hidden center which always keeps its distance. That center, it may be, exists not as the source of all the permutations of desire, but as a shadow or phantom generated by desire itself and by the hollow within each man's heart which keeps his desire unstilled.

Just as Hardy in his poems sustains in being the ghosts of the past, playing in this a role traditionally assigned to God, so in his function as artist-preserver he is the closest thing to a deity his universe has. He is an imaginary deity nevertheless, a God who exists only in the distance from reality maintained in literature by the fact that it is made of mediate words rather than of immediate facts. He saves things from that horrible parody of remembrance which is their continuation in the obscure surgings of eternity. He saves them by giving them clarity, pattern, and meaning. These qualities

are established in that "full look at the Worst" which
defies the unconscious cause of things by preserving the
sufferings of man as a rebuke to their unwitting source.
In the text from Shakespeare's *Two Gentlemen of
Verona* (I, ii, 114, 115) which forms a moving epigraph
to *Tess of the d'Urbervilles,* Hardy says to Tess: "Poor
wounded name! My bosom as a bed / Shall lodge thee."
The poet's words constitute that capacious, compassion-
ate bosom which offers lodging and repose to Tess's
story and to all the other stories he tells. His writing, to
give it a final definition, is a resurrection and safeguarding of the dead, a safeguarding within the fictive language of literature.

Like a tribesman caught up in his local culture, but
achieving, it may be, a partial insight into the way his
life has conferred meaning on the physical world, each
of Hardy's characters lives out his life moving toward an
incomplete illumination. Like an anthropologist detaching and in a sense creating structures of marriage relationship or totemistic symbolism from the relatively
unselfconscious day-to-day living of a people, the writer
gives a clearer form to human life. The critic follows
these. He tries to identify in the mass of Hardy's writings the hidden structures which will allow a compre-
hensive view of them all. The character ultimately
glimpses a covert design in his life which has been invisible while he has been living that life. The artist brings
that design into the full light of day. The critic is the
third in a series. He is a watcher watching the watcher

watch his characters. Dwelling within the works and outside them at once, he attempts to trace out the implicit patterns which give them form. Balancing distance against intimacy he tries to reveal the congruence of the various courses of desire woven through the web of life by Hardy's people.

Index

Index

See *A Note on Texts,* pp. xix-xx, for a key to the abbreviations used for works by Hardy.